Early Retirement

Promises and Pitfalls

Early Retirement
Promises and Pitfalls

Robert C. Williamson, Ph.D.
Alice Duffy Rinehart, Ed.D.
and
Thomas O. Blank, Ph.D.

 INSIGHT BOOKS

Plenum Press • New York and London

Library of Congress Cataloging in Publication Data

Williamson, Robert Clifford, date.
  Early retirement: promises and pitfalls / Robert C. Williamson, Alice Duffy
Rinehart, and Thomas O. Blank.
    p.   cm.
  Includes bibliographical references and index.
  ISBN 0-306-44324-4 .
  1. Retirement—United States. 2. Early retirement—United States. I. Rinehart, Alice
Duffy. II. Blank, Thomas O., 1947–   . III. Title.
HQ1063.2.U6W55 1992   92-17562
306.3'8—dc20   CIP

ISBN 0-306-44324-4

© 1992 Plenum Press, New York
A Division of Plenum Publishing Corporation
233 Spring Street, New York, N.Y. 10013

An Insight Book

Printed in the United States of America

Preface

One of the notable changes of our times has been the shift toward a more flexible approach to retirement. Because of the economy, notably the international marketplace, a number of industries have been forced to invite their employees to enter into early retirement. This trend comes on the threshold of burgeoning state and federal budgets along with a worsening of the economic climate. Consequently, it is difficult to predict the effect of these events on Social Security. Yet, should the present trend toward retirement continue, we may well ask if future workers will spend almost as many years in leisure in the postretirement phase of the life cycle as they will in the labor market.

With these questions in mind, the authors began their study in 1986, when Bethlehem Steel and other major employers of the Lehigh Valley—as well as the nation at large—were disengaging as much as a third of their work force, with cutbacks falling disproportionately on the middle-aged worker.

Our report is based on a questionnaire sample of 115 retired men and women in addition to interviews with an expanded sample, all of whom volunteered for this survey. This volume reports the responses from both the questionnaire and the interviews. Probably of most interest for both the general and professional reader are the vignettes of these individuals as they reflect on their careers and their adjustment to the act of retirement.

Acknowledgments

We are most grateful to the participants, who are given fictional names in the text. Their willingness to give us their time and share with us their feelings, evaluations, and life stories has greatly enriched our understanding of work and retirement and, indeed, of the processes of aging in late twentieth century America. We also are most appreciative of Diane Hyland's contribution to the construction of the questionnaire. We are especially indebted to Carey D. Patterson for her enormous and insightful contribution to the interviewing process. In addition we wish to thank Ann Van Doren for her secretarial help. We are indebted to JoAnne W. Hansz for an analysis of the health problems of a subsample of our retirees. We appreciate the permission of Wadsworth, Inc. to reproduce the figure from Robert C. Atchley, *The Social Forces in Later Life: An Introduction to Social Gerontology*, Third Edition, 1980.

Finally, we gratefully acknowledge the financial help and encouragement of the Lehigh University Office of Research. No less important, especially in the later stages, has been the support by Norma Fox, executive editor of Insight Books.

Contents

Part I
Introduction

Chapter 1

Aging and Retirement in a Changing Society

"Well, let's face it, from the time I was twelve, I worked all the time and supported myself. I put myself through college with my wife's help. I married her when I was twenty. Oh, yeah, we worked our way through Lehigh. I went to a junior college before, and then we came to Lehigh for a Bachelor's degree. For the Master's degree, the corporation paid tuition. Since I graduated from high school, I was on my own. Even before that, my father charged me board from the time I was thirteen. . . .

"I got very fed up when the company put me on third shift in early '86. I had worked on it in about '68 for one year and hated it then. At least then I was much younger, but I never did adjust to it. So when it came about again I was very disappointed. I even told them that I didn't want to work third shift. If I had to do something, I'd work second shift or around it, but I didn't like that either. I didn't go to school and get two degrees to work all shifts and do a lot of other things. But the announcement was made that I was to work third shift. I didn't think I was treated fairly. . . .

"When AT&T operated here locally they were at a reduced production level. Demand was falling. But at the same time, I didn't understand how corporate structure and finance justify their decisions. If I had been the vice president, I would never have set things up so that people like myself leave. . . . Retirement happened almost within a month. The company offered what they call the management income protection plan, and that's basically one year's pay over a two-year period. . . . Well, the rumors started in about August. I was becoming a little bit unhappy with certain things that were going on here, and so when the rumors started, I started doing some research. By the time the official offer was made on October 4, I was more prepared than I was before. I just had to confirm all the numbers. I checked with Social Security—I had dealt with their office before—to see if I was right about having forty quarters in order to qualify for retirement.

"I'm not unhappy with what I did. In fact, the longer I am out, the more I want to someday go back and thank a couple of people for shaking me up; because if they hadn't, I probably would have worked until I was sixty-five. My father worked until he was seventy. My feeling was, and still is, that I would have been much happier elsewhere. Even if it meant making less money, at least I would have been happier. I now toy with ideas. I'd like to be an investment counselor. I've brought myself to go out and look for a job. As it turns out, tomorrow I have one. I'm going to a pharmaceutical firm as a consultant. Something may or may not come of that, who knows. . . .

"Up until now, I really haven't made any changes in my standard of living. About the only thing that has changed so far is that we go out for lunch more often than dinner. I tend to play golf in a public course and not the big course. I used to go to Myrtle Beach every year for at least a week. . . .

"As for my hobbies, I can give you a list as long as your arm. I'm a woodworker, a machinist by trade, and a toolmaker by trade, so I have all the tools. I like to play chess, to read, to golf, to bowl. I do all the home repair. I did this whole room. I tore it down to the walls. I have a video camera and dabble in putting films together. We have a pool table in the cellar. I enjoy cooking. . . . I could keep going on. We garden a lot. In fact, we do a lot of canning. I help the wife can tomatoes, soup, sauce, and ketchup.

"If I wanted to get a job, I could probably go in and be a machinist. I could likely get a job as a carpenter. I've done plumbing, and I can wire. I rewired this house. We re-did the whole kitchen. I put a whole new service in for the dishwasher and the garbage disposal. Oh yeah, if I really wanted to do something, I could. And fortunately I'm in very good health. I really don't hunt and fish as I used to, though. I just don't get as much of a kick out of it anymore, but I do play guitar from time to time. I used to play guitar reasonably well, but you've got to practice, and I really don't spend a lot of time at it. I've only been out ten months, but I've really done some house-keeping. I must have maybe ten thousand files and spent three or four weeks last year coordinating them. I really feel like right now I'm almost ashamed of myself for having so many hobbies, toys, and such. Maybe I should get involved and do something for humanity. I'm just not ready to help humanity right now. It's really nice to live like this. For the first time in my life, I can live as the Rockefellers and the Vanderbilts have all of their lives. You have the choice when you get up in the morning to play golf, cook, go on a trip, read, or go to the library. One thing that's really nice about it, I think, is that I finally have a chance to read the stock market. I can now look at my investments; I can now look at my whole life—keep my letters up to date. I really started to change four or five years ago. I started running my life like a business, and now that I'm retired, I'm beginning to do that again. I think about percentages—what does this cost? What does this do for me?"

* * *

Jim Zimmerman, whose profile we have just seen, is a person who takes a dynamic stand toward most events in his life, including retirement. His story illustrates a few of the changes that have occurred in American society, how managerial change can occur in the corporation, how one may come to a retirement decision, what one may expect of retirement, and how to do it oneself.

Indeed, the twentieth century has been one of an enormous amount of social change. The first half of the century was marked by two world wars and the Great Depression. Despite a number of tumultuous international events, the second half has been one of comparative security. Most astonishing of all has been the pace of breakthroughs in medical technology, space travel, computers, and television. All this has resulted in an ever-higher standard of living, if somewhat dampened recently by inflation, fiscal deficits, and an overtaxed environment. Along with these developments is the cult of leisure as advanced societies have reduced the official work week from over fifty hours to less than forty. However, in view of transport time, our paper bureaucracy, and organizational demands, we have little more free time than did our forebears—all of which highlights the appeal of retirement.

In a century of vast social change, intriguing and often baffling questions accompany the act of retirement: When and under what conditions should one retire, and what kind of a future can one look forward to? There are pulls and pushes on one side for continuing to work, and on the other for leaving the workplace. Specifically, potential retirees ask, "What kind of income will I have?" "What will my benefits be?" "What is the best time to retire?" "How will I fill my time?" "How will it affect my spouse and my family?" "Will I miss my friends?" And so on. At the same time, society asks itself whether it can support all the retirees, who are likely to live twenty or even thirty years after they leave employment. Also, how can retirees be awarded the period of rest and freedom they deserve and yet be ensured of their sense of pride by remaining contributing members of society?

Answers to these questions affect all of us—retirees, potential retirees, those reentering the work force, those who get retirement benefits and those who "provide" them by participating in Social Security payroll deductions and pension systems. Consequently, we will consider some of the answers given by social scientists, policymakers, and those who have recently moved through the "retirement transition."

A demographic revolution is taking place over most of the world. In the advanced nations the process of a declining birthrate accompanied by a much greater life expectancy is well underway. In the third world it has just begun. We have seen life expectancy rise in the United States from forty-seven years in 1900 to seventy-seven in 1990. In 1900 only three million persons were sixty-five or older; today over thirty million are in this category. Early in the century, Americans continued in the work force almost to the end of their lives; today it appears that we may have the last quarter of our lifetime at leisure. Whereas two-thirds of men over sixty-five in 1900 were working, only one-sixth do so today. Moreover, the tightening of the economic situation in the corporate world during the 1980s brought on a wave of early retirement.

Indeed, many persons are abandoning their labors before age sixty. As we shall see in more detail, the technological and economic changes of the 1980s hastened the move toward early retirement. This trend has also been a product of the changing life style and value systems of post-World War II. In fact, these changes are part of a long-term historical process with their roots in the redefinition of personal and social goals that came with the democratic revolution at the end of the eighteenth century.

Changing Definitions of Aging

What has specifically led to our present policy on and expectations for retirement? That is, how does historical change affect us, including how we look at the upper years and how and when we decide to retire? Precisely how did we come to this notion of retirement as an expected phase of one's life? This development is based on both long-term and short-term forces.

According to David Hackett Fischer,[1] Western society, notably the United States, has moved through three major phases in its view of old age: First, the elderly were venerated during the seventeenth and most of the eighteenth centuries. One reason for this was the limited number who survived into the upper years. In fact, because of the high status of age it was not unknown for people to misrepresent their age in a direction contrary to what we see in our century.[2] Second, the cult of youth became marginally visible in the late eighteenth century but did not reach full bloom until this century. Third, the recognition of old age as a social problem emerged at the end of the first decade of this century. Significantly, 1909 saw the first public commission on aging (in Massachusetts), the first federal pension, and the coining of the term "geriatrics."

The recognition of the upper years as a normal part of life and of the right of the older generation to expect a pension was in large part a result of the social reform movement. These stirrings toward reform surfaced in the nineteenth century but assumed new heights in the Progressive Era of Teddy Roosevelt: the abolition of child labor, the women's suffrage movement, and a grudging recognition of organized labor. The New Freedom of Woodrow Wilson gave further impetus with, for instance, the acceptance of an income tax. No less important were other diverse factors—among them, the awareness that people were living longer and the desire of labor unions to eliminate the competition of older workers. However, despite gains in both private and state sectors, the dramatic change did not arrive until the Social Security Act of 1935. With that event, retirement was formally recognized as the right of every worker.

By the 1950s, labor unions were sufficiently strong to press private industry for supplemental pensions. This movement was strengthened by the climate of the times—the establishment of the AARP (American Association of Retired Persons) in 1955, the appearance of new publications such as *Retirement Planning News, Modern Maturity,* and *Senior Citizen.*[3] With the Great Society of Lyndon B. Johnson, the philosophy of adequate retirement benefits became officially accepted and was also symbolized in legislation on age discrimination in 1967. This same drift was evident in other advanced countries such as Britain.[4]

By the 1970s, at least two different and somewhat contradictory developments were evident—one permitting retirement at an ever-younger age and the other making it easier for older persons to remain in the work force. Spearheaded by the crisis of the steel and automotive industries, many employers felt the need to reduce expenses by encouraging early retirement. After all, younger workers can be brought into the office and factory, which means lower labor costs, as the beginning worker generally has a lower pay rate. This development fit in with the desire of many of the older workers for more leisure time. At the same time, the federal government was painfully conscious of a potential bleeding of the treasury if the tide of retirement were to reach full tilt. More important, the Social Security payments and surpluses as revenue had become a major means of maintaining a reasonably low deficit in the federal budget (that is, low until the national debt reached a catastrophic level in the 1980s). Groups representing the elderly, especially the Gray Panthers and AARP, resisted mandatory retirement, considering it insulting to older persons as a group. Consequently, Congress perceived the advantage that might accrue by easing up on age sixty-five as the formal entry to retirement. With the 1978 amendment raising the age of retirement to seventy we see at least the glimmering of recognition that any legally defined limit is arbitrary. (But the new law did not sit well in all quarters. For instance, fearing the expense of retaining senior faculty, university presidents successfully pushed the U.S. Senate into exempting professors from the new rule until 1982. High-level executives were similarly exempted from the new retirement age.) Finally, the 1986 amendments virtually eliminated mandatory retirement. (An interesting question is how will a company force out employees who insist on staying until, say, age eighty-seven!)

Again, two contrary movements are in force: one is the surge toward early retirement as employers offer incentives to remove older workers, and the other is the extension of the work age to seventy and beyond. An equilibrium between these two movements may be found someday. For the period of the 1980s the balance was clearly in favor of earlier retirement. However, in view of our longevity, as the new millennium approaches, society may discourage the worker from leaving the work force before his or her late sixties. A recent report suggests that the trend toward early retirement may be fading. Whereas in 1987, 25 percent of the companies surveyed were offering retirement incentives to cut nonmanagement jobs, only 20 percent were so inclined in 1990. Offering incentives to pare the more expensive management positions was even more sharply reduced.[5]

As a result of the changing age structure, the United States, along with other Western nations, may—or may not—be reaching an economic crisis in the retirement policy, as it relates to the total society. Presently only 12 percent of Americans are sixty-five years or older; however, by 2020, 17 percent are predicted to be.[6] If the average age of retirement remains at sixty-two or continues to decrease, we can see that an enormous dependency load will fall upon the American people—especially in view of the other dependent segments of the population, that is, the growing number living below the poverty level plus those who have not completed their education and are yet to enter into "productive activity." By the year 2000 it is likely that there will be one retiree for every three employed workers. Moreover, there is a continuous rise in both payroll deductions and Social Security payments, which are adjusted yearly for inflation. In addition are spiraling medical costs. Under Medicare an elderly couple receives an average health insurance value of over $4,000 per year, equivalent to more than a fifth of their income.[7]

This situation could mean a drive toward lower benefits for the elderly.[8] Increasingly, workers will likely have to look to private pension systems.[9] This impending crisis probably could be resolved if the fiscal system is prepared for it. However, as Senator Daniel Moynihan reminded us in 1990, we rather precariously have been using FICA payments to reduce national insolvency.

The answers to these questions remain beyond our control, but the experience of individuals who retire or who are thinking about it cannot fail to color our view of the future meaning of retirement and cause us to have a more cautious attitude toward our preparation, particularly financial, for that event. For all of us the road to retirement involves a number of decisions and reflects our total orientation to life.

How Do We Look at Aging and Retirement?

Several viewpoints have been proposed by social scientists over the last few decades in regard to what happens to us in the later years. What is successful aging? How can we make it successful in our own lives? The diversity of interpretations points to differences among people and variations in the styles of retirement. In Jim Zimmerman we saw a somewhat defiant but constructive response in meeting what he considered an impossible situation imposed by his employer and his subsequent retirement. Throughout this book we will present vignettes of individuals showing a wide variation in the general reaction to retirement.

Curiously, some of the approaches or theories suggest that successful retirement is mostly a matter of making a clean break from the world of work, whereas others indicate that continued activity, especially worklike projects, ensures happiness in retirement.

The first approach to become prominent was *disengagement* theory. In a research study of 275 persons ranging in age from fifty to ninety, Cumming and Henry saw a tendency toward withdrawal from both social contacts and general activity and felt that it was related to positive attitudes later in life.[10] In this view, retirement could be thought of as either a recognition for years of service rendered or that the person no longer fits into the world of work. At the time it was thought that the best response was to "go with the flow" and make a clean break from the world of work. Disengagement theory was supported by other research, not only from this country but from abroad. Some of the findings implied that disengagement was inevitable and universal.

Increasingly, however, the data were contradicted by other studies, which gave rise to other interpretations, most notably *activity* theory. In this view people tend to shift gears in late middle age and find substitutes for previous statuses, roles, and activities. In other words, they stay active but in quite varied ways. Older persons studied by Havighurst and his colleagues expressed a more positive orientation. Accordingly, innovation and adaptation characterize persons of retirement age. As persons move into their sixties and seventies they abandon their previous roles and look to new ones. Although not all elderly are able to make this kind of response, most find new activities in order to maintain their self-image.[11]

As the behaviors of older as well as younger people assume different patterns, it is not surprising that researchers prefer to frame their findings with labels reflecting the behavior they observe. Most of these approaches are variations of activity theory: *substitution* is the tendency to make a conspicuous shift in roles and activities in the later stages of the life cycle; *accommodation,* letting oneself take on a retirement role, suggests the flexibility observed in the majority of the postretirement population, even though this capacity can lead to negative as well as positive modes of reaction.

Perhaps the most favored variation of the activity theory is the concept of *continuity.* This theory assumes new experiences throughout the life cycle, while people themselves remain pretty much the same, at least in their personalities and value orientations. Change is integrated into the personality, along with the continuity of attitudes and values and possibly an expansion of leisure-time activities. Retirement becomes a challenge of adaptation and growth. Whereas activity theory relates to the concept of homeostasis—as never remaining in a static position of rest but constantly responding to new stimuli—continuity theory stresses evolutionary development.[12] We are continually attempting to maintain our self-esteem and lifelong principles and practices. We also respond through feedback to the needs of others. At the same time, continuity theory remains at odds with *crisis* theory, or the idea that the transition to the upper years is one of a series of dislocations.[13]

It is important to note that all these views assume that retirement is in fact a "normal" part of life. Older people react, one way or another, to the inevitable transition. None of these views especially invite elderly people themselves to take a very active role in creating a new life as they grow older, either by deciding to continue working or to make leisure living a *career*. Part of the reason for not recognizing these aspects is certainly historical: these models of successful aging were all developed in the 1960s, before the movement away from mandatory retirement *or* the development of a well-defined picture of a leisure-oriented kind of retirement.

Other Western nations are also assessing the meaning of retirement. Scandinavia in particular has pioneered in social policy for the upper-aged. The French refer to this period as *le troisième âge* (third age), and French Canadians refer to senior citizens as *les adolescents reciclés,* or recycled teenagers.

Thus, new ideas of retirement—its whys and its effects—are no doubt necessary. It is probably time for social scientists to be developing new theories of the meaning of retirement as a distinct phase of life that take into account the realities of retirement in the 1990s and into the next century. Although a new theory of retirement is beyond our purpose in this book, much of it will let one group of relatively recent retirees speak, allowing them to create a new view of retirement that is more dynamic and innovative than what has gone before, even though not all found the Golden Parachute they were looking for. For example, we saw the case of Jim Zimmerman as exemplifying the activity theory par excellence. In comparison, Tom Lorenzo, a blue-collar worker, is more a mix of activity and disengagement, having retired at age fifty-seven after thirty-seven years at work:

"I was born in Chicago, Illinois. I come from a family of eleven brothers and two sisters. Both parents were born in Italy. Waiting until my father got himself a job, my mother came to America in 1905, three years after he did. They settled here in Easton. In 1923, jobs weren't too plentiful, I guess, which is why they moved to Chicago. In that era, the mob started to take over. I asked my older brother how much he remembers of the city of Chicago—he was only twelve at the time. He told me of the time my dad and mom were working in the back of a grocery store, and the guy that owned the store was my godfather. When the mob came around to take protection money for the store, my father stood up to them and refused to pay, so they bombed the store. In another incident, the cops started shooting from the corner at one of the alleged members of the gang who was standing right on our front porch. They started to shoot at each other and one of the bullets went right through the windowpane, over my dad's head in the bedroom. Had he got up to look out the window, he probably would have been shot right there.

"So I guess they figured it was no place to raise a family, so they moved back to Easton. I was two and a half years old then. I went to Easton schools. My parents were from the southern part of Italy. I was there in the war. Yeah, I can talk Italian, but when you don't have the older people to talk to, you forget it. I was president of the Castel Society Club here in Easton in 1964. The people were mostly from Sicily. I was vice president of the social club and of the regular lodge. Sundays I would go there in the afternoons. Some came over on the same boat with my mom, and some with my dad. I used to play an Italian card game of Boss. . . .

"After high school, I started to work in Bethlehem Steel in '42, left for the service in '43, then came back to work for them again in '48. I started in the Saucon Heat Treatment, then went on to the Alloy Department. When I came back from the war, I was placed in the same department, then transferred to the Saucon beam yards. That's where I retired from.

"What led to my retirement was my wife's stroke. She's recovered, but at the time I had no idea what the future held. I figured that I had put in enough time to get out and I could keep my head above water with the pension I got (before I could collect Social Security).

"Retirement gives you more freedom, a chance to do things around the house that you want to do. You've got the time to take in some travels. When we had the extended vacation plan, my wife was working. I'd get my thirteen weeks, and I'd be stuck in the house when she couldn't get off work. Eleven out of the thirteen I couldn't go anywhere with her because she could only get off two weeks at a time.

"I had a friend that did the same thing. He sat down and figured out what his bills would be, what taxes he'd have to pay, and decided that he had enough to stay above board. Of course, he went voluntarily, but the company offered him a sweetener, a couple hundred dollars a month more on top of the regular pension, but that stops as soon as he hits sixty-two. No, I didn't get a sweetener when I left. There were about twenty who left even earlier than me and they didn't have a sweetener either.

"I could find a job now, but I'm not interested in working again. I didn't take a pension to go out and work for $3.25 or $3.65 an hour, because if I wanted to work I would have stayed in Bethlehem Steel until I was sixty-five. I had the option to stay on.

"Negative things about retirement are that sometimes you get bored, especially in the evenings. In the daytime, you can always find something to occupy your mind. But generally, in the evenings you experience a period of restlessness. I usually work in the backyard in the spring and summer. Sometimes the neighbors ask me for some help. Yeah, I belong to clubs, service organizations like the VFW, but even there they don't really have anything for members to go to and enjoy themselves. No social functions you can attend to enjoy yourself.

"My two children live nearby; my daughter lives up the street, and the other, my oldest, is in the area somewhere—we don't hear from him. You know how kids are: they make up their own minds. They don't care, one way or another. He's 38 years old. But we have six grandchildren, and we see them quite often.

"Generally, we go down to Myrtle Beach, South Carolina, in our motor home during the winter for two months. We usually come back in March. During the summer, if we're not on the road, we have a place up in the mountains, the Poconos, where we go to a trailer camp. We spend our summer weekends there. That's another relaxing part of retirement life—getting away from the humdrum.

"Well, I would say the majority of the men who retired came to accept it. A few, after they got out, missed the monetary value of a job. So on that basis, they felt like they should have been still working. Of course, your house is paid for and the kids are on their own, but for men in their fifties whose kids are still in school, or their wives aren't working, it could be a rough course. The most important thing that makes retirement manageable, though, is your health. I'm thankful for that."

The Determinants of Retirement

The term "retirement," as referring to withdrawal from employment, hardly surfaced during the nineteenth century. Only military or naval personnel were stipulated to be "retired." Paid work was always the norm for any able adult of whatever age after the Industrial Revolution. However, the notion of retirement gained momentum in the 1930s as a result of the need to distribute employment among as many workers as possible during the Great Depression. Still, as the work ethic was so much part of the saga of American life, workers were reluctant to leave employment. For example, according to one study, as late as 1951, steel workers felt really justified in retiring only if their health was impaired.[14] With the widening of Social Security in connection with the Great Society of Lyndon B. Johnson and the discovery that most retirees actually *liked* being retired (as long as they were reasonably healthy), retirement became a highly respectable option.

The ultimate meaning of retirement will be the focus of the chapters ahead, but at this point we note that in one context it represents a kind of *income transfer*. People reaching their sixties have for several decades been paying into Social Security and possibly other pension systems and now want to draw upon that and other resources. In fact, 90 percent of retirees draw on Social Security, 66 percent tap other assets, and 35 percent have a secondary pension, usually from their principal employer. Nearly a third of the upper-aged live on all three of these sources, and most on at least two, even though Social Security remains for most the basic ingredient.

As a consequence of our total pension system the stereotype of upper age as an economic disaster is something of the past. Indeed, whereas 36 percent of the elderly population were classified as living in poverty in 1967,[15] only 13 percent of retirees fall below the poverty line today, just below the average for the total population.[16] (It is significant that 20 percent of children are below the poverty threshold; however, children don't vote—retirees do!) The new affluence of the "third age" is revealed in still another statistic: the average income of all family units over age sixty-five rose beyond the rate of inflation by 55 percent between 1967 and 1984. Cutbacks in federal programs since 1980, however, are beginning to be seen in a slight increase in the percentage of elderly living below poverty level in the 1990s.

We may reduce our earnings after we leave our years of work, but Social Security, pensions, investments, and often an inheritance from a deceased parent may leave us economically as well off as or even better than before, with mortgages, college education of the children, and other expenses of adulthood becoming mere memories. In other words, the total effect of the Social Security system—at least for the decade of the 1980s—has been to perpetuate the distinction in income between more affluent and less affluent individuals as they move from the middle into the late years.[17] In retirement, as through most of the life cycle, women are twice as likely as men to be found in the poverty group, and minority groups are more than three times as likely as whites to suffer from want. In essence, from a financial point of view, retirement does not change one's relative "place" in the structure of income adequacy; white males continue to be quite well off, whereas women and minority group members continue to struggle.

Aspects of Retirement

Retirement assumes different forms. It can be approached objectively or subjectively, that is, how society or how the individual perceives it. It can begin early, on time, or late. It can be voluntary or mandatory. It can be partial or complete. We may choose it freely or be forced into it by poor health or by being laid off. Consequently, the distinction between voluntary and involuntary retirement is arbitrary, except when one is laid off by the employer. In most instances people retire because of a number of pushes and pulls. They are driven by the mandates or incentives offered by an employer, the state of their health, the need for release from tension, the desire for change, and perhaps a new set of activities, including a second career. They may choose to move from one kind of work to another, or from full-to part-time work. With all these variations, it is difficult to know exactly who should be classified as retired and who shouldn't be!

Throughout the life cycle we are operating under two sets of influences. One is the *structural,* namely society, the work setting, its rewards and pressures, the marketability of our skills. The other is the *individual,* that is, personality traits, goals, responsibilities, and definition of the situation. Among the structural factors are the following:

Economic. As implied above, the economic climate has considerable impact on the options we have. An inflationary cycle makes nearly everyone uneasy and tends to delay retirement. An economic reversal, whether for society as a whole or a given industry, results in layoffs, disproportionately directed toward the older and higher-paid worker.

The security of pension plans has come under increasing scrutiny. The ever-expanding demand on the Social Security system has worried some observers, especially those who look forward to the twenty-first century. A greater anxiety recently emerged when insurance companies were no longer considered as safe as they once were. Many retirees, actual and potential, were frightened by the threatened bankruptcy of the Executive Life Insurance Company in the spring of 1991, which puts pension funds at great risk.[18] These developments can hardly fail to affect one's preparations for—or concerns about—retirement.

Occupational. Generally, retirement is most desired by the manual worker, and least by the white-collar and professional worker. Consequently, blue-collar workers retire earlier.[19] However, the manual worker may be driven back to employment by the need for more income; the professional or managerial may return to the workplace because he or she finds it more exciting and/or his or her skills are desired. Others may "retire," only to shift to a different type of job, consultancy, or partial retirement that combines leisure with a reduced work load.

Gender. Women traditionally have retired before men, and most Western governments make a sex distinction in the retirement age. The difference in ages at retirement is compounded by the fact that husbands are on the average two to three years older than their wives. Moreover, recent decisions to remove more highly paid males from the work force have operated in the direction of men preceding their wives into retirement. In these instances most women prefer to wait until they are at the age in which they may receive the maximum in retirement benefits before retiring.[20] Because they are expected to outlive their spouse, women are more concerned about inflation endangering their future benefits.

Other structural factors include age, ethnic background, residential area—such as urban versus rural—religious affiliation, voluntary organizations, and type of employer—large versus small, private versus governmental. These factors will enter into our discussion in future chapters.

Individual, or subjective, factors involve the life experiences of the individual, whether values, attitudes, or simply fate:

Health. Research findings reflect the influence of health on decisions to retire. Illness becomes a major determinant of how long one chooses to remain economically active. According to one study, 12 percent of retirements are induced by poor health. Many older studies seem to show retirement itself having negative effects on health (and increased death rates!). People who have to retire because they are ill are more likely to be ill or die sooner than those whose health did not push them to end their employment.

The Time Dimension. The timing of retirement grows out of the person's sense of timing. One study finds that persons in middle age tend to make their first plans about retirement fifteen years before it happens. Hence, by age forty-eight to fifty, certain financial arrangements are made. These decisions are inevitably shaped by a number of other events happening in the person's life. The time factor also may operate after retirement. There seems to be a sense of elation for many retirees in the first months after leaving work. After the first year, that is, from the thirteenth to the eighteenth month, a letdown appeared in overall satisfaction in at least one study.[21] Robert Atchley proposes that people move through five stages following retirement: *honeymoon,* as they feel relief after the stress or monotony of the job;

disenchantment, when the halo effect of the liberation wears off; *re-orientation,* when options are reassessed; *stability,* as they settle in on various retirement roles; and *termination,* if they return to work or when illness or disability becomes a major preoccupation.[22] We should make it clear, though, that others have found little evidence of these "stages," and even Atchley makes it clear that only some retirees experience all or even most of these phases.

Values and Attitudes. Other factors influencing the timing of retirement are the views potential retirees have about work and leisure. Those who have a positive attitude toward work feel good about themselves and will remain in the work force despite a wide range of inducements. Correspondingly, those who feel that leisure is a just reward for working will seriously consider the first offer that allows them to retire without undue financial concerns. Other values play a part in the decision to retire; even general optimism or pessimism will set the tone for deciding whether to embrace the future or cling to the current situation, even if neither is completely to one's liking.

Early versus "On-Time" Retirement

The focus of our study is the trend toward early retirement, which is generally thought of as prior to the age of sixty-five. So fashionable has been this trend that articles have appeared in a number of publications, and an entire section of a 1989 *Wall Street Journal* (which cited a preliminary report of our study, among others) was devoted to this topic. As implied above, the phenomenon of early retirement tells something of the wealth of our postindustrial society, even though its members do not share equally in its economic assets.

Variations of early retirement include *partial* or *gradual* retirement, especially in the white-collar, managerial, and professional world. Likewise, *flexible* retirement suggests that employees have the final choice as to when they leave the workplace. These options all stand in contrast to mandatory retirement or a relatively fixed age for one's exit.

Also, in discussing early retirement we should always be careful to remember to ask, "Early for whom? Early by what standard?" Early retirement can be defined chronologically by relating to age sixty-five, but by that criterion the majority of retirements are early ones, making this age standard rather outdated. Alternately, some people who retire in their fifties are *not* retiring early, if by early we mean earlier than they expected or wanted it to be. Some who retire after sixty-five may still be early if they expected to work longer. In fact, one worker who took early retirement at age eighty-one in response to a recent state of Connecticut plan, which was studied by one of the authors, felt his retirement was "on time."[23]

Several studies give us a profile of early retirement. However, individual variations far outweigh any generalization. In a sample of early retirees (defined by chronological age) from three corporations, Dean Morse and Susan Gray found three-fourths of the technical personnel and middle managers feeling that their retirement came at the right time, one fifth "too soon," and 3 percent "too late."[24] Furthermore, those who took early retirement did not necessarily think of it as either permanent or complete retirement; employment options were available. However, a third of the blue-collar workers were frustrated by not being given adequate lead time. In addition, there was the disappointment of reduced income, faltering health, and lack of contact with their peers. Anxiety about medical bills was acute.[25] As many retired in the early 1970s, they were caught in the inflationary cycle of that decade. Still, most were more positive than negative about their retirement.

The most far-reaching analysis of retirement was made under the auspices of the Center for the Study of Aging and Human Development at Duke University. The research involved a number of studies, in addition to those made at Duke. They involved longitudinal monitoring of samples over a number of years, that is, studying the same people across time. These studies found structural factors like socioeconomic status and the occupation itself to have more weight in predicting when an individual might retire than his or her health or attitudes. In other words, adequacy of income and job satisfaction or dissatisfaction would determine when one is a candidate for early retirement.[26] At the same time, compulsory early retirement has negative consequences, especially when it involves markedly reduced income. Early retirees who are most likely to return to work are males, the self-employed, and those without pensions or other financial resources. It is a reflection on our society that minority group members generally find less trauma on retirement, as they are accustomed to a disadvantaged position. Or they may just feel escape from unpleasant work is a relief.

We return to the question of policy decisions. It seems that if society wants to reduce early retirement it should find the means of making the job more attractive, improve health conditions, including adequate medical insurance, and reduce the "sweeteners" or economic incentives to retire early. And, if society decides to slow down retirement beyond the normal retirement age, mandatory retirement and discrimination against older workers should be ended.[27] Moreover, programs designed to promote freedom of options could be directed toward blue-collar workers, as they are the most vulnerable to financial stress.

For most of us the principal task in preparing for retirement is calculating our future financial standing. Consequently, it is no surprise that white-collar, professional, and managerial men and women are the most successful in charting their course.[28] A number of companies offer assistance in planning for retirement in addition to giving financial incentives for early retirement, leaving the initiative and the decisions in the hands of the potential retiree. Unfortunately, he or she often finds constraints, financial or otherwise, in making plans for this new phase of the life cycle.

There is no final answer to the question of how we can adequately plan our retirement. Generally, white-collar workers and professionals seem to be more successful in their planning—what one investigator called the "dual economy" of the white-collar–blue-collar distinction.[29]

According to previous research, two-thirds of retirees are satisfied with their new status.[30] This ratio has risen as retirement has become more acceptable and attractive and in our fortunate society often can be started at a younger age, when one is more vigorous. In one national survey, the ability to adjust one's roles and relationships to others, active involvement in organizations and the community, and positive feelings about oneself are favorable to adjustment in retirement.[31] Successful retirement brings into play other factors: Is one psychologically ready for retirement? What has been the work experience? How does one view the aging process? What does leisure mean to the person? These all must be viewed in the context of finances, health, and marital and family situation.

The Research Design

The study that forms the basis for much of what we shall discuss emerged out of the awareness of the retrenchment of local industry, especially steel, in the Lehigh Valley (Allentown, Bethlehem, and Easton) of Pennsylvania, with its population of some 600 thousand. It was decided that a questionnaire and interview study were essential means of determining how the individuals were faring in early retirement, especially those in the middle to upper rank of occupations.

During the planning of the research, several factors became primary in the construction of the questionnaire: age at retirement, type of work, timing of retirement—early (before age sixty-five) or on time—length of the decision-making process, the retirement procedure and the last day of employment, number of years in the position and with the employer. No less crucial were other questions: Did the employee or management initiate the retirement? How difficult—or easy—was the retirement? How did it relate to preferred retirement age? With questions such as these we wanted to look more at both the structural and individual factors we have noted earlier.

We were also interested in measuring reactions following retirement. For instance, how did retirement change the individual? How does the person fill in his or her time? What new experiences, attitudes, insights, and activities emerge? How does the retiree perceive the future? How has the family adjusted? In addition were background variables, such as marital status, presence of children, educational level, religious affiliation, and residential setting.

In order to secure a sample, announcements were made in the press and on radio. These notices indicated that the focus was on early retirement, especially among upper-level technical and white-collar personnel; consequently, the 115 volunteers who completed the questionnaire were largely of that background. Of these 115 we interviewed eighty-seven retirees (30 percent of whom were women) plus twenty-seven spouses. The average age was sixty-three at the time of the interview (1986–87), and the average age at retirement was fifty-nine. Moreover, we reinterviewed twenty-two of these interviewees in 1990–91 to observe any changes. And in order to extend the scope of our sample we added twenty-five interviewees, whose ages ranged from sixty-one to eighty-one.

We chose an essentially white-collar group for our focus partly because many of the early retirement packages were directed toward that component of the work force and partly because other researchers had looked more at blue-collar occupations so as to examine the effects of income loss. As a result, those in our sample were less likely than those of other studies to have financial problems as a direct result of retirement.

The details of the research methods and the sample are described in Appendix A. Both the questionnaires and the interviews provide an intriguing set of data, which forms the contents of this book. For example, Part II explores the world of their work and other forces that become the basis of retirement. How do they look back on their careers? We also analyze how the retirees make an adjustment to their new universe. How do they manage their finances? What is the best and worst about retirement?

Part III turns to the specific kinds of adjustments retirees make. What new activities do they find or create? How do they now relate to their spouses? Their adult children? Do they keep their old friends or find new ones? We then turn to the question of how the retirees look at the world. How does personality affect the life course, including the later years?

Finally, in Part IV we see what kind of advice they would give to those who are about to enter retirement. We also discuss the implications of this study to the meaning of retirement.

References

1. David H. Fischer, *Growing Old in America* (New York: Oxford University Press, 1977).

2. Bruce Gratton, "The New History of the Aged," in David Van Tassel and Paul N. Stearns (eds.), *Old Age in a Bureaucratic Society* (Westport, CT: Greenwood Press, 1986), pp. 3–29.
3. William Graebner, *A History of Retirement* (New Haven, CT: Yale University Press, 1980), pp. 236–237.
4. John Macnicol and Andrew Blaikie, "The Politics of Retirement," in Margot Jeffreys (ed.), *Growing Old in the Twentieth Century* (London: Routledge, 1989), pp. 21–42.
5. Bob Baker, "Economy Puts Early Retirement Out of Favor," Allentown *Morning Call*, September 16, 1990, p. D1.
6. Alan Pifer and Lydia Bronte, *Our Aging Society: Paradox and Promise* (New York: Norton, 1986).
7. Timothy M. Smeeding, "Economic Status of the Elderly," in Robert H. Binstock and Linda K. George (eds.), *Handbook of Aging and the Social Sciences*, 3d ed. (San Diego, CA: Academic Press, 1990), pp. 392–397.
8. Stephan F. Gohmann and Robert L. Clark, "Retirement Responses to Social Security Changes," *Journal of Gerontology*, 44, S218–225, 1989.
9. Eric R. Kingson and John B. Williamson, "Generational Equity or Privatization of Social Security," *Society*, September-October 28(6), 38–41, 1991.
10. Elaine Cumming and William E. Henry, *Growing Old: The Process of Disengagement* (New York: Basic Books, 1961).
11. Robert J. Havighurst, Bernice Neugarten, and Sheldon S. Tobin, "Disengagement and Patterns of Aging," in Bernice L. Neugarten (ed.), *Middle Age and Aging* (Chicago: University of Chicago Press, 1968), pp. 161–172.
12. Robert C. Atchley, "Continuity Theory of Normal Aging," *Gerontologist*, 29, 183–189, 1989.
13. Virginia Richardson and Keith M. Kilty, "Adjustment to Retirement: Continuity vs. Discontinuity," *International Journal of Aging and Human Development*, 33, 151–169, 1991.
14. Philip Ash, "Pre-retirement Counseling," *Gerontologist*, 6, 97–99, 1966.
15. Malcolm H. Morrison, *The Economics of Retirement* (New York: Van Nostrand Reinhold, 1982).
16. Greg J. Duncan and Ken R. Smith, "The Rising Affluence of the Elderly: How Far, How Fair, and How Frail?" In W. Richard Scott and Judith Blake (eds.), *Annual Review of Sociology* (Palo Alto, CA: Annual Reviews, 1989), pp. 261–289.
17. Cary S. Kart, Charles F. Longino, and Steven G. Ullman, "Comparing the Economically Advantaged and the Pension Elite: 1980 Census Profiles," *Gerontologist*, 29, 745–749, 1989.

18. Janice Castro, "Is Your Pension Safe?" *Time*, June 3, 1991, pp. 42–43.
19. Olivia S. Mitchell, Phillip B. Levine, and Silvano Pozzebon, "Retirement Differences by Industry and Occupation," *Gerontologist*, 28, 545–551, 1988.
20. Lois B. Shaw, "Retirement Plans of Middle-Aged Married Women," *Gerontologist*, 24, 154–160, 1984.
21. David J. Ekerdt, R. Bossé, and S. Levkoff, "An Empirical Test for Phases of Retirement: Findings from the Normative Aging Study," *Journal of Gerontology*, 40, 95–101, 1985.
22. Robert C. Atchley, *The Sociology of Retirement* (New York: Schenkman, 1976).
23. Thomas O. Blank, "Retirement in Connecticut: A Study of State Employees," Travelers Center for Aging, colloquium presentation, April 15, 1991.
24. Dean W. Morse and Susan H. Gray, *Early Retirement—Boon or Bane?* (Totowa, NJ: Rowman & Allanheld, 1980), p. 21.
25. Dean W. Morse, Anna B. Dutka, and Susan H. Gray, *Life after Early Retirement* (Totowa, NJ: Rowman & Allanheld, 1983), p. 135.
26. Erdman B. Palmore *et al.*, *Retirement: Causes and Consequences* (New York: Springer, 1985), pp. 28–29.
27. *Ibid.*, p. 167.
28. William A. Campione, "Predicting Participation in Retirement Programs," *Journal of Gerontology*, 43, 591–595, 1988.
29. Toni M. Casalanti, "Participation in a Dual Economy and Adjustment to Retirement," *International Journal of Aging and Human Development*, 26, 13–24, 1988.
30. Robert C. Atchley, "Adjustments to Loss of Job at Retirement," *Aging and Human Development*, 6, 17–27, 1975.
31. Elizabeth Mutran and Donald C. Reitzes, "Retirement, Identity and Well-Being," *Journal of Gerontology*, 36, 733–740, 1981.

Part II

Retirement as a Process

Chapter 2

Retirement

Push or Pull?

"I was retired, or I was terminated, or however you want to put it in order to make it polite, officially at the end of February 1984. I turned fifty-five at the time. It was the best thing that ever happened to me. It was not a voluntary retirement. Let me fill in a little bit that might help you understand. I'm different from most of the others. Back in 1958 I was in charge of the new model development at Mack Trucks, and a man who had just finished his sixty-fifth anniversary and his last day of work died of a heart attack. I came home and said to my wife, 'I am not going to work until age sixty-five and die at work.' It really shook me. I said we're going to plan now to retire at fifty-five, and so at age twenty-nine, we started planning already to retire at fifty-five. So we were putting away money, saving, investing. When I retired (by then I was working for a large tool company) I had designed and built a new research center for the company—a two and a half million dollar building. I was working about seventy hours a week from the beginning of March until the end of September and I hadn't had a vacation. So I told the boss, who was vice president, that my wife and I wanted to take a vacation the end of October. What happened was that on October the first they transferred me from Research to Chief Engineer—yet I still had to supervise the research. He said, 'Well, there's some things you have to do before you can go on vacation.' On October twenty-eighth he listed seven jobs he expected done immediately.

"On October thirtieth, 'Walt, where are you? Where is the stuff I gave you?' 'Bill,' I said, 'It's impossible to get that done; we've had this vacation planned.' He said, 'I want you to come in right away, work tonight, work this weekend, and work until you get done.' I said, 'Dr. Zabriski, if there's no other way to do it, you can consider that I quit, if that's what it takes, but I am leaving on vacation right now. I've been really putting out a lot of time and work, and that's it.' So he asked me if that was the way that I wanted it, I affirmed, we hung up the phone, and I left on vacation.

"I came to the realization that my work was terminated. One thing that's very good with my retirement is that I have medical coverage for my wife and me for the rest of our lives. I get what would be considered a very small monthly retirement check, but it's something.

"I really believe that the company made out worse than I did. They're going through a bad time right now. In fact, the company is being sold, and a lot of the old timers are worried about what's going to happen. I think they have more of a challenge now. The business has been going downhill and I'm just kind of glad that I'm out of there. If there was anything that I probably can honestly say I miss it's the banquet. Every time that someone that I knew would retire or was separated, I was in charge of organizing his banquet or party. They never had one for me. That's probably the only thing that I really miss. The thing along with that was the way the separation went. I had a lot of close friends in the company. They'd come over and they wouldn't know how to talk to me or whether to talk to me. I really miss a lot of these people on a friendship basis. Yet the ones that were not quite as close with me at work, who were not in the same department, but who were friends otherwise, those I'm still fairly close with. But with the ones in the research department, more or less, I probably am hurt that the friendships and the closeness that we had has disappeared. Recently, on a visit to the plant, one of my friends came up to me and said, 'I've wanted to talk to you ever since this happened, but I don't know what to say. I think it was so wrong what they did.' I assured him that I'm happier now and everything worked out great. A couple of other people in the research department saw me walking through and around the area and came out to talk to me. They don't look happy, and I think part of what happened, due to the continued laying off of people, is that they don't feel secure to say they were my friends.

"Probably in the back of my mind I thought I could do consulting. But as I said, I don't think when I turned fifty-five that I would have had enough foresight or guts to quit a $45,000 a year job to go into consulting. So the fact that the decision was made for me worked nice. I still was on the payroll for three months after quitting, and during that time, some of this consulting actually started. Now that first year and second year I had a lot of time as far as consulting was concerned. I almost felt guilty a lot of times for sitting home and not doing anything. Last year I ran for county commissioner since I thought I had a lot of time to give. That started in the spring election, and by the time that fall election came around I told my wife that I hoped I wouldn't win because 'I'm afraid I won't have the time if I do.'

"My feelings after the termination were very mixed, obviously. Perhaps I felt surprised and frustrated a little bit, if not angry. But due to a strong religious background and faith in God, I have always felt that what happens God directs, and if I don't understand what is happening now, hold tight and things will work out well. I was very busy, and I find that whenever I get frustrated or angry about something, being busy takes my mind off of it and time goes by faster and things clear up.

"The best part of my retirement is that I can schedule my own work, do what I want to do, at the rate I want to do it, and therefore really enjoy what I do. I have not gone on a single consulting job that I haven't come home with much praise and self-satisfaction and knowledge that I had done a good job for industry. Another good thing about retirement is the time I get to spend with my family. We took our grandsons to Niagara Falls, and they had a ball. They're four and seven. They were good travelers. We've always traveled all the years we've been married, but now we're traveling more. We're also involved in more now. We like to help people. We are involved in church; we're volunteer staff over at the Presbyterian home near where Central Park was. I'm president of the Allentown Rescue Mission; she's vice president of the Ladies Auxiliary. I'm executive secretary of the Allentown area Sunday School Association and a volunteer driver for the cancer society. There's a lot of church activity and civic group activities between the both of us. If was funny, in my campaign for county commissioner, a flier listed all the activities that I was involved in, and somebody took one of the fliers and wrote on it. They didn't believe that I was involved in all the things listed; they thought it was a lie. They said that if I did do everything that I said I did, then I wouldn't have time to be a county commissioner. I've learned one thing with that little bit of political advice: people are very prejudiced and bitter, or have their minds set on things that they don't know anything about, especially politically. I have also gotten to the point where I probably feel that the newspapers are more of a hindrance to the solution of the world's problems than they are a help."

*   *   *

The decision to retire has hardly the intensity of the choice—or the promise—of a career or of when and whom to marry, but like these other episodes, retirement constitutes a major step in the life cycle, and one that only recently has become expected and planned for. In the case of Walter Koch, whom we have just heard, it was precipitated by a manager who could have stepped out of a previous century. Because of his resilience and ability, termination with the company had a happy ending for Walter. It is hardly so for all retirees.

As with all major changes in the life cycle, retirement arouses hesitation and fear of the unknown, even though it also offers hope and excitement. Rev. Don Siegfried put it wisely: "When facing retirement one has mixed emotions, as when facing any dramatic change in life, for example—marriage." The decision may be a preoccupation over a number of years—or over a period of weeks. For several of our respondents the decision came in a matter of days or even hours. As with most critical points in one's life, social background, deep-seated attitudes and values, and how one sizes up a given situation all come into play.

When trying to understand the effects of such a major event, it is important to consider both external and internal factors. On the one hand, there are *structural* influences: age, timing, the hurdles of potential income, health, the family situation, work conditions. On the other hand are the more personal, *subjective* ones: attitudes toward one's work, including the thought of leaving it and feelings about what one leaves behind: What are my plans for the future? What am I giving up? How do I feel about leisure? How do I think about the approach of old age? In other words, what does retirement mean to the individual? Specifically, what are the pushes and pulls leading to retirement? How do we perceive the work situation? What do we know of the experiences of those who have opted for retirement? No less important are the source and manner of the initiation of the retirement request, the resolution of finances, and the roles of the employer, agencies, family, and friends in preparing us for this event. At any phase of the life cycle we are likely to work through a number of decisions: What do I have in the bank? What are the possibilities for part-time employment? How shall I keep busy, and what will my friends think? And so on.

All these considerations must be viewed in the context of the individual. According to observers, three questions regarding retirement seem evident: (1) financial adequacy, (2) health problems, and (3) combinations of various factors.[1] As of 1980, about 40 percent of all retired workers left the labor force involuntarily because of compulsory provisions, 15 percent because of disability, and 45 percent chose retirement voluntarily.[2] There is almost always the debate between the planned and the actual date of retirement. Perhaps 60 percent are leaving the work scene within a year of the date they had originally planned, more often earlier than later. Since the mid-1980s the planning of retirement has been marked by a certain degree of uncertainty.[3] An increasing number of employees have been encouraged into early retirement, as mandatory age limits have been eliminated. Rather than facing the "inevitable" at a specific chronological age, the employee looks to his or her options with the approach of upper middle age, and consequently may calculate the mix of pushes and pulls over a long period of time to choose when the time is right. Still, the retirement timing may, in fact, be dependent on a particular outside stimulus, like a "Golden Parachute" offer, a package that is too good to refuse.

At the same time, there is no evidence that the anticipation of retirement benefits increases the rate of retirement.[4] For instance, the more generous provisions of the Social Security system in the early 1970s did not noticeably induce early retirement—at least at that time—even though the system permitted the elderly higher increases than wage earners received in this period of inflation.[5]

Whatever the circumstances, our findings confirm those of other studies; that is, retirement involves a number of intricately inter-woven variables.[6] Most of our sample had worked in an industrial setting (and usually in the same company) for nearly three decades. Most (58 percent) reported they had been very satisfied with their employment; another 26 percent were "somewhat satisfied"; and only 15 percent were dissatisfied. As we shall see, the reasons for dissatisfaction were long hours, psychological and physical strain, changes in the work load and process, changes in personnel, and perception of the younger fellow workers' desire to assume their position. Again, these complaints represent a minority of our sample but were acutely expressed in the questionnaire and even more in-tensely during the interviews.

The Mystery of Motives

Whenever we examine motives and perceptions we are always caught in the quagmire of cross-purposes and conflicting urges. We are also aware that the public motives are not always in accord with the private ones. In the days when the work ethic loomed, retirees often gave "health" as their reason for retiring, when in reality it was the desire for leisure that promoted their retirement.[7] In other words, rationalization also applies to the act of retirement.

The participants in our study were asked to check a list of reasons for their retirement and to rank them in importance. Their responses are seen in Table 2-1. Five principal motives are apparent: the pension system, health, work stress, pursuit of leisure, and finances. A considerable number of other items were listed by at least one person, for example, an offer from another employer, wanting to become self-employed, finding a new career, concern for the security or advancement of other employees, and the desire to move to a different climate. It is significant that the motives represent a balan-cing between the *positive* (moving toward a goal) and *negative* (escap-ing a bad situation). In a sense, the individual is making a decision according to a *rewards/cost* formula.

Imagine sitting down and making four lists. List No. 1 is headed "What is good about work?" List No. 2 is headed "What is bad about my work?" Lists Nos. 3 and 4 are the positives and negatives about

Table 2-1. Motives for Retirement*

	Number checking as most important	Percent checking among top four
1. Attractiveness of pension program offered	24	49
2. Health concerns	14	33
3. Stress of work	12	43
4. Leisure opportunities	8	50
5. Personal financial situation	4	50
6. Nature of the job was changing	3	27
7. Mandatory age policy	6	7
8. No opportunity for advancement	2	14
9. Employer's financial situation	2	11
10. Family matters	2	8

*Based on questionnaire responses.

retirement as you expect or imagine them to be. Now that you have the four lists you can assign weights to each item. Even though you know these weights won't be too accurate, they can be enlightening. The negatives about your work and the positives of retirement are the "rewards" to be gained by retiring. These can be directly compared to the positives that will be missed when you retire and the possible negatives that may come along with retirement, which together are the costs of retirement. Let us give a not too untypical example:

Work
Positive
   The paycheck   20
   Feeling that I'm a useful member
     of society   5

Negative
  Long, hard hours   20
  An overbearing boss   10

Retirement
Positive
  Time to enjoy the leisure pursuits
    I've wanted   35
  Renovating the house   10
Negative
  Missing my friends at work   5
  Having an unstructured life   10
  Getting in the way of my spouse   10
  Waiting until my full pension begins   10

As we can see, the points favoring retirement total 75, whereas the points for not retiring are 60. Presumably the candidate opts for retirement, but he or she is likely to make further calculations and may come to the same conclusion or possibly a different one. No one pretends that the point system is very accurate, but it is one means of trying to objectify our situation and motives.

The reasons given by a particular retiree for his or her retirement are probably more complex than our above calculation would indicate. For instance, in Table 2-1 the difference between the two columns shows that although only eight in our sample consider "leisure opportunities" to rank as the single most important of the choices offered in the questionnaire, no less than 50 percent of the retirees place it among their four major reasons for retiring.

Likewise, in the informal setting of the interviews, the retirement decision is usually portrayed as a subtle combination of factors, professional and personal. For example, Ruth Schuler, a former psychiatric social worker for a state mental institution, gave her explanation for retiring:

"I had given it some thought. I didn't think that I really wanted to quit working; I've always enjoyed working. I just kept thinking, 'I don't want to retire,' because I just could not see myself at half-work. I used to say to myself, 'I don't want to go to work today, but if I were staying home, how much fun would that be?' But then, about a year before I retired a year ago last June, I got thinking maybe I was ready. I got an estimate on what I would receive from my state pension and I decided that 'yes, I could do that.' It was almost my take-home pay. I thought I could manage on that and that there's more to life than getting up and going to work every day. I decided I wanted to retire and that my daughter deserved it because I have always worked. I had taken three months off when she was born and then had gone right back. Once I made my mind up, that was it. I never looked back. It was the right thing. Financially, I could do it and emotionally I was ready for it. I didn't do a whole lot of planning for it. I wasn't telling anybody, but I was tired of my job; I was getting very restless; the job was no longer very appealing."

Her adult daughter added this interpretation:

"Mother would sit with the calculator figuring our her pension. It would drive me crazy, and I would say, 'For God's sake, if you hate your job . . . ' It was really getting to be a problem. They were tending to hire young people with education but no experience, and she's sitting there with experience. And these kids would really irritate her, the things that they would do, such as, the young supervisors would not touch any of the patients. So my mother and the friend she worked with would be 'lugging' these people, sometimes three on each arm, some blind, some autistic. So, she wasn't very happy that last year. She would come home upset and I would think, 'Oh, here we go again.'"

In these remarks we see the combination of several forces: the overlap of irritation with changes on the job with the arrival of younger, less experienced personnel; the recognition of financial adequacy; a desire for more time with family; and preference for other activities.

As noted in Table 2-1, stress was in third place in the motives prompting retirement. However, in the interviews, when the respondents poured out more or less spontaneously their motives for choosing or accepting retirement, stress of work took first place for thirty-six of the eighty-seven retirees (41 percent). One-fourth (twenty-one) spoke of health, being laid off was mentioned by fourteen, and leisure opportunities by twelve. In the interviews only eleven retirees saw fit to mention the attractiveness of their pension plan, whereas it appeared as a primary motive in the questionnaire.

Overload in the Work Setting

As we shall see in succeeding chapters, much of the drive to retire arises from the thought of a new leisure. Yet, by adding together the several sources of discomfort on the job listed on the questionnaire, we see that 29 percent ranked negative rather than positive reasons for retiring—that is, the several sources of *stress*—as their primary reason for retirement, and over four-fifths ranked them among the top four reasons. This finding is hardly novel. In a study by Morse, Dutka, and Gray, 30 percent of their blue-collar sample of 894 retirees named pressure and treatment of older workers as a major factor in the retirement decision.[8] Also, in a sample of professionals, alienation and stress played a conspicuous role in the retirement decision, high school teachers being particularly affected.[9] Also, according to the present study, stress definitely applies to middle management and the professions.

As stated, the impact of on-the-job stress became more evident during the interviews than on the written questionnaires, as subjects could elaborate on their feelings. Over 40 percent of our retirees spontaneously spoke of feeling considerable stress in their last several years of employment. This tells us something about how white-collar employees perceive conditions in the work place. Similarly, in a 1987 Gallup poll of one thousand adult workers, 45 percent cited pressures on the job as their reason for retirement. However, in our study this tendency is of special concern, inasmuch as our sample of men and women were employed in sought-after, high levels of responsibility. Even many who said they "loved" their work explained that toward the end of their employment the work situation became less comfortable, more troublesome, threatening, or disillusioning. Among the specific descriptions of perceived conditions (in descending order of importance according to the interviews) are (1) pressures from above (layoffs of others or overload of work) and from below (the sense of encroachment from younger employees breathing down their necks), (2) politics on the job, (3) cues that bosses were dissatisfied, (4) drudgery, (5) fear of becoming passé or of being so perceived already, and (6) changes in the nature of the work situation (new bosses, new colleagues, new assignments, new organization, and low morale).

Some bitterness can be sensed in the following typical explanations selected from the interviews. From Chapter 1, we remember the case of Jim Zimmerman, who had twenty-three years with AT&T: "I must admit that for me the last two or three years really were trying. They weren't fulfilling. I don't understand yet why I was taken from some of the jobs, transferred, and then all of a sudden put on third shift." His experience is not unique. A biologist in a federal agency recalls the Nixon years as a "constant turnover of management personnel with counter-directives." Similar problems were voiced in other areas, such as the public schools: "a lack of leadership so I never knew where I stood as a teacher."

Charles McLean, an engineer at the Fuller Company who took early retirement at age fifty-seven after working twenty-six years, spoke of: "never-ending change in policy and little consideration of the human being." He had started at the bottom as a "helper" and union man and worked his way up through various levels to the position of "numerical control programmer." He cited three causes for his retirement: his health, seeing his father die of a heart attack at age sixty-seven after only two years of retirement, and his growing dissatisfaction with the attitude of new management. He saw these management problems not only in his own industry, but from talking to people in other workplaces:

"The new management knew nothing of my job, but they would give me an approximation of how long it would take to do the job—nowhere near long enough. It was unreal; you tolerate this and go along with it. All industry when they hire you pay you five dollars an hour and expect to get seven dollars worth. There was a day when there was gratitude and you enjoyed going to work, but not with the new philosophy, which I saw over the last seven years. The reason is not competition but incompetence. I have seen highly intelligent engineers with the company for thirty years replaced by cronies who were brought in by the new president, people who knew nothing whatsoever about the work. . . . Another thing that occurs is what has happened to a number of companies in this area—they are owned by conglomerates who in most cases come in, rape the companies, and then leave or sell them. They worked us six days a week and even tried to make us work on Sundays. The plant manager even said one day, "If you're not willing to work ten hours a day, seven days a week, shake my hand and we'll part friends." So that's just what I did."

Al Johnson, a former bank treasurer, retired at age fifty-eight partially because of poor health, found he was becoming "bored":

"Unfortunately, I came from a generation that thought the company was involved personally with each person and that only Madison Avenue types were cutthroats. But I found that the whole thing has now become that way. The one thing I'll pass on to anybody who will listen is—don't be loyal to the company. You see, the top-level management changes from time to time, so whatever relationships you have are changed. I think my generation had misplaced loyalties. Now I think that anytime you have an opportunity to move further along faster by taking a different job, all things being equal, don't let loyalty to your employer influence your decision."

Management, Layoffs, and Politics

Several in different ways expressed deeply felt criticisms of management in regard to the atmosphere in the workplace and the way the retirement process or event was handled, including such a simple thing as the *insensitivity of management* to one's work and loyalty, or for one's longtime service to the company, including overtime or special projects. This finding relates not too happily to a statement made by a Lehigh University professor of management, who is quoted as explaining in a seminar the employer–employee relationship thus: "The company requires an employee to fulfill a role. The employee expects salary, benefits, and a sense of pride and belonging in return. A social and psychological contract between the parties thus takes effect the day the employee joins the company."[10]

The interviews indicate that it is the rude breaking of this contract that hurts the person forced or persuaded into early retirement. The employer appears not to show a reciprocal sense of loyalty to the employee. In reality, management could be caught up in a shift in the economy. On this point, Ralph Small, a Ph.D. in electrical engineering, who was with Bell lab for over thirty years designing transistors and integrated circuits, said: "We were all encouraged to retire at sixty-five, even though the law said it should be seventy. It was clear that our work was being produced in Korea at a lower cost. We were offered a sweetener with the notion that if we didn't take retirement at that time our chances could be less favorable next year. And, after all, they could hire young technicians at half the price they were paying us."

Retirees from Bethlehem Steel were especially annoyed at the discrepancies they encountered. Retired manager Terry Jenkins said, "I can remember the many years I worked at Steel when people didn't have to retire, actually until about 1960 when they put in forced retirement." Michael Ritter, who was in personnel at Steel until he retired at age fifty-five, recalls:

"Indirectly, I found that many of the vice presidents and other upper executives could retire when they wanted and with very fat deals. It was a fairly well-kept secret. Such is the way things work in a corporate tyranny. Then came the days when we in personnel had to shuffle people around the different plants and sections. It was especially bad after the fabricating division was closed down. But the worst was yet to come. The bloodletting really got to you. Then I knew it would eventually come to me. There was an awful month of wondering, and then I said to myself, 'It's my turn.' It was an awful month of decision making. I was relieved when it was over. I simply saw too many injustices done. Of course, they were necessary, but the inequality of it all really bothered me."

Also, John Hines, who was pretty near the top himself, reflected on how a former president of Steel "received on retirement a much more plush health insurance policy than anyone else did." Indeed, the complaints of the middle-range executives were possibly more bitter than the complaints of those lower down the ladder. Still, other managers simply took a rather philosophical attitude. For example, Alan Adams retired in 1982, not because he had to, but because "I didn't want to see the end of the company."

Politics was the word used by several in a variety of occupations to describe distress in the workplace. It was the only reason that Carl Stouffer, a deputy warden of a county prison, could give for a shake-up by the state which demoted him to lieutenant, after nineteen years during which he often gave overtime on Saturdays without extra compensation. His indignant wife added, "That was a slap in the face. He hadn't done anything wrong. He's even worked when sick, never missed a day. I used to get so angry—he wouldn't stay home, he was so conscientious. And that's how they rewarded him!" He went on to say, "I would have liked to have another year to get in my twenty years, but it would have been awfully frustrating because you never knew when the axe would fall. In the beginning I liked my work; at the end it was drudgery."

Politics was a major problem for civil service administrator Willard Schulz in municipal government of Philadelphia:

"Around 1961 stuff began to get very political—lots of political interference. Then about 1982 they began to try to move me around. I was approaching fifty-five. The situation had become so political that it was very difficult for a person who is a professional administrator to maintain any sense of reasonableness in the kind of things that were going on. Decisions should be made the way the general community thinks, not for special interest groups. These groups became the real authority. Certain people get into politics for power; they get elected and reelected to get positions of authority to take care of a few people for favors."

Of course, it is difficult to separate the political climate from the usual interpersonal tensions on the job. As one engineer phrased the matter: "Somehow you know when to retire by the facial gestures of those around you!"

The Never-Ending Pressure

Overload for workers was frequently mentioned, as would be expected in this period of reductions in force and in cost. Bruce Shoemaker, a mailman for almost thirty years, took early retirement with a lowered pension because they "are pushing, pushing, pushing. Every time they'd add more territory onto my load and expect me to do it in the same amount of time. Though I enjoyed my work, it just snowballed. And I thought, 'I'm going to get out and enjoy myself while I can.' The old fellows I'd worked with for years were all getting out, and I felt I didn't need this; I might as well enjoy myself."

Work overload was also reported by Cliff Thomas, a supervisor at Bethlehem Steel, where layoffs were occurring:

"They said if enough didn't leave the company voluntarily (taking the early retirement incentive of half pay for twenty-one months, plus their pensions), they would have to reduce the force at their discretion. I chose not to be one of those. Ordinarily we were a two-man office but, when my boss retired a year before I did, he wasn't replaced. So I was doing maybe not quite double work—not quite, because the work load was being reduced. On days when you were busy you worked through lunch hour and a little overtime to get it done; after vacation you'd have twice as much because it wasn't being done by anybody else."

Computer programmer Jim Dowd, who was employed for twenty-eight years at Steel, took his retirement at age fifty after this harrowing experience:

"Gradually they told me to get out. One time, all of a sudden, they gave me an annual individual evaluation and I got very low grades. I was graded on things I had never been reprimanded about. Then they did something unusual; they said they were going to give me evaluations each of the next two months and see how I was doing. So I worked very hard, took work home, and I did really good work the next month—and again I got poor grades. And it dawned on me that maybe they were setting me up, getting the paperwork ready to look as if I weren't cutting the mustard any more. My lawyer agreed with me. 'They're going to lay you off one of these days and the paperwork will show that you can't do it any more. They'll show that they gave you three months to shape up and you didn't.'

"They were just going to put me out the door, a layoff with no benefits at all. But because I put in my application for retirement pay they decided three months later to give me my pension. Those three months were terrible, because they baited me with looking over my shoulder all the time, giving me tasks very difficult to do in the time allowed, hoping I'd blow my stack and become insubordinate so I could be fired for that. I did everything right, right up until the last minute. When I left, it wasn't nice—they came to me a day early, before the day they had scheduled, and said, 'You may go now.' They watched me clear out my desk and walked me out to the parking lot and took the sticker off my car. It was almost as though I were a criminal. They do that to most everybody, especially in computer work, who might be able to sabotage the files.

"I was happy because I didn't have to be there anymore but not happy about the way it ended. They just said, 'Okay, it's time to go,' and in about five minutes I was pushed out the door. During those three months, I couldn't believe that I was so sure that I wanted to get out, so positive about it. I was sick of the place. I got my retirement benefits, so I won."

And a chief clerk in a supermarket described stress in her workplace thus, after forty years at work: "It got to the point where it was very stressful at work. Others still there tell me to be glad I'm out. The management makes it harder for employees today. All they hire is part-time workers, no more full-time workers."

The machine setter Mario Moro, who retired at age sixty-one from the manufacture of microchips, described his conflicts in this way:

"I was tired of work, completely fed up with the work procedure. I just looked forward to retirement and the many things I wanted to do and didn't have time for while I worked. Once retired, it seemed as if working previously was just a big nightmare. The company treated me fine; if you treat someone fine they'll treat you fine, too. I just didn't like the stress involved with my work. I understand this prevails in all businesses today. Management just won't take any excuse. You can't get anywhere; your hands are tied. I was in charge of people and of very delicate machinery. It was very stressful. I had been working six to seven days a week. . . . The later years in industry got to be very much pressured. People in upper management, running the business, are college grads who have only the knowledge of books and not the experience, and you can't reason with them about problems. Because they have a better education they don't listen to you. Things don't get done; they just sit on a decision. Money and time are wasted. You can take just so much of that. . . . Also, I belong to the union but I don't sanction everything they do. For example, everything is seniority with them regardless of whether the person is qualified. I think that is terrible."

Separately interviewed, his wife's quick answer to why her husband retired early was "pressure—thirty-five years. Job pressure. He wasn't interested in doing it any more. He found people were just not so conscientious and he found that difficult to deal with. He felt his responsibility to support his son was now over and that he could afford to retire."

Nor was pressure from overload limited to industry or business. A suburban high school guidance director, for example, told how her responsibilities kept increasing: "But nothing was ever taken away and I didn't get any help. It was getting frustrating. The school district kept talking about money. I was one of the higher-paid employees and they could hire someone younger at a lower rate. I got the subconscious feeling that I was a heavy load on the district."

While it was overload for some, others saw the *decline in work load* as an ominous warning. For example, Matt Boyd, a coordinator for a government agency at Steel, saw the signs and decided to get out and into some other employment.

"They had gotten rid of quite a bundle of their employees, and literally the handwriting was on the wall. They had consolidated departments, they had dissolved departments, and it looked as if the Safety and Health Department was not going to survive. I felt it was in my best interest to get out and get my second career going before I hit the magic age of fifty and would not be wanted anymore. I had seen any number of people who had taken the so-called sweetener and it seemed as if those in their forties did fairly well in finding other work, but those who hit fifty had a real significant problem. So I got out and got into a second career as a consultant, because I wasn't going to survive in there."

But not all complaints about stress in the workplace were against higher-level personnel. For example, a former school psychologist, who retired fourteen years earlier at about age fifty-four, gave four reasons for his retirement: (1) he was tired of helping others make decisions; (2) a new principal in one of his three schools was harassing him, and his devoted secretary got married and left; (3) four members of his family had died of cancer at a fairly young age, leading him to think about his own chances; (4) a union "came in and started pressuring me to join or they'd see that I'd lose my salary differential above that of teachers. I'll tell you three words I used when I retired. I was disenchanted, disillusioned, and discouraged. The work had lost its savor."

Self-employed professionals tend to delay their retirement into the seventies or beyond, and they often convince their partners (or sons who have joined their practice) to permit a part-time involvement. But in time they, too, must give up. Nathan O'Hara, M.D., said, "At seventy-four I had had it. A seventy-hour work week plus professional meetings." Others have their own reasons for leaving. For dentist George Davis the decision was not difficult: "I had several reasons for quitting. Insurance rates were tripling. Also, government regulations such as disposal of waste, the AIDS epidemic with all that glove business, and worst of all, when patients began asking 'Would you mind if I scheduled my next appointment with your son?' "

The Financial Imperative

As each of us gets into the nitty-gritty of the retirement decision, the dollar sign becomes the big "If." There is the pencil-and-paper game as to Where will we be financially? What are our needs? Do the children still need help, or in a crunch would they help us? How much shall we have left for travel or a vacation home? Or eating out? Will either of us have to enter a nursing home?

Our sample stands in contrast to the national picture in regard to financial resources. In a national survey, 15 percent of households sixty-five and older had no income other than Social Security. Generally it is unmarried or widowed women and minority groups who suffer the most in these years.[11] The most secure appear to be married white men, and the least secure are widowed or deserted black women. As with most major decisions, a number of doubts enter our minds. As Don Siegfried noted in counseling one of his fellow ministers on life after retirement: "You cannot convince him that his expenses will be lower. Taxes will be less; professional expenses, his driving, books, clothing, all of these are going to be lower than they are now. I think he has too many grandiose ideas. I cannot convince him of this but it's true." After a severe illness, Don himself was tempted to retire in 1981 at the age of sixty, but said "no" for three reasons: "One, I was not yet eligible for Social Security—that's my most important reason; two, the people in my church had been very good to me and my wife, and I felt we owed it to them to go back if we could; and three, I was just not ready psychologically to do this. I had to prove to myself that I could go back and work. I was very happy doing what I was doing."

Generally the first question for the potential retiree is "Am I eligible for retirement?" The second is likely: "What will my pension check be?" The relationship between Social Security and the company pension (if there is one, and over 90 percent of our sample did have one) can be a complex one. Inevitably, the financial arrangements in early retirement may differ greatly from company to company and within the same company from one year to the next. Or the payoff can vary with rank. At least, the plant employees at Steel whom we interviewed felt that they had a less favorable settlement than did the managers, who in many instances left before the "depths" had been reached, when interest rates were close to 15 percent, with the likelihood that their settlement would guarantee them a handsome sinecure for life.

The formulas of age and service varied markedly for our sample. Bethlehem Steel preferred age fifty-five and thirty years of service in order to qualify for full benefits at retirement. But this formula depended on whether it was before or after 1982, when the parameters generally became more rigid. Other industries had their own formula. Carl Hoffman reports:

"To be eligible you had to be within the ages of sixty to sixty-five and to have been with the company fifteen years. They gave us two months to decide. For almost a solid week we had seminars where they presented us with the picture of retirement, what your benefits would be, and how these could change, what your investments might be, and all that. The deal was that you get 60 percent of your salary the first year, 50 percent the second year, and 30 percent the third year. At that point you could pick up your retirement benefits as if you had reached sixty-five without any penalty."

Other factors can affect the financial settlement. In one instance, Black and Decker bought a tool division of General Electric. Tom Schmidt was involved in this takeover and would have liked to stay to age sixty-five, but as with many others was forced out at sixty. However, he did at least find himself with two pensions (which together were larger than what he was later to receive from Social Security): "The G.E. check is much larger, but I get a good check from Black and Decker considering that I only worked there a couple of years or so. I am one of the lucky ones. Some men got very little from G.E. as they did not make the thirty-year requirement—several missed it by only a few months."

Companies on the edge of financial ruin can pose special problems. Deborah Schulz worked for a major metropolitan newspaper and was let out when the paper closed. "We're planning a class action suit because the pension fund was not properly funded and we got almost nothing." Fortunately, her husband, covered by civil service, was luckier.

One problem facing the retiree, especially the married one, is the distribution of the pension, that is, the plan the principal wage earner elects in order to protect the spouse. Adelaide Williams is a case in point: "My husband happens to have a teamster's pension, which is a very good one. We realized that he is ten years older than I am, and so he chose the 50/50 option. Now with the addition of Social Security we are quite comfortable and I will receive half of his pension if he dies before I do."

Individual Variations

Not everyone could be described as seeking retirement because of increasing stress and overload. For at least half of the sample the urge for retirement was the lure of leisure and a situational change—the positive "pull" being dominant over the "push." For example, we interviewed Carmen Ricci, surrounded by her impressive artwork, mostly beguiling seascapes, and looking incredibly young for eighty-one. Her work career was largely in her twenties, and after marriage she was a homemaker—which for most women is far more than a forty-hour week. Then at age sixty-one, after the death of her husband, she returned to employment outside the home. Finally, at age seventy-nine she decided she had had enough; the pull had become strong:

"I was born in Orvieto, Spain—that lush mountainous country in the northwest of the country. But before I was ten years old my father was getting nervous that Spain might enter World War I, and he had heard that the United States was looking for skilled machinists, so we took off from Vigo—always on the alert for German submarines—and landed at Ellis Island. An agent from Bethlehem Steel was the first to grab my father, and so it was off to South Bethlehem where we made our home. It was all very strange for us, but we got help from a number of people. Coming from Spain we just thought any church would be Catholic, but the nearest one was Baptist, so we started there. It was great, not least because I had classes in weaving. Anyway, I graduated from Liberty High.

"I didn't know quite what to do, but right after I got out of high school I was tutoring the students at Lehigh University in Spanish (all of them passed their course!). My family had a rough time in the 1920s and worse in the Depression. But soon after I finished school I thought New York would be the place for me. After all, it's surrounded by water so maybe my ship might come in! At least it would be different from little Bethlehem. At first I lived in the Bronx.

"I had a number of odd jobs, but before long I met Tony, a young Italian-American. We were married, and I was back to the Catholic church. Tony had the feeling that I should not work. It wasn't so much that he was macho, because he didn't feel that it was fair for a woman to do all the housework, cooking, and mothering, and have to work outside the home. Also, he was a severe diabetic, and somehow he didn't feel he could give himself the injections, so that was another job for me. And one by one came three daughters. Finally, we left New York to live in Elizabeth, New Jersey, but it was a low-lying area, too damp and with a lot of animal life—mosquitoes, at least—so we moved to a nice home in Jamaica, Queens, right up the street from where Donald Trump grew up.

"But I had to do something. Anyway, I was not happy with the way Roosevelt had built up the welfare state; I wanted to see people become more self-reliant. So I got very active in the Conservative party in New York. I started going to the meetings, but by the 1960s I was running for office from Jamaica, first for local office, and then for the state assembly, finally for Secretary for the state of New York. Of course, I didn't have much of a chance as a Conservative, but . . . South Jamaica gave me almost 100 percent support in the election.

"Well, my husband died in 1968. I knew that I didn't want to sit around the house, so with my Spanish I became an interpreter in legal offices and in court. I got to know a lot of lawyers, who needed me for bilingual cases. This led to my becoming a private investigator.

"By the late 1970s life was getting too rough in New York, and I settled for other work, like selling in a boutique. By the 1980s it was even grimmer in the New York area—I was robbed, beaten. Later my car was stolen. Finally, one day in October 1988 I looked out of the window and saw what I thought was my ladder being carted off by a stranger. I immediately checked and found that he had taken it out of my garage. I said 'This is it!' I quit my job in the boutique, and left for quiet, safe Bethlehem.

"I loathe New York, but it's part of me. I'm always buying the *Post* to see what's going on. Of course, I still go in on the bus to see my daughters and their families as well as friends, and they all come out here from time to time. I have another daughter here and her children—I have nine grandchildren and seventeen great grand-children, so you see I keep busy. We're a very close family. Two years ago I went with my youngest daughter back to Spain. Nothing of my old Orvieto was there, only the cathedral. The house we lived in and my school were gone. But that's the way it is all over. Nothing is the way it used to be. . . . Also, my younger sister lives in Bethlehem with her paraplegic son. Ten years ago he was struck by a hit-and-run taxi driver in New York. Now thirty-five years old, he's an invalid for life.

"I fortunately have good health and am involved in AARP and St. Ann's Church and painting. I went back to that after being away from it since I was thirty. I work in acrylic, oil, and even charcoal, but I like watercolor best of all. . . . I'd like to do some volunteer work. Especially, I would love to read to children. But with all my work— I'm a compulsive housekeeper, I love cooking—I just don't have the time. Besides, I still have to dabble in politics!"

This chapter has focused more on negative factors like stress than on the positive features of leisure and new horizons, partly because many of the testimonials in the interviews went in this direction. As we shall see in Chapter 3, a number of ingredients went into the final decision. It is, after all, the predominance of either push or pull that drives us to retire. For some, retirement can be a decision over which one has little control, as it was for many in industrial America in the 1980s.

References

1. Toni M. Casalanti, "Participation in a Dual Economy and Adjustment to Retirement," *International Journal of Aging and Human Development, 26*, 13–24, 1988.
2. Paul E. Zopf, Jr., *America's Older Population* (Houston: Cap and Gown Press, 1986), chap. 6.
3. Joseph F. Quinn and Richard V. Burkhauser, "Work and Retirement," in Robert F. Binstock and Linda K. George (eds.), *Handbook of Aging and the Social Sciences*, 3d ed. (San Diego: Academic Press, 1990), pp. 307–327.
4. Pauline K. Robison, Sally Coberly, and Carolyn E. Paul, "Work and Retirement," in Robert H. Binstock and Ethel Shanas (eds.), *Handbook of*

Aging and the Social Sciences, 2d ed. (New York: Van Nostrand Reinhold, 1985), pp. 503–527.

5. William J. Serow, David F. Sly, and J. Michael Wrigley, *Population Aging in the United States* (New York: Greenwood Press, 1990), p. 108.

6. Elizabeth L. Meier and Barbara B. Torrey, "Current Retirement Trends," in Malcolm M. Morrison (ed.), *The Economics of Aging: The Future of Retirement* (New York: Van Nostrand Reinhold, 1982), pp. 61–97.

7. Christopher J. Ruhm, "Why Older Americans Stop Working," *Gerontologist, 23,* 294–298, 1989.

8. Dean W. Morse, Anna B. Dutka, and Susan H. Gray, *Life after Early Retirement* (Montclair, NJ: Allanhead, 1983).

9. Keith M. Kilty and John H. Behling, "Predicting the Retirement Intentions and Attitudes of Professional Workers," *Journal of Gerontology, 41,* 219–227, 1985.

10. *Lehigh Alumni Bulletin,* Winter 1989, p. 15.

11. Robert L. Clark, "Income Maintenance Policies in the United States," in Binstock and George (eds.), *Handbook of Aging,* pp. 383–397.

Chapter 3

The Ultimate Decision

Former bank treasurer Al Johnson illustrates the kinds of decisions that several of our retirees had to make. Again we see the balancing of pluses and minuses involves a range of questions regarding health, finances, family concerns, and leisure pursuits:

"Banking is a rather routine thing unless you're in certain types of departments, such as International, where I was for awhile in New York. It was hard work, big numbers—like over a million dollars—but I guess maybe I'm unusual since I was bored ten years ago. I retired in 1984. The only reason I'd go back to work is if I suffered a loss and had to put food on the table. Then I wouldn't go back to banking, probably. I would prefer to do labor, because I think it's more rewarding and you can actually see your results.

"I also got sick with cancer, and the illness made me realize that I possibly could die without ever having enjoyed retirement, if there is enjoyment in retirement, which I didn't know either. But I assumed that it couldn't be worse than doing a boring piece of work. So I said, 'What the hell am I working for? For appearance's sake?' I've aged considerably since I had that disease, but I used to be very young looking, and some people were amazed when I retired. People say to themselves, 'I'm getting bored and I only have x number of years left on this earth.' Then they plan to change and come to that realization pretty early. Before you know it you're sixty-five. I was thinking when I was thirty-five, forty, that I wanted to be independently wealthy by the time I'm fifty-five. You know one thing to practice? It's easy, the last ten years, the way the interest rates ran, the thing to do was set some aside each year, and no matter how hard it was, x dollars are going to be an investment. The way you start is on day one of the year—borrow that money. You figure you're going to put $15,000 into investments this year; then you're forced to pay the loan off. At the end of the year, hopefully you'll have the $15,000 paid off and you'll have $15,000 additional. If you can't do that much, do it with a little less, and at the end of the second year, maybe you'll have something, which will make the next years easier if you wanted to borrow more to increase your equity. That's what I used to do, though I'd borrow $50,000. . . .

"I had made up my mind while I was in the hospital that if I did not enjoy what I was doing, I was going to start to enjoy myself. I didn't need a lot of money to live on; most of my responsibilities were over. You know I had five kids. On the day I retired, my father-in-law died, so I picked up a mother-in-law. He died the weekend that would have been my last week at work. That's one of those things. I think the more I read in the paper, there's a lot of people doing the same thing. She will be ninety next birthday and she's in good shape, good health mentally and physically.

"See, I'm really a frustrated gliding instructor. I do a lot of flying and parachuting. I had intended at fifty-five to give up banking and teach gliding. But I have no depth perception anymore, so that sort of stopped that. And then when I was fifty-five I got this cancer. I was seriously ill, so I made up my mind to get myself physically back together while I was still working, and then do nothing. I'm one of those people that if I'm bored, it doesn't eat at me."

*   *   *

Perhaps the foremost question is: When is the best moment to make one's departure from the work world, or at least from a given employer? In Al's case the decision was compounded by health problems, questions about longevity, and frustration at not being able to do what he would ideally have liked to do.

Moreover, the mere prospect of having to *adjust to changes* in finances, personnel, equipment, or procedures in the workplace is the determining factor for several retirees. For example, Arthur Zavecz, after twenty-five years of teaching, took the incentive for early retirement in 1982 at age fifty-five, causing his income to drop from $22,000 to $16,000. He said the offer was made because the state was seeking ways to help school districts get rid of higher-salaried teachers so they could hire two teachers at lower pay! "For me it was a fortunate combination. I met the requirements of the combination of age and years of employment, a new principal was coming in, they were going to get the ninth grade back into our high school, and the administration was getting so worried about any kind of liability. It would be confusing; . . . I was already dissatisfied with a lot of things at the school, and school morale was terribly low. For me, it was a battle to keep going those last few years."

Leaving while still being wanted was another part of the retirement decision. At least five persons, in addition to the cases of stress noted in Chapter 2, simply felt ready to retire. This was partly because of working conditions, but their reasons had less emphasis on felt stress and more on an inner conviction that they did not want to stay until perceived as "old hat." They decided to leave while they were still wanted—a kind of protection of self-concept and public image. Interestingly, this response came more from public school personnel than from any other occupation, possibly because they work with the young. For instance, Neal Rossi taught for thirty-three years, retired at age fifty-two—when his wife was very ill—and since has chosen various kinds of part-time work of a different nature: "I had enough. I didn't want to go out like some teachers did after just hanging on and on until they became terrible teachers." And another male teacher, who retired at age fifty-five with twenty-three years of experience, expressed the same concern: "I wanted to leave being a good teacher. I didn't want to be the old crab in the classroom."

Arthur Ferraro, an engineer who retired at fifty-two and within two months was hired as a laboratory instructor at a nearby college, explained:

"I had always thought that in my middle fifties I'd like a change of career, to try something different. I felt that if I stayed until fifty-five then I'd just be saying, 'Well, I might as well stay six or seven years more.' I didn't want to get in that situation. I liked my job until the day I left; I don't think in thirty-four years there were more than a handful of days when I really felt I didn't want to go to work. But I wanted to continue that way. I didn't want to just be there. I've seen others over fifty-five just counting the years until retirement, some looking forward to it, some not."

Pressure and Escape

Whether for the white-collar clerk, the professional, or the foreman in the shop, pressures mount. For some, there is the last straw. For others, retirement can be a simple unfolding of events or occasionally well planned. But few retirees completely escape some anxiety during the period when making the final decision, especially if there is excessive pressure to decide "then and there." For that few, retirement may be the happiest day of their life, despite their possible immediate resentment.

Work-Related Stress

As we have seen in the interviews the strongest push toward retirement was stress. These indictments of management and the ambience of the workplace itself, not only in big business but in local banks, schools, colleges, and hospitals as well, offer food for thought to employers faced with carrying out individual or group layoffs. Are these negative changes in the work situation real and typical? Are they peculiar to the sample in this study? Or could it be they are figments of mental, physical, or emotional changes occurring in the aging process? If so, in a sense "the fault, dear Brutus, is in ourselves." We may ask the same question in regard to the following section on health and fatigue as naturally age-related causes of early retirement. Admittedly, part of the stress was due to the tensions and indecisiveness within corporations, and the popular press corroborates the views cited here in the participants' reports of age discrimination in the workplace. As the average age of the sample was merely fifty-nine years at retirement, however, the question of physical and mental breakdown was not relevant to the retirement decision of these retirees.

In conclusion, one can identify in these interviews two related but distinct sources of stress: first, the awareness of change in the workplace (new personnel, equipment, methods) and in the market-place (necessitating cutbacks in costs); and second, the specific methods used by management to reduce costs, especially labor costs. The message to management is that if concentration on the bottom line is inevitable, the method could be less harsh. Our older population is now asking for at least a "kinder and gentler" approach, a more humane procedure for being eased into retirement, including the decency of a longer lead time before the grand exit by forced retirement at any age. Responses by this group on the questionnaire and by those in the study of Connecticut State retirees supplement this point.[1] One of the few structural factors that had clear effects on postretirement satisfaction was the longer the period of time people had between the decision to retire and the last day of work the more likely they were to be satisfied.

Health and Fatigue

Health has often been cited by retirees as a reason for retirement, and it is a genuine concern. It also seems a respectable explanation for leaving employment in a work-oriented society. But in the 1980s it was no longer as salient a motive as before.[2] From Chapter 2 we learned that the pension plan offered by the employer is the most important determinant of retirement. On responses to the question-naire, *health* ranked second as the single most important motive for retirement and was mentioned by nearly a third in the interviews. Among physical ailments, the most prevalent were heart troubles, cancer, other debilitating diseases, and bodily injury.

Perhaps even more than others in our sample, nurses are subject to these physical breakdowns. For example, an obstetrics nurse, who worked twenty-one years on the graveyard shift, became so geared up that she couldn't slow down, even while driving her car. She slipped into the habit of sleeping only three to four hours because she felt sleep was a waste of time. In addition to her other problems, she is overweight, and now has two "worn-out knees" from being on her feet all those hours.

The most dramatic and remarkable story was that of Gordon

Wald, who at sixty-two enjoyed doing electrical installation work on high-rise structures:

"I wouldn't be retired if I hadn't had a heart attack last January. Then I had five bypasses done in August, just two months ago, and I feel great. At the time I was working in New York City. It's more interesting work there—all those high buildings. I worked on the World Trade Center, the Verrazano Bridge, Shea Stadium, and the like. It's very exciting. That day I was on a twelve-hour day and some thirty-five stories up. When I came home that night, showered, and sat down and lit up a cigarette, I told my wife something was happening to me inside, then I passed out—no more than an hour after I had left the job. They rushed me to Bellevue Hospital, where they kept me ten days. I'll tell you that knocked me out worse than anything else. I was wounded in World War II, yet that heart attack beat me down to nothing. I could hardly do anything. The doctor advised me never to go back to work, and no lifting or climbing—and that was my kind of work!"

Fatigue, boredom, and *loss of motivation* at work often emerged in the interviews. Undoubtedly, these problems could be related to declining health and vigor, both part of the aging process, as well as to conditions of the workplace. In any event, the interviews were sprinkled with remarks such as "More and more I found myself chewing Maalox" or "Almost every day I would get a headache around four o'clock." General fatigue and loss of motivation could interact with somewhat reduced ability for the body to spring back to produce effects such as these. Indeed, several retirees, albeit in self-defined good health, found that their growing disaffection with work lay within themselves more than with their work situation, as we see in the remarks of Arthur Ferraro, who at age 52 retired in order to follow a second career in college teaching:

"It wasn't because I was getting older or that I wasn't learning things as fast. I was learning new jobs all the time, but the motivation was going down. I think when you're in a technical job you have a lot of burn-out. You push and push and push and you burn out. I think you get a little jaded. I found myself getting tired of hearing the same problems. I thought, 'What good is it going to be if I continue being so supercritical of everything because I've heard it all before with different names, different products.' Your attitude gets different in the middle fifties. You might not feel so good as you did before. Mentally you're beginning to say to yourself: 'It's time for me to retire.' Maybe it's harder even to do the things you want to do because it's getting harder to motivate yourself. You even begin to use the rationale that your retirement will open up a place for a young person. That's one of the things in the piles of things you're thinking, though not at the top. . . . Your mental attitudes are different in your late fifties and sixties from what they were in your forties to middle fifties. I think it's mental attitude. Not all people want to stop thinking or stop doing things, but as you get older you find reasons not to motivate yourself."

Oliver Burke owned a good-sized hardware store for twenty-nine years and retired at age sixty-five. He recounted his feelings this way:

"Really, what it comes down to is that we (his wife was co-owner and worker) just had had enough. I worked for fifty years; I started at fourteen in my spare time working more than playing. I only went through high school; that was still the Depression years and there just wasn't money, and nobody encouraged me to work my way through college. Then over the years with the big boys moving in, the individually owned store got more and more difficult. Things started to shrink; so about a year before we actually retired we started to plan actively. It became 'Let's quit while we're ahead.' "

Being Laid Off

Dismissal was the third most frequent reason for retiring given in the interviews. The event can arrive after a continuing state of agony: "You see those pink slips appear on someone's desk. Then you wait from day to day, week to week, knowing that you, too, will find your pink slip." In Chapter 4 we examine the trauma of these experiences.

The ringing of the bell sometimes falls hardest on the professionals who are deeply involved in their work. Ralph Buckingham, Ph.D., an engineer at Bell Lab, found himself forced out at age sixty-four and felt acutely depressed. He sent out some 200 applications for employment, but finally found that what was available was of less financial return than taking early retirement or involved a major geographical move. He finally found solace in reading in a variety of scientific fields, but still resents that his research capacity is not used. Another case is engineering professor John Mueller, who was annoyed that he was forced out at age sixty-seven. If he had been born six months later he would have come under the new law that would have permitted his continuing to age seventy. He was sufficiently angry at the college (which might have granted him an adjunct status, i.e., part-time teaching) that he seldom returned to the campus, to which he had been so committed in the past.

The trauma of Aldo Carlucci at Bethlehem Steel is almost a classical case:

"I was part of a group of seventy-five laid off or retired on that one day. I had thirty-five years with them. I'm fifty-nine years old. I started at the plant on a wage basis. In '59 we were out on a long strike without pay. I learned that once in the office force—a white-collar job on salary—you were good for life; it was generally understood that your work was guaranteed. So I got into the research division for the last twenty-five years or so. And that's the way it was until they started laying off in about 1982.

"From a thousand employees the division dropped to 200. You hope it's not going to be you, but as we saw this happening everybody's morale was very poor because you didn't know from one day to another. A lot of people condemn the company for the way they did it, but there's no good way. . . . They told us on Friday 'You'll be paid for a month but you can go home now.' That's just as well. If we'd hung around, how much work would we have put in?

"I was ineligible for the lump sum settlement; they stopped that some years before. I guess I got thirteen weeks pay besides, because that's in the contract. After that I could start my company-paid pension. I get a thousand bucks per month pension. Another thing I had taken advantage of is a savings plan where they contributed a certain percentage. That's something I can tap later."

The closing of the Mack Trucks plant in the Lehigh Valley prompted many retirements and left a hostile attitude in Mike Kohler and even more so for his wife Jane, who was forced out by the closing of Black and Decker: "It's a case mostly of mismanagement, and finally they realized the heyday was over but would not own up to it. We're in a competitive market, and you can't go around wasting a whole box of screws.... As for Mack, it may move South but they're going to face the same problems of trying to copy the Big Three, when they simply can't assembly-line the process."

These negative remarks must be viewed in the context of the wider satisfaction that most retirees feel on leaving their work. In an interview, people are more able to relate various negative incidents in detail than is possible on a questionnaire. A great deal of ambivalence does surround retirement, however, because the individual is shifting gears and leaving a situation of both pleasure and distress on the job for an appealing but uncertain future.

The Pursuit of Leisure

Half of the sample indicated that "leisure opportunities" (see Table 2-1) was among their top four motives for retirement. Seemingly, the retirement experiences of friends and colleagues had a strong effect on them. Several claimed that people who retire earlier, when still physically well, seem to be in better mental health during their retirement years, a finding well supported by research studies. Still others referred to their experience of having family members who worked until sixty-five or over and died soon thereafter without time to travel or be with tleir families, or do things they'd always wanted to do. These persons are determined to avoid a similar fate. It is significant that when asked in the interview and on the questionnaire what is the best part of being retired, the response was a resounding emphasis on the joys of leisure.

Timing and Planning

The question of when to retire is, then, a product of the forces surrounding us and our reactions to these events. As noted in Chapter 1, the average age of retirement for our questionnaire sample was fifty-nine, with a range from forty-five to seventy-three. Nearly nine-tenths retired before age sixty-five. In other words, the sample can be labeled as one of "early retirement," as the age of sixty-five is generally thought of as "on-time" retirement. Indeed, most of the sample had planned to retire before they reached their sixty-fifth birthday. But if the retirement comes suddenly or at a different time from anticipation, there is not the time to prepare for it.

However, retirement planning is often vague. Take the case of nurse Dorothy Schmidt:

"The hours at the college were terrible—weekends and nights—even though I had two teenage children. I really liked all phases of nursing, but there's such a great change in that field. . . . I finally decided to retire at age fifty-eight because of a work-related ruptured disc from heavy lifting, which I shouldn't have done as head nurse, but I'm always one to think I'll join with everyone else in working. But it was harassment on my last job in a retirement home that really did it. I was perfectly able to handle my job, except heavy lifting, yet one day the director of nursing came by and said, "You know, I wouldn't have had to rehire you." So that really got to me! That, after so many years of dedicated service. . . . To add to that, my husband's plant was closing at the same time. . . . All I get now in partial pension is $137 a month, but we can manage on my husband's pension. . . .

"I didn't do any advance planning about retirement because I hadn't anticipated it happening. I thought I'd have another seven years. In fact, I used to tell everyone that I was going to work until I was eighty. . . . But I have several job offers and the hospital wants me to come and work on a part-time basis. . . . I'm of the opinion that people should keep going as long as they can. If those brain cells start dying you're in trouble. I don't even like the word 'retirement' because I think it refers to lie down or give up."

Our respondents varied markedly in their plans for and approaches to retirement. Let's take a look at some of the questionnaire data. A fifth (20 percent) had planned to retire before age sixty, 37 percent between ages sixty and sixty-four, 33 percent between ages sixty-five and sixty-nine, and less than 1 percent at age seventy or over. Nearly 9 percent had had no plans about the age of retirement. To differing degrees most of the sample retired somewhat earlier than they had anticipated. In this respect the timing was not too different from that found in other studies, notably the Morse and Gray sample (see Chap. 1, ref. 24) in which three-fourths felt that the retirement had come at the right time.

A number of studies point to a somewhat nervous period of anticipation as plans are being made toward retirement. Curious events and delays can occur as the individual plans for—or is forced into—retirement. We recall from Chapter 2, Walter Koch's unhappy departure from his company. In a different vein, nurse educator Alice Stratton recalls her ambivalence about ending her teaching and administrative role:

"My husband was retired for about three years, but I continued to work because I liked what I was doing. Every year he would say to me 'When are you going to retire?' And I kept saying 'Just one more year.' I don't think he was impatient but he really wanted me to retire, especially as I didn't take summers off. Finally I convinced myself that at sixty-seven I should do it even though I could have worked until seventy. Yet I still thought about it for a whole year, even knowing that I should give a year's advance notice. Finally, I went to the dean, but I still held off writing that letter."

In part the anxiety depends on the economic climate—inflation, interest rates, employment opportunities.[3] The latter is important as nearly a half of our "retirees" were interested in working at least part time. Usually toward age fifty, financial considerations become relevant, although explicit discussions with the spouse surface later. In other words, planning begins perhaps fifteen years prior to retirement.[4] It is interesting to note that employees have a fair degree of *savoir-faire* regarding the retirement process. For instance, in one survey two-thirds of the workers planned their retirement strategy two years in advance of their actual departure, whereas the remainder felt unclear about their plans.[5] Financial questions loom large in the planning, especially the question of bridging the gap between retirement and the onset of Social Security payments, at least for those retiring before age sixty-two.

Our retirees were asked what planning, if any, they made in approaching retirement. Over two-thirds (68 percent) said they did some planning. Predictably, financial considerations appear to be the principal concern: 20 percent listed this reason as their first priority, followed by planning for leisure activities (6 percent). Irrespective of the ranking, no less than 71 percent checked "financial" and 37 percent "leisure," among the five factors of planning listed on the questionnaire. Of lesser concern were future plans for employment or possible change of residence. Quite a few did not appear to plan *at all* in any systematic way. Of course, as we observe in the interviews, specific plans become intertwined with a variety of motives.

The report of Steve Kovacs illustrates as well as anyone we interviewed that determination may resolve the dilemma of those who do not really want to retire. Despite his sense of disillusion he immediately began to plan and act:

"When my parents first came over here from Czechoslovakia, they bought a little grocery store in Yonkers, New York. It went very well for them, but then of course things got very, very tough, I guess around 1929. The stock market crashed, so they moved on for one reason or another. I guess it was then that my dad decided to go to school and go to a seminary in Illinois. . . .

"I was born in Akron, Ohio. We moved to Steubenville, Ohio, and then in 1936, when I was eight years old, we moved into the Oakcrest area. My dad was a Slovak Lutheran pastor and he was having problems hanging onto the church, for all kinds of political reasons. The worst problem was that we had a big family. There were eight kids. So he came here and rented a farm so we could get through the depression by raising our food. He worked hard at it. It was a fifteen-acre farm, and about three acres were on the west side of the house. The rest of it was across the road. We tried to buy the farm from a Hungarian. For $15 a month, we had eighteen acres, would you believe that! We moved out during the Second World War.

"I was in products engineering. My specific job was in integrated circuits. My task was to work in high-vacuum technology, and we put the coatings on top of the integrated circuit chips to protect them from the environment so they would last a long time. In addition to that, whenever they needed help I would work on some of the underlying layers that were built upon the integrated circuit chips, too. It was very interesting. I loved it. But the job that I had when I was offered the retirement was, I think, the most challenging and most interesting one I had the whole time I was working there. It made the decision doubly tough. I was in that position since August of 1980, and I retired December 1985. So it was over five years that I was in that particular job. I saw it was coming, so about nine months before the retirement offer was made, I asked for a transfer to another department that was just starting out in a new and interesting field. It was quality assurance, and actually it's like being a pathologist. I'd get the failures and I'd look at them and find out what the trouble was, in a specific area of quality assurance. You'd have to maybe use chemicals to take the layers off. I liked that the best. I was in that about nine months. . . .

"My move to retirement goes back to the breakup of AT&T. People down in Texas came out with a radio-telephone system, and up until that time, AT&T had a monopoly on it. They took it to court, and that was the first case that AT&T had ever lost because of outside competition. So I think that was even before 1972. They changed the retirement formula from time to time, but most of the time you had to be at least, I think, fifty-five years of age and/or have thirty years of service. When I was there in 1972 I already had worked there twenty-one years. It was getting bad; I thought there might be other opportunities someplace else, and I used vacation days to look for jobs—that's how bad it was. You know, they had layoffs and they wouldn't tell you whether you'd be next or not. At first I didn't accept early retirement. I said, 'I've got two children to get through college yet.' . . . But I was even having trouble going into work in the morning. As of November 1, 1985, they said you could retire early and they would give you one year's salary to spread over two years. At that point, I had discussed it around the supper table with the family. My wife and I agreed that it was too early and I couldn't retire. A number of times I mentioned it because I was really very unhappy over there, not being treated like everybody else. I always feel if they treat everybody the same, you don't feel too bad. About the second or third week in November I wasn't sleeping well at all with the decision I had made. I'd wake up thinking about what it was going to be like after this cutoff date if I didn't take the retirement. I thought about all the things I wanted to do yet, and being a go-getter, I decided I'd better go out and try it on my own. . . . From the time they told us that we could retire until the time I did was forty-five days. I felt better right away. I really started sleeping better and felt better about the decision. I worked only a week or so after I made the decision. We really had to rush the paperwork through. With the offer that they made—the one year's salary over two years—and my pension meeting almost the other 50 percent of what I was getting paid, we could maintain the same standard of living for two years. . . . My boss told me he was very happy with what I was doing. He wanted me to stay, but he could not, because of what was happening, guarantee that I would maintain the job that I had. There was a good possibility that somebody else who was there longer, had a degree, and had more experience with that particular line of work might come in and bump me out. So there was no written guarantee for anybody over there really.

"They offered me all kinds of advice; they had meetings to get you prepared for this. I wasn't planning to retire, so I didn't go to the meetings. But they did give some of them later. For instance, after we retired, they had whole-week seminars which cost the company $1,500 for each one of us who attended.

"I'm not critical how the company handled my retirement. I am critical of everything that went on before that. As a matter of fact, since I've retired, I've been trying to maintain a positive outlook on everything that happened. I don't want to dwell on the negative, because in trying to get my own business going, I don't want anything like that. I've lost—and this is what helps me make a decision—some very dear friends of mine who were much younger than I was—they never had an opportunity to retire. . . .

"I had some ideas for some patents and did a patent search myself in the Patent Office in Washington. I picked the one that I thought might have the best application and would be marketable. You get into too many legal complications if you do something relating to AT&T, having been an employee of theirs. As a retiree, I would still have to give the company the patent.... I've also got other ideas. The first month I was retired, I went out and formed a company. I registered the sole ownership in the state of Pennsylvania because with all the ideas I had swimming around all these years, I felt I had to find an outlet. Also, I have some ideas for wholeselling items which I find on the market which are under-advertised. I found out that there are some items out there that have more applications than the company knows about. So you find these things out by accident sometimes. I have a couple ideas with these two products I'm working on. I want to go out and actually sell them door-to-door wholesale. That's another thing that I'm trying out, and I hope to build it up into something that will give me some income by the time December rolls around and the payments stop.

"I learned how to drive a school bus and I drive it whenever somebody is sick. I drive about two or three times a week.

"It looked to me that out there in the marketplace, as far as the U.S. is concerned, there was going to be a lot more homes built. I thought I'd take a look at the building and supply business, so I worked at that for about three months before the weather got bitterly cold....

"The postretirement seminar encouraged the retirees to go ahead, that you didn't need to put a lot of money into your own business, and to try things a little bit at a time, slowly. That's the kind of direction I'm trying to go in. I haven't gone back to them yet for more advice because I'm also working with the people over at the Small Business Center at Lehigh University. I want to work out a small business plan with somebody over there as soon as I can sit down and talk with them. I did talk to them about doing some consulting work in the area that I was involved with at AT&T, and they lined me up with one small outfit up in Lehighton. I helped them out a little bit....

"I'm feeling better about myself. I think the family is feeling better about me, too. I used to come home from work and I was emotionally and mentally drained. I know I used to sit there and eat, and eat, and eat. It was all nervous energy. I think I'm better off now.

I don't have that nervous energy. I don't eat as much, and I don't feel that compulsion. I never really gained weight with all the eating, though. I'm lighter now by six to eight pounds, and I exercise more.

"I really haven't gone through the list of things I'm involved with. I'm involved with church work, and I was on the financial committee there. I also sing in the choir. I'm thinking of going back and trying to get the flight person to reinstate my flying status. I've been flying ever since I was 16. I was in the Air Force for four years during the war. Then, photography is a hobby. Never a dull moment. I've got thousands of slides and photographs to file."

*   *   *

As we can see, Steve Kovacs was committed to continuing a working life well into retirement, and a reinterview with him in 1991 showed him to be successful in this attempt; he has two businesses— one in maintenance of medical equipment and another in computer consultancy.

The Process of Retirement over Time

How long does the retirement process last? The average estimated period between the day of decision and the last day of work was about four months. The clustering of the time interval varied thus (percentages are approximate due to fractionalization):

Less than a week	5%
1 to 3 weeks	20%
1 month to less than 3 months	26%
3 months to less than 6 months	19%
6 months or more	31%

As shown, for half of the respondents the retirement process was less than three months, but for many the urge had been brewing for months or years before. In other words, the decision to retire may not be articulated until long after a vague need has surfaced. Some precipitating event then brings the motive to consciousness. Older employees (over age sixty-five) were more likely to give notice in advance, whereas the younger (under age sixty) were inclined to retire at the offer of the employer.

Other things being equal, sudden retirement was more difficult than planned retirement. Generally, women found retirement less difficult than did men.

Inevitably, we ask how age, planning, and timing affect the success of retirement. Several statistical relationships emerge in the findings from the questionnaire:

1. Age at time of retirement is significantly related both to satisfaction with one's last work and to satisfaction the individual finds with retirement. In both instances, younger retirees are more satisfied than are older ones.
2. Whether one retires early or on time has little prediction as to satisfaction. However, timing as related to one's expectations and plans relates significantly to several factors. That is, those who retire earlier than they planned have lower scores on (a) happiness as compared to five years ago, (b) satisfaction with retirement, and (c) satisfaction with how the retirement was handled.
3. As mentioned earlier, the length of time between the decision for retirement and the date of retirement itself is related to (a) satisfaction in retirement, (b) overall life satisfaction, and (c) happiness as compared to five years ago. In all cases, the longer the period of time for planning and adjustment, the more satisfied and happier is the retiree.
4. To no one's surprise, those who feel retirement was more difficult than they expected have lower levels of life satisfaction, happiness, and retirement satisfaction.

Sense of Control and the Self-Image

A sense of control is important in how the individual looks at the retirement decision and process. Two-thirds (66 percent) thought they had initiated the retirement, and one-third felt that the employer was the center of control. A major finding of our questionnaire study is that the feeling of having initiated the retirement decision oneself is positively related to both (1) satisfaction in retirement, and (2) satisfaction with how the retirement process was handled. Our sample was largely of salaried employees and managers, who may feel more financially free to initiate the retirement decision than do hourly wage earners. Consequently, this correlation helps explain the predominance of happiness in retirement found in this study, as we shall learn in Chapter 4.

Of the 115 retirees who answered the questionnaire, 59 percent were very satisfied with the way the employer handled the retirement decision, 21 percent were "somewhat satisfied," and 20 percent were "somewhat" or "very dissatisfied." How an individual perceived the handling of retirement depended partly on his or her feelings toward the job situation (as with many of our findings, this relationship showed statistical significance).

As an example of satisfaction, we point to a former employee in management retired at age fifty-six after thirty-four years with Steel, which he had joined after he left college. He made the retirement decision only because it was his last chance to be provided with the so-called Golden Parachute, or lump sum settlement plan, often referred to as the "sweetener" or the "carrot." He had identified closely with his company, taking pride in the quality of the product, yet he is now even happier in the employment he found after that first retirement:

"I don't harbor any animosity toward the company. I can understand why they did it, and, in fact, I think maybe the lump sum setup was bad for the company's costs. I would like to praise them for making available to us a two-day seminar with an organization that discussed with us where the job market is, how to find a new position, how to write a growth-oriented resume, and tips on handling interviews. Our wives were also invited. This was followed by a three-to-four-hour personal session to help us draft our resumes. That plus all the services of the company's Center on Career Continuation (which the company had started when they began huge layoffs) I found most helpful, one of the real big pluses. It was done in such a professional way, including typing, duplication, mailings of our job applications, and unlimited use of their phones."

As already reported, however, several retirees elaborated on the traumatic nature of their separation experience. Surprisingly, most of these were at employment levels and in types of business, industry, or higher education where one would hardly expect such treatment from longtime employers. In one case, Kenneth Kline, a middle-level bank manager, age fifty-eight, was called in by his thirty-three-year-old vice president (recently armed with a M.B.A.):

"When he called me in he closed the door, which I didn't think was unusual. He said, 'It's time for your evaluation.' I said, 'Oh.' He said, 'I want you to read it.'... I couldn't believe what I was reading. I have been with the company all these years, and never anything negative, and I always got a very respectable raise. In fact, the letter had a demotion in it. I said, 'What's this?' He replied, 'It should have happened a year ago, but your immediate superior at that time didn't have the guts to tell you. He admitted that he always had a yellow streak in his back and couldn't bring himself to level with you. Incidentally, that's not all the bad news; we're transferring you to a branch office, and a woman will replace you here.' I said, 'You know my background, and I really don't know why exactly you are doing this to me, because I always had a good relationship with customers, never any complaints, no problems with the employees.' 'Well,' he said, 'This is not the day of being able to demonstrate one's talents to customers or employees; this is the time of big corporate business. I'm afraid you will just not fit into that particular picture.' Then I said, 'Well, Bill, I really would like to work until I'm sixty-two, if it's possible. I'm not proud—you already demoted me.' He replied, 'Really, nobody wants you in the bank.' Startled, I said, 'You're kidding.'... After a moment he came back: 'Why aren't you getting hostile?'

"Early the next morning the phone rang and he asked, 'How are you this morning, Ken?' My reply: 'About as good as could be expected.' I went on to explain that I would take the move to the other branch. At that point he became belligerent: 'I can assure you that at the branch I'll still be your boss and I'll be on your back the way bees are to honey. I'll give you three to six months to meet my goal, and if you don't, you'll be out the door with nothing.'... The next week I had some angina pains and after a couple of weeks the bank called and said they could arrange to give me my pension now instead of at age sixty-two. . . . A few months later the phone rang and it was Bill: 'The reason I'm calling is that you left in such a hurry that the bank did not have time to present you with a plaque and retirement gift. Could you find time to come and see me this week, and I would like to present it to you personally.'"

Ken decided he would forgo this ceremony, but seeing Bill some weeks later on the street he asked jovially: "Where's my gold watch?" Bill answered: "You don't get a gold watch, you were only with us thirteen years." It is hoped this kind of episode is rare. However, one spouse spoke of her husband's experience in another Lehigh Valley bank: "You know, when people look back, they often say: 'It never should have happened. I mean he gave his full life to that bank and in the end there was no gratitude.' I don't think there is such a thing anymore as loyalty to a company, because they can turn around and forget you completely. And you can give them your whole life."

Let us turn to another case—and hardly a unique one. A manager at Steel was told one morning by his superior to clean out his desk by afternoon. However, as implied above, in this instance the upper management did at least offer him and other retirees a variety of vocational counseling and placement services.

In contrast, Tim Trueblood, a senior staff accountant who retired at age fifty-two after thirty years with Steel, described the separation process this way:

"I ended up being the only one left of the old 'gang,' and the new gang just wasn't like the old-timers. The entire office changed—the personnel, the job responsibilities. It just wasn't the same. I feel I was eased out. . . . I could see from the ledger that the company was going downhill for the last three years. But I didn't know it was happening to me until it happened. You could tell the day before by such a clue as that your pass to get on the computer was suddenly removed. Then you'd know that tomorrow is it. When that happened to me, I sat down, put my feet up on my worktable, called a friend and said, 'Guess what happened.' We laughed. I was perfectly relieved! They did for me something that I didn't have the guts to do for myself. . . . We had heard stories that in another department a manager would call all the employees into a conference room, tell them there was going to be a layoff, and when you got back to your desk there would either be a pink slip, or not, on your chair. Some sections were given three months notice, which was better than what I got."

The hurtful impact from the lack of a sense of control in the retirement decision was described by several others. For example, Linda Eisenhard, who had worked eighteen years for a bindery, lastly as a proofreader, related the following ambivalent feelings and dilemma for many women, who are generally more taken for granted by employers than are men:

"Some seven years after the company was bought out, anyone in office work or any executive over fifty-five with fifteen years of work was asked to retire. I tell you I was really shocked when they came and offered it to me, because I had no idea. I had planned to work at least to sixty-two or sixty-five, and I was in fairly good health. When they offered it, I just couldn't believe it! I couldn't work the rest of the day. I was pleased because my husband was already retired, and yet shocked because I had no idea that they were going to do anything like this! There were no rumors or anything. I felt I was doing a good job and yet when I heard that they were offering it to others who had been working longer than I or who had come in with the new owners, then I didn't feel too bad. Then I knew it wasn't just me. I couldn't wait to tell my husband; I was excited. He said immediately to take it. He and I get along real well, like to do the same things. He'd had a year of being at home by himself, so I guess he was ready for me to come home. . . . I accepted it the next day, because you had to make up your mind within thirty days. It wouldn't be offered again until normal retirement age. My last day was two months later. They're paying me a so-called supplement till age sixty-four, when my pension starts. But if I had not had a husband, I never could have retired on what I got: I would have had to keep on working. What they give in pension to women is not enough to carry you through. The men's earnings there were better for the same kind of work."

Walter Koch, whose retirement history was our introduction to Chapter 2, gave his notice at age fifty-five because of extraordinary work overload and impossible time demands. He applied for retirement, and to his surprise his request was accepted during his two-week vacation:

"I don't believe we had been home five minutes when the phone rang and my boss told me not to come to work tomorrow but to come to his office. So, the next day I went up to the vice president's office, he handed me a paper, and I stepped outside into a vestibule where I could read it by myself. He gave me two or three options. I immediately decided that the best was to take the retirement. . . . I walked down to Personnel, passed a few people on the way. It was hard to say good-bye to them, so I went down there as quickly as I could go and signed the papers. It all started at eight o'clock. By ten o'clock I had gone up to the research department, cleaned out my desk, and was home to tell my wife."

Nonetheless, retirees generally felt that they had ample lead time to prepare for their exit. In reality, most of our sample were looking forward to retirement. Consequently, they reacted positively to the period of anticipation.

In conclusion, our study has pivoted on several major concerns of the retirement decision: the pension package, health, work stress, finances, and leisure opportunities. In addition, the question of the self-image and feelings of control are possibly the most salient finding in our study of early—or any—retirement. Our 167 respondents who contributed to this study represent many different modes of how to adjust. Although some of them wanted to retire more than did others, few if any of them were completely passive in the process of moving from full employment into a different phase of the life cycle. These issues set the stage for Chapter 4, where we explore the process of adjustment, specifically the *internal*, or subjective, aspects, as the retiree struggles to find a sense of purpose. Chapter 5 examines the thoughts the retirees have on their years of work.

References

1. Thomas O. Blank, "Retirement in Connecticut: A Study of State Employees," Travelers Center on Aging, Colloquium presentation, April 15, 1991.
2. Joseph F. Quinn and Richard V. Burkhauser, "Work and Retirement," in Robert H. Binstock and Linda K. George (eds.), *Handbook of Aging and the Social Sciences*, 3d ed. (San Diego: Academic Press, 1990), pp. 307–327.
3. Kenneth F. Ferraro, "Cohort Analysis of Retirement Preparation, 1974–1981," *Journal of Gerontology, 45*, S21–31, 1990.
4. Linda Evans, David J. Ekerdt, and Raymond Bossé, "Proximity to Retirement and Anticipatory Involvement: Findings from the Normative Aging Study," *Journal of Gerontology, 40*, 368–374, 1985.
5. David J. Ekerdt, Barbara H. Vinick, and Raymond Bossé, "Orderly Endings: Do Men Know When They Will Retire?" *Journal of Gerontology, 44*, S28–35, 1989.

Chapter 4

Adjusting to Retirement

Is retirement a trauma or an escape? For Lewis Fitzgerald it was perhaps half shock, half challenge. Being retired at age 48 inevitably meant a second career. He had the mental resources to cope with his new phase of life, and a revisit with him nearly four years after the original interview revealed that he was managing reasonably well in his new venture as entrepreneur:

"I started with Steel after graduation from Lehigh. The Loop [an eight-month program of acquainting new personnel with the plant operations] had started, and some years later they had a small graduating class. They wanted to fill the auditorium in order to impress the vice presidents who were coming to speak, and that's when I got the opportunity to go through the Loop program. It was a good experience. I had already been working for them for ten or twelve years.

"After twenty-three years, I guess I was caught up with the frustrations of working in a downtrodden industry for several years during their decline. I always had an optimistic point of view. I thought of the survivors; at least I was on the bottom rung of the ladder going out. Then every few months they'd lay off a few more, and then the responsibilities of the people that were left down there were changed. Not too many knew what was going on. We were wondering would we make it to the next month or would we make it to next Friday. That was hanging over our heads and became our small talk during the day.

"My annoyance was that for eight years I was bounced around

among about six different departments, which changed my responsibilities all the time. I had to work for smaller crews, and finally I was given the responsibilities that four or five people had taken on before. So we had to streamline our systems. One day they called me up and said they wanted me to come to a meeting tomorrow to let me know where I fit into the reorganization. I hung up the phone and wondered what it was all about. Someone next to me asked if it was a morning or an afternoon meeting. I said, 'What's the difference?' They said the morning meeting is for people who are leaving. This was a morning meeting, and I went in there with about fifteen other people. They wished us a good morning, but it wasn't going to turn out that way, and they started reading the benefits. I was one of the few that said I was ready to graduate, to turn over a new chapter. You didn't have any option of retiring or terminating, but I was one of the few that was thankful that the decision was made and the indecision had ended. I didn't have to worry anymore.

"My feelings at the time were mixed. One, I was elated that the decision was made. I felt that at this point in my life and with the business contacts I made just prior to that announcement, I had an optimistic future for greater potential than I had before. I said to myself, 'Okay, now my destiny is in my hands. I'm not in a work situation where somebody's putting a ceiling on my worth.' I ended that meeting shaking hands, with the feeling that I was better off than the others. In other words, I wasn't married to the steel company.

"I dallied with the decision about doing a job search, but I wasn't really going into it as I might have. I suppose after twenty-three years of working, I may have taken somewhat of a vacation. I took about a year when I was really enjoying the kids, taking them to the pool in the afternoon, and not working a strenuous schedule. Finally we were at the point of hurting financially.

"There's a pension system, but I have to wait until I'm sixty-five. I was up in the Church Council of Allentown, and I picked up a pamphlet on food stamps. I looked to see if I qualified for my size family. My pension is just a shade above what would qualify me for them—$1,200 qualifies you for food stamps, and my pension is $1,294. That's an eye opener. When these kids get ready for college, that pension's barely going to buy a bag of groceries. Right now it's nice.

"When I think about the way Steel handled it all, I know what they went through in their decision making. I was in that position, where I was the decision maker that had to lay people off. If I had to lay off one person out of four, it was hard to pick whether the youngest one went, the oldest one, the least productive one went, or where you draw the line. How do you draw the line? I can appreciate that they were caught up in that wrenching feeling of decision making. It comes down to the fact that the decision has to be made, so you make it.

"They had the Center on Career Continuation, and they brought in an outside concern called Mainstream Access. The initial stage was to take you through a week-long program where you're developing yourself and exploring your reactions to the experience. There is a big world out there and you are something, and you can go in a lot of different directions. They did a lot of personality explanations about people who are introverts and extroverts. I went through the programs, and my wife sat in on them, too. Then they had a clearing house for job placement. They put notices on the bulletin board for available jobs, they had phone books for other cities, they had resume-writing help and a typing service. They also had a course for entrepreneurs, people starting their own business, which was interesting. I went through that, too.

"Well, happiness, is a state of mind, and I've always been happy. I think that I'm this way now because the pressure is my own creation, and the pressures of outside concerns are less.

"One of the other things that our world is saying is that finances alone don't make a successful person. Many of the very wealthy people like Onassis and Howard Hughes may have had money, but they didn't have a good balance in their lives. The key word is balance. We have to strive to get our family, our physical conditioning, our religious life, our social and community life, and the finances all in good balance. That's a better kind of life to lead. One of the things I want to do is help people get what they want. So I'm involved in the public TV auction, helping people collect the gifts that they donated. I'm involved with the Lions and headed up their Easter flower sale, and with the Lehigh Alumni.

"I have a nonstructured schedule, and so I can take off an hour or two here in the middle of the day to talk to you or take off to take the kids up to the pool. But then I might be working until two o'clock in the morning or getting up at four o'clock. I'd spend a couple hours driving around town doing different errands, so I pick up the time at night. My wife thinks that I'm working more, but it's off and on work."

* * *

The process of adjusting to retirement raises a number of questions: How much of our status and our happiness is a result of our work role and work image? On leaving the role, do we become more depressed? More lonely? Is our health affected? How shall we use all that free time? What can we do to make the retirement years more meaningful?

There appear to be two primary aspects to the adjustment process: our feelings toward retirement and the specific actions we choose in adjusting. This chapter examines the various ways our respondents look at their new world of retirement.

Identity and the Social Setting

Nearly all the participants in our study grew up in the Lehigh Valley—the metropolitan area of Allentown, Bethlehem, and Easton, Pennsylvania. This area represents a conservative life style, based as it is on proximity to the Pennsylvania German heritage, the dominance of fairly traditional industries—such as textile, motor transport, and steel—and a strong religious participation. As reflected in our sample, the population is largely of European descent. The United Steelworkers union did not permit Afro-Americans to work at Steel until the mid-1950s, and Puerto Ricans have moved into the Lehigh Valley in recent decades to provide a pool of unskilled and semi-skilled workers.

Despite its pattern of basic industries, the community is not without a touch of intellectual atmosphere, with six institutions of higher learning within a ten-mile radius, as well as other sources of "culture"—an above-average press (at least in one of the three cities), museums, live theaters, and a musical focus, including Musikfest, the

Bach Choir, and the Allentown Symphony Orchestra. Moreover, on the economic side, the 1980s saw the transition from heavy industries to more contemporary new enterprises and an influx of white-collar workers.

Our sample inevitably draws upon several traditions identified with upper-age persons—a low divorce rate, religious values, and political stability. In addition, educational attainment was a goal for most of the respondents. The strong work ethic of both Pennsylvania Germans and the new immigrants is also reflected. At the same time, most, but hardly all, felt a sense of liberation in moving on to a stage of leisure and freedom.

The Initial Shock

For perhaps a fifth of our retirees, retirement was a moment of exquisite bliss. For others it was either a kind of suspended ambivalence or an unforgettable trauma. For several, leaving the workplace had been preceded by weeks or months of uncertainty, tilted more to pleasant anticipation than to distress, or perhaps surrounded by a degree of black humor. "At Steel we never knew whether or not to bring our lunch on Friday."

For more than a few, "Black Friday" in March 1984—there were other Black Fridays—seemed like the end of the world. Betty Carlucci remembers all too well: "When he came home that day, well, we both just cried. We knew it was coming but we didn't know when. I just felt bad for him." Aldo was one of those who needed the structure and recognition even more than the pay of the job.

Over half of our retirees felt a sense of relief on retirement. As noted, at least one study has pointed to initial enthusiasm in the first year, followed by a period of letdown by the second year of retirement.[1] Other studies indicate a period of uncertainty and then a period of growing satisfaction with retirement.[2] Neither for our very recent retirees nor for those who had been retired some years did we find a prolonged crisis—except in a few cases—in the life cycle at the time of retirement. Nor did those retired for only a short time differ appreciably from those retired for a considerable number of years.

Are We Ever Satisfied?

A notable finding of this study is the degree of contentment with retirement. Although the retirees varied in the amount of time it took and the means used to reach this state of adjustment, over two-thirds (69 percent) answered on the questionnaires that they were "very satisfied," 22 percent were "somewhat satisfied," and only 9 percent rated themselves as "dissatisfied." Other surveys reported in the daily and popular press, by such organizations as the Commonwealth Fund, the U.S. Department of Labor, and *Modern Maturity*, often indicate contradictory findings on the degree of happiness among retirees. These data depend on factors such as blue-collar versus white-collar status, voluntary versus involuntary retirement, perceived quality of work conditions, financial condition, and health. Satisfaction also depends on the timing of retirement. For example, according to a study by Philip Wirtz and Ivan Charner,[3] among six thousand retired union members, 23 percent felt they had started retirement too early. Most studies of retirees, retiring both early and on time, show that well over half are satisfied with their new status.[4]

A number of factors fed into the overall positive attitudes of our set of retirees. As would be expected, among those in our sample who had wanted to retire, only 10 percent regretted their date of retirement, whereas among those who had not wanted to retire, 35 percent felt it was too early. Also, this negative attitude toward the retirement date was more than three times as prevalent among those who felt they were *worse* off financially. As our sample was primarily of salaried personnel, many had satisfactory retirement benefits and perhaps larger savings and investments; consequently postretirement feelings were more optimistic. (A blue-collar sample might have displayed more relief from work pressure, but more concern with finances and what to do with leisure time.) The higher rating on overall happiness in our study suggests, as with other surveys, that a volunteer sample attracts the more eager or optimistic members of our society. Rationalization, or the reluctance to admit that retirement might have been a mistake, is also relevant. Then there are the decisive and pragmatic: "I never look back. Whatever happens, I go on from there."

The retirees seem to fit the model of continuity; that is, the act of retirement fits into an ongoing structure in their lives. At the same time, retirement is a many-faceted event. It's a question of family relations, finances, health, and a myriad of other factors. In one study, the degree of community activities was the most important variable in the feeling of well-being for both retired and working men.[5] But primary to the social or civic involvement is the question: How does the loss of our occupational identity affect us? After all, the work role is all-important in probably every society of the world.

As noted in Chapter 3, satisfaction with retirement proves to depend on a cluster of factors. Among these factors are degree of work satisfaction, timing of retirement, feeling of having initiated the decision, feelings on how the employer handled the retirement process, health, income, and several personal and interpersonal factors. We may turn to the remarks of Nellie Jones, who headed an employment office. Although only partly dissatisfied with her job pressures, she chose to retire at age sixty after thirty-one years (interestingly, two people were hired to replace her). She explains:

"At first you wonder if you are doing the right thing. You do have lots of doubts. But once I made the decision, I was not going to back away. I didn't regret it one day. But for others, it can be different. This is basically a one-industry city, and I'd have men who were laid off come into my office who didn't know where to turn. They were worried whether they could make their mortgage payments or educate their children. These were people who sat in the office and actually cried because they'd never been laid off before. Many were relatively young men, under fifty. And they felt partially responsible for what had happened, even though it was really a class action. . . . At least for me the best thing about retirement is being able to do whatever you want when you want. Even in the first month I can't say there's been a day that I regretted being retired. . . . I never thought that I would be so happy."

A statistically strong relationship is found between retirement satisfaction and judgment of how the employer handled the retirement process. Thus, among the less happy are those who spoke of an initial feeling of being "hurt" when told they could or must leave before they had planned to. Interestingly, even after several years, anger is more often expressed by the wives (reacting to the way their spouses had been let go) than by the husbands: "We were both hurt. I could *see* my husband was hurt." He, however, said that he was "frustrated." This gender-based difference is part of our culture. For example, contrast the following excerpts from separate interviews of John and Esther Mueller talking about the initial adjustment. He was a college professor forced to retire at age sixty-seven (prior to the effective date of the legal basis of mandatory retirement at age seventy); she was a high school teacher still employed. Note here the role of attitudes and activities in their adjustment. When asked if the mandate to leave the work he enjoyed had hurt him, his subdued answer was, "No, I didn't feel that strongly. I wasn't particularly pleased with it but that's the way it was so I just accepted it." In contrast is his wife's analysis of the initial adjustment period:

"He was very annoyed and very angry. He did not want to retire. He loved teaching so much, and I felt bad for him. He didn't really know what to do, and I, too, in a way, blame the college. I was angry at the college because they could have used him, not for any remuneration, just to use his knowledge and his mind. I wanted to write a letter to them. They could use him even to teach a class. My (adult) daughter and I prayed so much that he would be able to use his mind. . . . All he was doing was working on the farm; he cleaned up the yard, sawed wood, took care of the animals. My daughter and I became very worried when he'd go down to the local market, have a cup of coffee, and sit with the old cronies who gather there. We did not want him to become part of that kind of mentality. Now that I'm about to retire I'm glad, because we can do things together. It was really very bad because here's this man who has all this knowledge. Also he was going to write a book but never got the impetus or the energy once he retired. I began watching the papers for ads for volunteer work for him. Finally he got consulting work and that sort of brought him out. He goes to lectures occasionally. Another thing that pulled him out was getting on the school board. He goes to all their conventions and loves it. He is also very active in the church and teaches a class for children there. Then he became involved in helping me in the student contests for the state History Day. But curiously, it was his decision to raise bees that saved his sanity.

"At the college they should do something to make people feel appreciated for all the years they put in. You have all this experience and they're cutting you off when you could go on. We're so different from the Orientals, who value age. We do not value age nor what it represents. We are losing a wealth out there, though volunteers give a lot of it."

The Search for Happiness

Not only did we ask the retirees how satisfied they are now in retirement, but we asked each to compare his or her degree of "happiness" today to five years ago, when most were still working. Again, their responses show a positive adjustment in retirement:

Very much happier	37%
Somewhat happier	31%
About the same	20%
Somewhat less happy	10%
Much less happy	3%

In other words, the process of adjustment produced a mix of *positive* and *negative* reactions but an *overall* balance toward the positive for the vast majority. Often a new lease on life was called for. After his career as senior vice president of a utility company, Mark Chamberlin decided to move to the country, raise fruit trees, collect antique machines, and take up square dancing. Another retiree suggested, "It's best to take a sabbatical the first year." A frequent remark was, "What I really miss is the opportunity to use my skills." More than occasionally a blend of images from the past pervades the feelings about retirement. One former teacher lamented: "I miss the coffee breaks with staff more than the kids in the classroom." Several found their adjustment in a kind of vigorous defensive reaction. For instance, when a number of Steel executives discovered that the "package" no longer included the maximum health insurance, they organized REBCO (Retired Employees Benefits Corporation), which became a pivotal anchor of their postretirement activity. Several hundred blue-collar retirees were also caught up in this movement. Betty Carlucci spoke of her husband Aldo: "When Steel was going to cut the benefits, they took them to court. He signed up on that too. We now have a medical program."

In most instances the retiree came to terms with his or her departure. Marjory Trueblood describes both her and her husband Tim's trauma at his being dismissed at age fifty-two after thirty years as senior accountant at Steel. She describes a series of shifting feelings, moving from a strongly negative emotional response to a more passive one and then to a positive emotional adjustment:

"There was so much pressure the five months before he was laid off! The night he told me I cried and I remember we didn't sleep much. There was an upheaval in our lives, even though in the end he was happy to be out. . . . When friends called it was like somebody died in the family. They didn't know what to say. In the beginning it was real anger on my part; that disappeared right away and then it was sadness. It took a month before I got adjusted. At least it's relief that he's finally happy."

Perhaps none of our retirees had as difficult a time as did Juan Garcia. His illness seemed to develop in him an ego-strength beyond what most of us could probably develop:

"I was born in 1934 here in Easton. My family had come from Mexico during the First World War. Quite a few families came here in order to work for Steel and the railroad. More of them lived in Bethlehem. I was the only Mexican in my school here and only once in a while did I have any trouble. But even in the Depression my Dad found a job, at least intermittently.

"After high school I worked a while as a laborer for the Central Railroad of New Jersey, but I decided I wanted to be a policeman. I took the course and scored high enough to be qualified. Once on the job, I found that I went from traffic control to other routines and rose in the ranks and made it to sergeant. I enjoyed being with my fellow policemen. We are still good friends. Somehow, though, I noticed that they were against minorities. I often wondered if I wasn't an exception, and probably underneath they also looked down on Hispanics, too.

"I was usually up before six A.M. as I was in charge of the platoon. Later I was president of the union. I got into a lot of activities. For one thing, I organized the medicorps here in Easton and until recently I was in the ambulance corps.

"A few years after I was on the force I got married. It worked out the first four or five years, but she found someone else. I got custody of our two children, who are now on their own. Soon after the divorce I began to have problems urinating. I went to the doctor and found it was diabetes. It was about that time that I got married a second time. She, too, had been divorced. . . . The injections helped for a while but the disease got worse. About six years ago I was going downhill fast, and I lost my left leg, and there has been some loss of sight. So I had to retire at age forty-eight in 1982.

"It has been rough, but I try to be philosophic about it. People have been helpful, but not always. I remember one winter day when I was removing snow and fell on the ice—not a single passerby offered to help me up. . . . I spent a lot of time in the hospital and got to know a number of the nurses. A lot of them are single and need help with repairs around the house, which I do for them. I do pretty well with my prosthesis. . . . My police buddies still drop in on me. And I spend a good deal of time with my family. My own children are grown but the teenage son of my present wife is still with us. Also, I have a lot of brothers and sisters, and most of them live nearby. My eighty-two-year-old mother lives with my oldest sister. . . . Well, you can see I just don't have time to feel sorry for myself."

The Life Cycle, Crisis, and Planning

From the forties into the fifties, many individuals reach a point of evaluating their accomplishments as compared with their aspirations. As Daniel Levinson notes in his examination of a sample of men in midlife, there are doubts about oneself, one's career, and one's marriage. Three tasks appear to be central in this midlife transition: (1) ending one phase of adulthood with an appraisal of what is to be done, (2) changing the unfavorable aspects of one's life and evaluating new options, and (3) wrestling with the meaning of the life cycle, for instance, the confrontation of youth and old age. Many of our sample had just been working through this phase of the life cycle. As expected, retirement is less traumatic when the individual is relatively satisfied with the retirement procedures and has a chance to find substitutes for his or her career.

Figure 4-1 illustrates how we move through given periods of adjustment over the years. Young, middle, and old age have varying cycles of mood, energy, and self-reflection. Hope, satisfaction, and despair alternate. Achievements and failures give rise to points of transition. Ashley Montagu feels that at heart the middle-aged are trying to recapture the magic of childhood: to explore, to love, to learn, to wonder—typical urges of the child.[6] However, our data suggest that most retirees—who generally still consider themselves to be middle-aged—have a relatively passive life style. In other words, the Jim Zimmermans and the Walter Kochs are not necessarily typical retirees. Studies of the psychological reactions (including responses to the Thematic Apperception Test) among samples of individuals in the late fifties and beyond show that they tend to have a low profile; that is, they are more likely to be in the background than in the foreground of what is going on.[7] Often people in their fifties and sixties do appear relatively passive in the face of changes, but it is difficult to know whether this is because they are entering a new phase of their lives or whether people in that age group today have always been somewhat less assertive and active than those younger than they are.

As persons have their own rhythms of development, there is little agreement as to whether a midlife crisis exists. The evidence suggests that men are more vulnerable to self-doubts than are women. In any case, retirement may be a result or even a cause of crisis. Certainly this period is one of exploring options, some being more pleasant than others. Moreover, according to Susan Littwin, the generation born in the 1920s, because of their recollection of the Great Depression, are better prepared for this transition than those born later, especially in the 1950s and 1960s, who have been reared on an

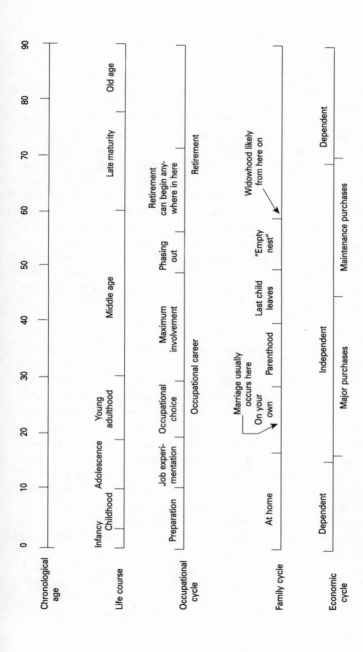

Figure 4-1. Relationships among age, life cycle, occupational cycle, and family cycle. The relationships vary according to individuals and with occupation, social class, and ethnic group. From Robert C. Atchley, *The Social Forces in Later Life: An Introduction to Social Gerontology*, 3d ed., Wadsworth, Inc., 1980. Reprinted by permission.

unrealistic combination of prosperity, high-paying jobs, and the make-believe world of television.[8]

All life events relate, of course, to our social interactions. As Jay Mancini points out, each of our decisions or activities affects in some way our communication to others—family, co-workers, and friends. We begin to define our situations differently from what we did before.[9] All this has become easier as our society has accepted the idea of retirement—even early retirement—as a respectable identity. Even those who have not come to accept a new self after retirement can somehow manage to maintain a portion of the self-image or what they perceive to be their identity to the other person. For instance, the ex-vice-president of Allstair Aluminum Corporation still maintains some of his former status even if he has to use the past rather than the present tense: "I was vice president. . . . " Still others enjoy their new relationship to the world. For instance, John Hines, a former vice president from Steel, was happy to move out of the pecking order: "It's kind of nice not to have to worry whom I'm talking to, in what circles I can move, with whom I play bridge, what kind of car I drive. I got kind of tired of that stuffiness."

The transition to retirement is for most persons not a sudden affair. Whereas earlier studies indicated that less than 12 percent of retirees had made specific preparations for retirement, later research finds that the preparation is in progress over a lengthy period. One study of 816 male workers in the Boston area, using informal means rather than the usual questionnaire approach, found that a majority were making plans for retirement over a period of fifteen years or more.[10] Asking friends "what is it like," making financial investments, changes in buying habits—all are subtle or deliberate means of moving toward that fateful day. The degree of planning is partly shaped by the economic climate.[11] Those retiring during the inflation of the 1970s made more elaborate preparations than did those of the more comfortable 1980s. But whatever the socioeconomic situation, we apparently move through the life cycle with an awareness of the transitional character of each stage, and moving out of the workplace is no exception. Even "early" retirement apparently affords to most people an adequate time to play out the pre-transition process sufficiently.

However, even when one has the time, there are a number of

complicated questions. To whom does one turn in seeking advice regarding financial or employment possibilities during the retirement process? Inevitably, most of our sample relied on their family, friends, or colleagues to give advice. A third of our sample found their employer offering counseling, or at least suggestions, either about finances or employment opportunities. Only 9 percent of the sample turned to agencies, and 8 percent found their unions useful in making the transition.

Time, Place, and the Perception of Difficulty

The length of time to adjust depends on each individual. Nearly half (46 percent) felt they adjusted within a month; 18 percent, a month or two; 11 percent, three months to a year; 5 percent, more than a year. In other words, for the majority adjustment comes sooner rather than later. Yet, 21 percent say they are "still not used to it," even three to four years after beginning retirement. We tried to zero in on that important minority, but in fact found little explanation for their inability to adjust quickly. Clearly, there is a complex interplay of events and probably a lifelong pattern of slower-than-usual adjustment to change. Early in the chapter we hinted at the conservative life style of Lehigh Valley residents and their comparatively slower acceptance of innovation. However, in any region the older population generally finds change more difficult than does the younger.

In view of the popular mythology about aging, younger people often think of the reactions of elders—including adjustment to retirement—as problematic. However, research indicates that this age group has a coping ability equal to that of the young.[12] Indeed, the virtues of endurance and patience are hardly alien to the senior population.

The feeling of difficulty in making the adjustment is, naturally, a strong index of satisfaction. A third of our sample found the transition easier than they expected, a sixth found it more difficult, and a half said "it's about what I expected." We discovered that in some instances expectations can harm adjustment: "I was so anxious to get out. The pressures were building up. All I heard was 'we've got to make a profit.' Then once retired I realized that it wasn't all so simple.

Inflation was more than I thought it was going to be. The kids' tuition was going up. I had gotten a false idea of what my pension would be. . . . " Naturally, those who found retirement easier and those who experienced it as expected were much more satisfied than the relatively small group who found it harder than expected.

Those who are suddenly forced or enticed into retirement without much lead time—either by their poor health or by the action of the employer—seem to take longer to adjust. Conversely, the period of adjustment is shorter for those who over time had felt a distinct shove from management or from younger colleagues or for whom the last few years of work became disagreeable (more stress and fewer satisfactions). For them the sense of relief in escape from work can result in near euphoria.

The variables of time and age assume various forms, and each of us processes time according to our individual needs. Matt Boyd spoke for many of the younger retirees when he said, "You've got to find a new niche before you're fifty." Indeed, for many, the meaning of time is different at sixty from what it was at twenty-five: "Each day means a lot more to me than it used to; I've only got so many days left in my life." Then there are those who look upon life in a more immediate sense, such as Aldo Carlucci, who says: "You get up the next day, you know you're not going to go to work and what are you going to do with your time, and things like that. You go through a lot of soul searching until things iron out." Recent retiree Gordon Wald, a construction electrician comments: "Well, trying to find things to occupy myself is more of a problem than I anticipated. It's just like when I go for a walk I want to have a destination to go to and that's what I did this afternoon. I walked down and had a haircut so I'd have a reason for being there. I haven't really done the walking that I had planned on doing. I should go down and see the ducks at Muhlenberg, but I ain't done that yet." After years of long days at his hardware store, Oliver Burke remarked, "It's a big change, and my personal feeling was how am I going to be able to handle this in spite of all the jokes about waking up in the morning and thinking I don't have to work anymore." For Jim Dowd, after the stress at Steel: "No longer is someone saying to me, 'Where is that report you promised last Friday.' But there's less stress outside work, too. If I go to the bank, I don't care if there's a line or someone steps in front of me. I don't care if it takes forever. Before, my time was so limited."

Also, the timing of retirement with respect to the seasons can be important: "It's a lot better when you are dumped in the spring or summer; never retire in the winter." Another said: "The worst thing about retirement is winter." Also, a former social worker commented, "Somehow I just find myself more accepting of new things in my life during springtime or even summer. I'm sure glad that I left in June, not January." Still another mused: "At least when you get out in spring or summer you have the long days and you can go on a trip to kinda break-in retirement, or at least you can play golf. I was never very good on skis."

If the consciousness of time and age is a major component of our identity, location is not far behind. The Lehigh Valley itself provides a setting that is midway between the metropolis and the rural. Residing in suburbia or a mid-size city appears to be favorable to adjustment in retirement.[13]

In his book *Prisoners of Space*, Graham Rowles notes: "Feelings about places are intimately linked with the events of the individual's unique biography."[14] Or, as another observer explained, "We ourselves give meaning to the environment."[15] This tendency seemingly becomes more intense in the later years. As one retiree said, "My husband wants to move, but I could never imagine leaving here. We know all the neighbors, and it's where we saw our kids grow up." At least three of the retirees had moved to the Lehigh Valley from elsewhere, especially a major metropolitan area, and never felt completely at home: "I think it was the change in life style that bothered me. I know he resented it, and we had a nice life, though not luxurious, in New York City. Then we had to come back here to this place and get it in shape, leaving a good job and the beautiful people with it. We both loved New York. But I've always been one to do what you have to do. It's one more phase of our life." In a similar tone, Ed Volpe, a retired vocational school administrator, notes: "Living here on the South Side, which most people think of as a depressed area, gives us a feeling of continuity. I suppose I'm ready to leave, but my wife says no. We've been here our whole married life, our children grew up here. Maybe my retirement would have been harder if I had moved away. I don't know." On the other hand, Alan Adams, a one-time executive, said, "The year I retired from Steel we decided to sell our house in Saucon Valley. What do we want with a two-acre estate? We're now in a more modest house that suits our phase of life—but there's still room for all the kids when they come home."

The Best and the Worst

In order to assess our subjects' feelings, on the questionnaire we asked what is "best" and what is "worst" about retirement. The responses are listed in rank order in Table 4-1. The number and unanimity of positive responses far outweigh the negative.

As implied in Chapters 2 and 3, *time* and *freedom* dominate their answers. Many retirees emphasized *freedom to get away* from something (usually an employer-fixed time schedule). Others wrote the

Table 4-1. Best and Worst Aspects of Retirement*

Best		Worst	
1. Time related		1. Left question blank or could think of "nothing that is worst"	29%
a. Freedom from schedule, clock, routine, deadlines, or "freedom to do what I want, when I want"	51%		
		2. "Loneliness" or miss people associated with former work	16%
b. Freedom to travel, pursue other interests (old and new), do volunteer work, be with family and friends	39%	3. Financial concerns	12%
		4. Inactivity (including social activity) or boredom	11%
2. Release from on-the-job "stress," pressures, need for decision-making	17%	5. "Not enough time"	5%
		6. Age related: health and deaths of family or friends	5%
3. Chance to enter new work	6%	7. Other	14%
4. Improved health	5%		
5. Other	5%		

*Based on 115 questionnaires; multiple answers possible.

positive phrase "freedom to do what I want when I want"; these retirees are looking *forward to* enjoying the time to undertake some specific activity. According to their answers to the questionnaire, the next best thing is getting away from the stress, pressures, responsibilities, or the boredom of work; for those retirees it is *escape from* something negative more than enjoying freedom itself.

And in the interviews, when again asked what are the best and worst things about retirement, the responses were much the same as in the questionnaires, with the positive comments dominant in roughly the same order. However, in the interviews, new horizons were more the theme rather than past pressures at work. During the interviews, a resounding cry was the "joy of no time schedule"—the sense of freedom after years of hearing the alarm clock and having their time structured by the job: "It's great to look out at the falling snow and know I can stay right here in bed." Rev. Don Siegfried summed up his feelings: "I now have the fun part of the ministry. I've always enjoyed working with people. Preaching I also enjoyed, but I don't have to worry now about raising budgets and doing all the correspondence or the silly leg work that goes with any job that you'd have."

As seen in Table 4-1, far below the sense of freedom and the release from stress, according to those who answered the questionnaire, are the satisfaction found in postretirement employment and health. A very small percentage felt that their health improved after retirement. These are primarily persons who while working had experienced heart trouble, operations, ulcers, frequent colds, or headaches. (We shall return to this subject later in the chapter.)

The most common answers to a similar question about the *worst* aspects of retirement in descending order of frequency, were (1) loneliness or missing colleagues, (2) financial concerns, (3) what to do with one's time, (4) not enough time, and (5) age-related troubles (health and deaths of family or friends). Interestingly, "missing colleagues" appeared less often in the interviews. As the interview followed the questionnaire by several months, it seems possible that some retirees adjusted gradually to the loss of friends as time went on. Or, possibly, they had made new friends who were as satisfying as the ones from work had been. This regret of missing interactions often came from those who served the public. For example, dentists and doctors said what they miss most is the contact with their patients, especially during the first year or two after retirement.

In other words, the process of adjustment is a mix of *positive* and *negative* factors, and in some instances, over time, the negative ones could become less so.

What Do They Miss Most?

Questionnaire responses to a checklist of what the retirees miss from work mirrors and amplifies the open-ended question about the worst aspects of retirement. The major adjustment the retiree has to make is moving from the recognized and often socially stimulating world of the job to the often more private life. On the questionnaire, the retirees checked the following items that they specifically miss:

The people they worked with	65%
The feeling of being useful	41%
Status and respect of others	38%
The stimulation of the work itself	34%

Most checked at least two items. Loss of contact with fellow workers was the most frustrating aspect of retirement for two-thirds of retirees. During the interviews, by contrast, these items were mentioned by considerably smaller proportions. Surprisingly, given this sample of professionals, even when directly asked to talk about whether they missed using their skills, their status, their sense of identity, or the work itself, only a handful answered "yes." There may be psychological explanations for this difference between what is anonymously written and what is spoken face-to-face. After all, the interview is a less-structured process than the questionnaire.

A few agreed that something is missing. For Hank Nelson "the worst about retirement is your loss of self-esteem. That's why I'm working even if I don't make all I'm entitled to because of the limits set by Social Security." Another put it: "Even though leisure may be respectable when you are retired, it takes a long time. It's part of the Puritan ethic or the Benjamin Franklin notion that idle hands are not worthy."

Coping with Loneliness

Only 16 percent identified "missing colleagues and others" when asked about the worst aspects of retirement, but nearly two-thirds (65 percent) checked that response on the checklist. That, however, is not the same as "being lonely." When asked outright on the questionnaire about "loneliness," over two-thirds (72 percent) indicated no change in their overall loneliness. However, nearly one-fourth (24 percent) felt more lonely. The feeling of loneliness was found to be negatively linked not only with retirement satisfaction but also with general happiness—in both cases with strong statistical significance.

Listen to what Tom Lorenzo, a steel laborer from Chapter 1, has to say about the loss of contacts and adjustment: "In a sense the job was good. You do miss it, especially in the first six months. You sort of want to mingle with the guys again. You miss that togetherness of the co-workers you had. I served as a trustee of the local union for three years and as vice president for three years, and then as president of a labor council for five years. All this I really miss." Tom would not call himself lonely. But a few did, among them Betty Little, the former supervisor of a social agency, widowed at age thirty-eight with children. She envies men socially:

"A widower is at a big advantage socially. Everybody wants him for dinner. A man can go anywhere by himself, whereas a woman is more hesitant. Everybody wants an extra man, but about an extra woman they think, 'Oh, my God, we don't want her!' Men may have a harder time at home and most of them remarry. I think women feel loneliness more acutely than men because men can go out and find someone to be with. Or if a woman does get a date, the men want you to act like you've been married to them for twenty years—on your first date. I miss talking to men, as I could in the office. Also finances are very different for a widow. If you have your health and if you are a couple, that makes a big difference because there is someone there to help take care of you. Look around the malls, see all the couples together walking and talking. I think they all look happy."

Occasionally a sense of loneliness may stimulate the individual to do something for others. Bill Flynn, a retired professor, took care of an elderly couple as he empathized with their isolation. The childless Thomases adopted children in the Third World and volunteered their help to the lonely residents of a nursing home. These expressions of compassion we will explore in later chapters.

A point that should be made is that "loneliness" can mean different things at different levels of intensity. Although the percentage in the questionnaire and comments in the interviews both indicate a willingness on the part of a sizable minority to express some sense of loneliness, seldom are they talking about the nagging despair of being alone in the world and isolated. Rather, they seem to be indicating a loss of contact with specific individuals, but that loss is placed alongside a relatively healthy level of interaction and involvement with significant others. It is a relatively specific, relatively minor loneliness that resulted from retirement, especially for the men. The loneliness described by Betty Little, on the other hand, transcended retirement; it has to do with the roles of single men and women in society. Unfortunately, retirement took away from her one acceptable way to interact with men outside the role constraints of dating.

The Search for Financial Security

Lower income and cutting down on one's spending can be a challenge for both the retiree and the spouse, especially if they feel their income is greatly reduced or have health costs for the care of themselves, parents, children, or other relatives. This responsibility and the fear of one's own old age often cause resentment:

"When my husband's mother was his age (sixty-eight) she was traveling all over the world! We will see that she is never alone, and that means we must give up *our* lives. . . . Getting old today is scary because you work all your life with money going toward your retirement so you can enjoy your life at that time. Now we have to think 'What's going to become of me if I get ill and can't be taken care of at home?' Now we aren't saving toward enjoying retirement; we are saving in case we become ill and must live in a nursing home!"

Among those who spoke of financial worries was Jim Zimmerman, a former AT&T department chief, who retired at age fifty-five after learning he was being demoted to the third shift, as we saw in Chapter 1:

"My income level has dropped in round numbers from the $60,000 range to $20,000. The company is paying me what they call the management income protection plan—one year's pay over a two-year period. That bridges the gap. But it's going to be a rude awakening next year when my income drops. I will still have five years to get across until I can get Social Security. So financially I worry; the house is not paid for. The worst thing about retirement, I'd say, is giving up the income. The change is drastic."

One interesting development with Steel was in the lump sum settlement given to those who were invited into early retirement. One foreman received $184,000, which he then invested in high-income blue chips and the like. He comments: "What is curious is that the company provided no guidance about what to do with this money, at least as far as I know. And there were a couple of guys who put their money in the wrong places." In fact, many of today's retirees are financially cautious, inasmuch as they grew up in the shadow of the Great Depression. Roland Eisenhard notes how times have changed in this respect: "I try to impress on my son-in-law to take out an IRA. But what does he do for last year? He puts it into an overseas international mutual fund and says 'I'm not afraid to take a chance. If I lose all of it, I haven't lost more than $2,000. If it makes money, great.' See, I'm the cautious type. I grew up in the period where you didn't gamble your money. He's earning more now as a teacher than I did when I retired. It hurts, but it's not really envy that I feel."

In the interviews the majority of our interviewees rarely spoke of financial concerns and instead talked of much travel abroad, dining out, golf at the club, and no noticeable curtailment of their spending habits. More typical of the way retirees in this study handle their income is seen in this statement by a manager who was abruptly laid off in 1984 from a $48,000-a-year supervisory position and has been in consulting work for three years: "I did not get angry, as I probably would have if I had had a financial problem staring me in the face. I did a fairly good audit of my finances and figured out if I have to use so much a month, how long will it last? And, if I don't live to be 106 I'll be O.K. So I wasn't worried. And the work I'm doing now more than compensates for any feelings I went through. I enjoy it so much more."

Only a few of the blue-collar workers or wage earners expressed a sense of doom about receiving only the minimum Social Security check or the lack of a pension from a former employer. Most felt that they lived in a just universe. Despite his usually dark view of his situation, Tom Schmidt noted, "I got a pretty good deal when Black and Decker took over from G.E. The younger guys got nothing of their G.E. pension fund." And Gordon Wald said: "Because I'm not doing anything, I don't deserve anything." Adelaide Williams, in particular, had no problem adjusting, as she and her husband moved into their trailer court: "When I stopped working our income was cut by about 45 percent. But our income is adequate. Besides I just love making things. I sell my handmade bags at fifteen dollars. I've always been very creative, even when I was a kid. In high school I went to the Baum Art School, but then as a housewife my creativity took other directions."

Health and Retirement

According to earlier studies, health was a major determinant of the age at retirement and of adjustment in subsequent years. More recent research has shown health to be a somewhat minor factor.[16] In a national survey, a fourth of the respondents mentioned health as their main reason for retirement, but further analysis showed it to be interwoven with other motives.[17] In a comparison of white-collar (using a number of our interviewees) and blue-collar retirees, JoAnne Hansz found that nearly 90 percent of the white-collar retirees rated their health as "good" or "very good." However, the blue-collar retirees were found to have less control of their job loss and had more psychological stress before and after retirement.[18] In response to a direct question on the questionnaire about self-rated health, the majority (53 percent) indicated no change in their health after retirement: almost a third (32 percent) felt better, while 15 percent report their health is worse. A lack of health concerns related positively to retirement satisfaction, statistically speaking. In the interviews, pre- and postretirement health problems that limit activity appear in third rank among the "worst about retirement," although not for a large percentage.

Over a fifth of our sample mentioned a history of heart or cor- onary problems for either themselves or their spouses. Colin Fisher, an electrician at Bethlehem Steel, comments: "My heart problem was the basic reason for retiring. I talked to my insurance agent, and he showed me the statistics on the life span of ex-steelworkers—the earlier you get out the better chance for your health." The saddest example is Robard Young, who started work in Woolworth's at age fifteen, went into the army, returned to Woolworth's as a cook, then advanced to trainee-manager and manager. At the age of twenty- eight he went to Steel in the foundry division and planned machine operations and at age fifty-one retired because of several heart at- tacks and operations:

"When I went back to visit the plant a few weeks after I retired, I found that for maybe the week afterward I couldn't stop thinking about being back at work: Why are they doing it this way? Why don't they do it that way? During the first year every time I went I seemed to miss it more, so I made up my mind not to go back, and I haven't. You see, I found out they obviously weren't my friends; they were colleagues and co-workers.

"My medicines cost me $1,500 a year and I keep wondering how much in the future. Right now we're making it and managing to get away on vacation every year for a few days. You have to keep in mind your income is not going to go up as it was when working. I know the future is not going to be good, but the steel company does have a good health plan."

Cancer was reported by several of the interviewees, usually in connection with a spouse they had lost. Barry Lichtenweiner had not only lost his wife to cancer, but he, too, had it and held in remission:

"That's why I do a lot of volunteer work through the Visiting Nurse

Association. First I went to their bereavement program, which lasts over twelve weeks and was most helpful. In our group there were eight people, seven women and myself (I did feel a little self-conscious at first). It was a place where you could talk—everyone has the same problems and you can express your feelings. To this day we meet once or twice a month at our different homes, often for dinner. I volunteer and go around to sick people and talk to them or help out while the spouse gets some relief."

Alcoholism became a health problem for at least three who admittedly were heavy social drinkers prior to retirement. Dorothy Schmidt spoke of her husband, Tom: "His drinking is perhaps a bit heavier than when he was working. Actually I think he got started when he went into World War II when he was only eighteen. He doesn't drink during the day, but sometimes he doesn't get out of bed. . . . There are times he talks of ending his life. . . . All I can do is pray a lot."

There were a few other cases of acute depression. Also, one woman attributed two months of sickness and sciatica to being upset about retiring at age forty-five. Whereas men reported more heart trouble, women spoke more of arthritis and of work-related health problems, such as leg pains or back trouble.

On the whole, health was at least satisfactory for most of the sample. In fact, one interviewee who went to a dinner for the company's retirees commented: "They looked younger than when I saw them at work." Almost no deterioration of health was said to be *caused* by retirement. Yet the declining health of their friends or older relatives caused a degree of anxiety.

The Impinging Factors

We have pointed out how a multitude of conditions surrounding one's employment and its termination can affect how one feels about retirement. As we saw in Chapter 3, the perception of personally having initiated the retirement (66 percent thought they did), of having sufficient lead time to plan for and adjust to the idea of upcoming retirement, and of the employer adequately handling the retirement were all positive features for satisfaction in retirement (with statistical significance). All are structural factors related to the retirement *process* itself. We have also reviewed the individual's feelings related specifically to the period of *adjustment after* retirement. Activities, social networks, family support, values, personality—all form the context of adjustment in retirement, shaping feelings and behavior.

One may ask about another structural factor. Is the residential setting relevant? A national survey of the upper-age economically advantaged confirmed that they were more likely to be suburban or noncentral city dwellers.[19] Although those in our sample living in a suburban area were generally happier with their career, perhaps because of more affluence, retirement satisfaction and adjustment were not affected. However, a midsize urban area, such as the Lehigh Valley, may not show as sharp a demarcation between urban and suburban as would major metropolitan areas. Several respondents did poignantly describe the importance of place for them, whether continuity or change of place was the result.

Associations and Organizations for the Retiree

We have clearly seen in both data we collected and our review of other studies that most retirees adapt to—we should probably use a more active and creative word like *manage*—their retirement years well. They do so in ways as varied as their personal work experiences, personalities, and life situations as they begin to be "retired." Many simply continue the same activities they have grown accustomed to in the past. Many take at least some time to pause and reflect and then plunge forward once more. A fairly large number engage in new activities, either in combination with past pursuits or as a new vocation, which itself might be a new work experience or the job of being a "person of leisure" or a busy volunteer. Nearly all are doing their part to create a different kind of world, a different way of relating work to leisure, as they pioneer retirement as an expected and completely normal part of the life cycle.

When we looked at the types of activities that became more frequent in later life (as will be revealed in Chapter 6), we saw that many retirees increased their involvement in a number of individual or family-centered endeavors. These included housework and yardwork, hobbies, and time with family. Quite a few also increased activities that are more organizational in nature, namely in work, volunteering, and social organizations.

In the next few pages, we explore a few of the ways that organizations or associations can aid the retiree in deciding what directions to pursue and in attaining goals he or she has set. First, we will mention a few national organizations; interested readers can then begin to pursue the specifics of what is available in their own communities with this as a guide.

A national organization with which most readers are probably at least somewhat familiar is the American Association of Retired Persons (AARP). The membership of AARP is now over thirty million persons, who may join beginning at age fifty. Despite the name, there is no requirement of being retired to be a member of AARP, and so virtually anyone over fifty, many of whom will be in the work force for many more years, can participate. Dues are a mere five dollars per year, which include opportunities for discount programs, a wide-range of information resources, and a subscription to *Modern Maturity* (which, because of the membership, has one of the largest circulations of any magazine in the world!).

At the national level, AARP sponsors research related to aging and publishes many consumer-oriented materials that are likely to be of direct interest to all readers of this book. The scope of its concerns includes, among others, work, housing, consumer affairs, physical and mental health, problems of age discrimination, political action, and minority affairs. (If you aren't a member, the address to contact is AARP, 1909 K St., N.W., Washington, D.C. 20049.)

Also an important organization at the local level, AARP has over 3,500 chapters across the country. Certainly one obvious place to begin to explore social opportunities—and find out about volunteer activities—is one's local AARP chapter. The organization is so large that many cities provide a choice of chapters for membership and participation.

The second largest national membership organization of older persons is the National Council of Senior Citizens (NCSC), with a membership of nearly five million and over 4,500 clubs. Although membership in NCSC is open to all older persons, it is more closely tied to labor unions than AARP, and thus most members are long-time union members. (Its address is 925 15th St., N.W., Washington, D.C. 20005.)

A different sort of "national" organization in the sense of its penetration into the entire United States is really a collection of regional organizations that developed from and are in part supported by the Federal Administration on Aging. This is the so-called aging network of Area Agencies on Aging. The Older Americans Act amendments in the mid-1970s required that each state have a unit on Aging and a set of Area Agencies based on political or geographic regions of the state (counties, large cities, or areas like "southeastern"). If a state didn't have such an arrangement it would be ineligible for federal money for programs related to aging. Not surprisingly, every state quickly made sure it had such a network!

Area Agencies on Aging are primarily planning and managing systems for delivery of social services in their regions. Many of these services, like home health care, meal programs, chore services, and supportive services, are not likely to be of interest or need to most recent or aspiring retirees for many years to come. However, what is likely to be of value is that Area Agencies on Aging are also clearing-houses for a wide range of information of interest to all Americans over the age of sixty (the cutoff age for most of their programs). They can often provide information about volunteer opportunities, for example, or agencies that specialize in helping older persons find work. They are knowledgeable about all kinds of organizations for and about older persons.

They are well worth contacting, whether you are a lifelong resident of your current area or, even more so, if you have recently moved. Most telephone directories will have a listing under social service organizations or senior services, but if that route doesn't work, the state's office or department on aging, which may be in the directory's government listings, can send you to the area agency in your region. Also, the Administration on Aging (330 Independence Ave., S.W., Washington, D.C. 20201) or the National Association of Area Agencies on Aging (Suite 208, 600 Maryland Ave., S.W., Washington, D.C. 20024) can provide specific information about the area agency in a particular area.

Work-Related Organizations

Although for many (mostly younger) people it may seem odd to talk about work in relation to retirees, we know from this study and many others that a sizable minority of those who retire from one job find another (about 40 percent). Of course, for most retirees work is a sometime thing, either part time or seasonal, with maybe 10 percent working full time. In our study, 42 percent had worked for pay sometime since retiring. In most studies, a relatively small percentage of those *not* working would like to be.

Job seeking in the later years can be a lot like dating; it takes some time to adjust and redevelop skills that the older person did not anticipate he or she would need anymore.

Fortunately, for many older persons who wish to work, the job often seems to find the retiree as much as the other way around. One's previous employer would like some consulting or part-time assistance, or another employer hears about the skills and experience of the retiree and makes an offer. Some employers, especially larger corporations, provide extensive outplacement services that include assistance with job searches, especially for early retirees. But if a retiree wishes to work, and where and how are not obvious, how can he or she go about finding a job?

There seem to be two answers to that question. One answer is to use regular job-finding channels, like the newspaper or employment agencies. This may yield a job; unfortunately, it may also yield age-based job discrimination. The Age Discrimination in Employment Acts make discrimination toward "older" workers (workers over forty) illegal. The Acts are administered by the Equal Employment Opportunity Commission of the federal government. If you feel that a job is being denied you because of age, you can file a complaint (EEOC's number is 1-800-872-3362). Age-bias complaints are in fact frequent these days. Individual victims can often get representation through their local legal services or legal aid society. In fact, such services may well have a person whose a specialist in aging and/or job discrimination.

The Department of Labor administers a Senior Community Service Employment Program through local service agencies that assists low-income persons above the age of fifty-five in finding employment.

There is often an alternative job-finding organization, however, that is not likely to bring a retiree face-to-face with age discrimination. Usually called the Senior Job Bank, this organization specializes in placement of persons over the age of fifty or so. The Senior Job Bank develops positions with employers who are interested in the skills and experience of older workers, and it also often helps older job applicants with resume writing, preparations for interviews, and other job-finding skills. The Senior Job Bank can help older "job-daters" get over the uncertainty about what to do and where to look.

Finally, many state employment offices, and sometimes Area Agencies on Aging, have specialized programs to provide new skills to older workers to make them competitive for new jobs. In some cases, retirees from more traditional jobs may find themselves filling jobs that didn't even exist when they began to work, such as computer data entry!

Volunteering

As with work, volunteering is as varied as the skills and interests of older persons. Also, as with work, volunteer opportunities often seek out the retiree. Many older persons have been volunteers for many decades; they may simply devote more time or energy to the same organizations as they have in the past. Alternatively, some retirees may have felt they didn't have time to do much volunteer work before or are looking for new vistas of volunteering, so they may need a bit of guidance as to how to go about getting matched to volunteer placements that can utilize their skills.

Again, there are programs in place in many communities that can aid in searches for volunteer activities. One of the most well known and extensive is RSVP, the Retired Senior Volunteer Program. A federally and locally supported program, RSVP serves as a liaison between older persons who would like to volunteer and a wide array of organizations that need volunteers, such as libraries, schools, hospitals, and community agencies.

RSVP can find volunteer opportunities that are permanent, or it can keep a pool of "temps" for older persons who want more flexibility. Persons in the pool can spend five hours doing a mailing for a social service agency one week, a telephone survey another week, or not take on any activity for awhile, when other interests come to the fore. Seldom do RSVP offices complain that they have too many volunteers or that some don't want to have a regular ten-hour-a-week schedule; they are happy to have a wide variety of people in the pool to match by skill, schedule, and interest to the never-ending needs of most nonprofit agencies.

Related to RSVP but more specialized is SCORE, the Service Corps of Retired Executives. In conjunction with the Small Business Administration, this program matches retired executives, with their reservoir of managerial experience, to small businesses, whose owners are often in danger of being in over their heads because they are young and inexperienced. Truly consultants in every sense of the word, SCORE volunteers are credited by many who have received assistance with making the difference between success and failure of a business.

Both RSVP and SCORE are part of the ACTION program of the U.S. government developed as part of the National Older Americans Volunteer Program, a 1969 addition to the Older Americans Act. Two other popular programs under the same umbrella are Foster Grandparents and Senior Companions. Both of these volunteer programs match up older persons with those with special needs or disabilities; the primary difference is that in the case of Foster Grandparents the others are children, while Senior Companions work with older disabled persons.

Of course, ACTION does not have programs that are only solely directed toward older volunteers. ACTION has other VISTA (Volunteers in Service to America) programs for volunteers in the United States and overseas service with the Peace Corps. Both programs accept volunteers of any age for placement into service positions. In both cases, volunteers get a subsistence allowance.

Many AARP programs at the state and local level are staffed by volunteers. Specialized training is given to some by AARP, such as in the CHISS (Consumer Housing Information Services for Seniors) program, which uses volunteers to provide information about housing options to older persons in need of alternative housing arrangements.

Every nursing home and hospital always welcomes volunteers of any age and skill level, from the teen-age Candy Stripers to older volunteers. Working with programs and activities, providing books, and just being "friendly visitors" are common possibilities for volunteer work in these institutional settings. Also, local governments often have advisory boards for their social service and health departments; those who sit on such boards can have a hand in forming policy that can better the lives of people of all ages in their communities.

As the above shows, volunteer activities and organizations to match older persons to volunteer sites can range from formal to very informal, be age-specific or simply available for those of any age with the time and commitment to be involved, and require time and skill commitments at every level.

Social Organizations

Similar to the case with work and volunteering, many retired persons know just where to turn for social involvement and stimulation. They may intensify involvement in their existing social networks—family, friends, church groups, and social clubs. Yet, some may not have such networks or would rather find additional outlets for their social participation. Others may feel a strong need for being part of a group that has as part of its common ground the experience of having retired. In these cases the retiree may turn to organizations that are composed primarily of retired persons.

One central organization for many retirees—AARP—has already been described, and AARP chapters are excellent sources of social activities. Another focus for recent retirees who are members of unions is the retired-member arms of their unions. Former employees of large corporations often can become part of the "retired X Corporation association."

Another place for socializing often overlooked by recent retirees who feel they are too young for it is the local senior center. Senior centers vary greatly in terms of their membership; although it is true that some are oriented to much older persons, many senior centers have facilities that can serve for both socializing and activity purposes, such as woodworking shops, art classes and so on. Many of these centers are closely aligned with their region's Area Agency on Aging.

Educational Organizations

A final set of organizations to be considered can fulfill many aspects of later life interests. Lifelong learning programs have been expanding at a rapid pace. These range from the totally informal sharing of knowledge to formal presentation of academic courses.

Many colleges and universities allow persons over the age of sixty to take regular courses for little or no tuition. Even expensive private schools should be approached for their special programs; for example, Lehigh University, where all the authors formerly taught, allows persons over the age of sixty to take summer courses for five dollars alongside the "regular" students, who are paying over $1,500 for the same course!

Perhaps the best approach to education for many older persons is the Elderhostel program. Elderhostel (80 Boylston, Suite 400, Boston, MA 02116) is a nonprofit corporation that coordinates a large number of courses offered by colleges and universities. Over one thousand institutions of higher education across the United States and in over thirty other countries participate in this popular program. The institutions offer short courses on a huge variety of topics in sessions designed especially for older participants. Many campuses provide very inexpensive housing during weeklong Elderhostel sessions when regular classes are not in operation. Similarly, school districts often have continuing education programs at school sites; while not especially for older students, they are primarily for persons well beyond typical college age who are taking courses for enrichment. Another option is home study courses. Some are offered through state universities, while others are programs of organizations that are specifically directed to home study. All of these opportunities can be explored in your own locality.

One final point deserves mention: older persons can not only participate as students in many of these programs; they can also be the instructors. Many recent retirees have a great amount of experience and know-how and make excellent instructors on everything from pottery to foreign policy. Those with an interest in the process of education can combine volunteering (or possibly even paid employment) with involvement in that process on a lifelong basis.

Adjustment to retirement, then, is a series of experiences. It is the realization that we are entering yet another phase of the life cycle, and that we are not as young as we might like to be, especially in a society that so handsomely rewards youthfulness. But armed with the triad of good health, financial resources, and plans for using the new leisure, retirement can be an enjoyable phase of life; and, indeed, retirement was a negative outcome for only a sixth of our sample. In the next chapter we look at what the retirees thought of their lifetime of work.

References

1. David J. Ekerdt, Raymond Bossé, and Sue Levkoff, "An Empirical Test for Phases of Retirement," *Journal of Gerontology*, 40, 95–101, 1985.
2. Stanley Parker, *Retirement and Work* (London: Allen & Unwin, 1982).
3. Martin Tolchin, "23% in a Study Feel They Retired Too Early," *New York Times*, April 16, 1989, p. L27.
4. Erdman B. Palmore *et al.*, *Retirement: Causes and Consequences* (New York: Springer Publishing, 1985).
5. Elizabeth Mutran and Donald C. Reitzes, "Retirement, Identity and Well-Being: Realignment of Role Relationships," *Journal of Gerontology*, 36, 733–740, 1981.
6. Ashley Montagu, *Growing Young* (New York: McGraw-Hill, 1981).
7. Donald E. Gelfand, *Aging: The Ethnic Factor* (Boston: Little, Brown, 1982); Pat M. Keith, "Depressive Symptoms among Younger and Older Couples, *Gerontologist*, 27, 417–422, 1987.
8. Susan Littwin, *The Postponed Generation* (New York: Morrow, 1981).
9. Jay A. Mancini, "Leisure Lifestyles and Family Dynamics in Old Age," in William H. Quinn and George A. Hughston (eds.), *Independent Aging: Family and Social Systems Perspectives* (Rockville, MD: Aspen Publications, 1984), pp. 58–71.

10. Linda Evans, David J. Ekerdt, and Raymond Bossé, "Proximity to Retirement and Anticipatory Involvement: Findings from the Normative Aging Study," *Journal of Gerontology, 40*, 368–374, 1985.

11. Kenneth F. Ferraro, "Cohort Analysis of Retirement Preparation, 1974–1981," *Journal of Gerontology, 45*, S21–31, 1990.

12. Suzanne Meeks *et al.*, "Age Differences in Coping: Does Less Mean Worse?" *International Journal of Aging and Human Development, 28(2)*, 127–140, 1989.

13. Toni C. Antonucci, "Social Supports and Social Relationships," in Robert H. Binstock and Linda K. George (eds.), *Handbook of Aging and the Social Sciences* (San Diego: Sage Publications, 1990), pp. 205–226. Also Donald C. Reitzes, Elizabeth Mutran, and Hallowell Pope, "Location and Well-Being Among Retired Men," *Journal of Gerontology, 46*, S195–203, 1991.

14. Graham Rowles, *Prisoners of Space: Exploring the Geographic Experience of Older People* (Boulder, CO: Westview Press, 1978), p. 199.

15. Robert L. Rubenstein, "The Home Environments of Older People: A Description of the Psychosocial Processes Linking Person to Place," *Journal of Gerontology, 49*, 45–53, 1989.

16. Palmore *et al.*, *Retirement*, p. 47.

17. John C. Henretta, Christopher G. Chan, and Angela M. O'Rand, "Retirement Reason Versus Retirement Process: Examining the Reasons for Retirement Typology," *Journal of Gerontology, 47*, 1–7, 1992.

18. JoAnne W. Hansz, "Examination of the Effects of Early Retirement and Job Loss among Men on their Physical and Emotional Well-Being," Master's thesis, Lehigh University, 1988.

19. Cary S. Kart, Charles F. Longino, and Steven G. Ullman, "Comparing the Economically Advantaged and the Pension Elite," *Gerontologist, 29*, 745–49, 1989.

Chapter 5

Reflections on a Career

"I [Victor Karlovsky] have a younger sister and a younger brother, who is semiretired because he and I jointly own a bar and restaurant in Bucks County. We keep the restaurant open four days a week. I help out there three days a week—I'm retired—and he only works one more day a week than I do. We've had the bar for about twenty-one years. I did this on weekends. I would leave my regular job whenever I got out of the office on Friday and go straight to the bar to work there Friday and Saturday.

"I was managing a loan office in New Jersey. Then I worked in a nation-wide New York bank in the financial services division. I was in security, that is, internal control, where any problems we had with our employees were taken care of. You had to investigate, question, and all that kind of stuff. We found fraud and embezzlement, prostitutes, drug pushers, and child molesters in our employ. One worked in the French Quarter of New Orleans. To every derelict that came in she'd make a $5,000 loan, give them fifty dollars for showing up, and usually the proceeds went to her bar.

"With these types around, I'd be sitting here watching a football game on a Sunday afternoon and get a phone call saying we had a problem in Phoenix, get on a plane. My territory was all over the U.S. and Puerto Rico. So you never knew where you were going to be any day. I was afraid for my life a couple times. It was to the point that I'd hire people to start my car. It was interesting. I always, well, way back when I was a kid, wanted to be a private eye. . . . I might add that I was in Special Internal Security in control work for five years, but my total in the finance and banking industry was twenty years.

"I had started out working in a local home loan office after I got out of Lehigh, went with Howard Finance and eventually got promoted to the home office in suburban Philadelphia. That's when I got that bank job that I mentioned.

"What brought me to retire was that my brother died young. You hear a lot of people saying, 'I'm going to keep working while I can still work.' My philosophy is, 'What are you going to do, retire when you're ready to die?' His death triggered it. I was diagnosed as having emphysema; that gave me a little scare and that clinched it. I always thought about early retirement, and my brother's death gave me that impetus. I had a follow-up physical, and I don't have it. That didn't make me unhappy. Better to have some breathing abnormalities or some congestion, but the fact that it was not emphysema was a big relief.

"In the history of our family, the males unfortunately don't live very long. My cousin died when he was in his early fifties, two other male cousins died in their fifties, and my father was sixty-seven when he died. I figured this was a trait. I have an older brother. He was just seventy-three a couple of weeks ago, so I'm not taking any chances. I decided to retire at age fifty-six. I planned. I made some pretty good investments when I was younger and saved a lot of money, and I can live comfortably without that hassle. Of course, I get a little bit of income from the bar.

"As soon as I turned fifty I was thinking about it. I counted the days. I was like a prisoner who was getting out. The last six months were pretty tough. I didn't want my superiors to let my underlings know that I was retiring. Of course, finances were part of the picture. In fact, the pension that I get now from the bank is like found money because our company had a profit sharing plan, and upon retiring or severance employees get a lump settlement. After acquisition by the bank, we also got their retirement plan, so I had the best of two. I was covered under the profit sharing as well as by the overall pension. Being a bachelor, I've been able to save. I could invest the profit into different CDs. So actually, when I knew that I could live in the same style I had been accustomed to, and I knew I wouldn't have any burden, I thought, 'Why not?' I live off the income from my investments. I touched the principal, yes, but not to live on. The outside of the house was sided, the whole interior has been gutted, a new fence was put on. So now, with the kitchen, I've gone through maybe $40,000 worth of improvements on my property.

"You can imagine the day I drove from my headquarters upon retirement; it was like—I couldn't make a comparison—but getting into the car and just driving away and not even looking over your shoulder. I had a thirty-five-mile-a-day ride. That was an hour or so each day. It was in suburban Philadelphia, and as I drove away I thought, 'Oh, I don't have to do this anymore!' I was telling everybody that the first thing I was going to do the first day of my retirement was go to bed with a big hammer and when the alarm clock rang, I would smack that thing to smithereens. I never did smash the alarm clock, but I did let it ring and I just sat there and smiled.

"But it's not to say that it's all perfect. The lack of schedule is the worst thing, because I see myself getting disorganized. Just take a look around this place. Things piled here, there. That's just correspondence. This is like my 'in' basket, except at work by the end of the day there was nothing in the basket, everything was in the 'out.' It gets me. There's no impetus. Maybe I miss being bossed around. But that wouldn't be the reason either because when I managed offices, before I got the promotion to the home office, everything was orderly, everything was done on time. I always had to work for somebody, but I had a lot of freedom. I had that office and I wouldn't see anybody from the home office for four or five months at a time, just oral communication. I can't understand why I can't get myself channeled into getting off my butt and being organized.

"I traveled a lot before. But now I can spend as much time traveling as I want to. My big escape is travel. I've seen all of the Caribbean, South America, Europe. I haven't seen all of the U.S. that I want to see. The Orient has no fascination for me at all. I want to go to the village where my parents were born, in Poland. My mother had a couple of sisters and brothers, but I think they're all deceased. But our cousins still live in the village. I've never been there. I want to hit the good parts of Europe that I missed before, like Germany, Holland, and the Scandinavian countries. I did Rome, Paris, and London. I can't travel during summertime because of gardening and yardwork, so I have to go in the fall—I figure by the fall of this year. There's also my interest in Little League.

"I would never move out of here. Rather than go to a retirement home or that type of thing, if I was infirm or something like that, I'd have someone come in. Loneliness? Don't think that's an issue— maybe if I didn't have all the friends and relatives that I have. If it got to that point, I might consider selling everything and going into a senior citizen-type dwelling, a condo or something like that, where I would be joined by people my own age. But most of my friends are younger, so I don't feel fifty-eight. I don't think like a fifty-eight-year-old. Once I feel my age, maybe I might reconsider."

* * *

Victor Karlovsky's job is hardly a typical occupation, but it does point out the kind of strain—and fascination—that some jobs embody. His profile also shows a certain degree of verve and independence that a single person has more chance of realizing than does a married person. But, as we saw in Chapter 2, strain can emerge in a number of occupations and at different periods of one's work history.

In this chapter our retirees reminisce about the decades of their working lives. What motivated them to work in the particular field they chose? How would they describe the pattern of their careers— satisfactions and rewards, obstacles and frustrations? How did they relate to management? We also inquire a bit into the relations between blue-collar and white-collar workers. How do professionals and semiprofessionals fit into the system? What obstacles and successes does one encounter in a career?

Work, Career Choice, and the Socioeconomic World

Early in life we become aware of the different kinds of work. We also learn that a variety of motives drive human beings to work. Most of us work for money, self-satisfaction, service, companionship, and for still other motives.[1] Among our sample, composed as it is mainly of managers, professionals, and technicians, the psychological rewards are more important than the monetary, because the latter are assured. A retired dentist who had resisted the enormous increase of fees that came after many companies and unions adopted dental insurance plans said: "It gave me a lot of satisfaction to know I was helping people." This commitment to service was especially evident among the nurses. However, for a Bethlehem Steel lawyer the rewards were also internal but in a different way: "The challenge was always there, and once I was forced out of Steel I was determined to find a new career as a legal consultant." The blue-collar workers expressed less of this enthusiasm; for them monetary rewards are presumably more important than the psychological ones, but a mix of both applies to nearly all workers.[2] One type of reward does not preclude the other.

One may ask how one's specific occupation affects retirement. According to our data, little relationship is found between type of occupation and retirement satisfaction. Although the motives to retire and the kinds of satisfaction in retirement differ between persons, the differences between upper blue-collar workers, white collar workers, and managers were not significant.

Beyond the reward system is the sense of identity that work provides.[3] For most occupations a feeling of growth emerges. One gains in knowledge and pride. There is also the variable of time. The young worker looks upon himself or herself as involved in "becoming," the older worker as possibly "having been."[4] Through much of our career we are aware of both success and failure—both of which have a great deal to do with our sense of competence. Self-perceived confidence has been shown to be the most critical source of self-esteem, at least in the workplace.[5] A network or circle of friends is also a predictor of satisfaction on the job.[6]

The very choice of one's occupation draws upon a number of sources, as we shall see in this chapter. Not least is the importance of a model. Evelyn Cohen remembers how she wanted to go into a medical career because of her admiration for a doctor. Retired psychology professor Ted Neff said he always wanted to teach because "I had an inspiring teacher in high school. When I went to Williams College my professor of French had a keen interest in every student. I felt the same way in my career, but as the years went on I wasn't quite so ambitious. Student quality declined and by the time I retired I was content to reach at least one student in each class."

Moreover, the percentage of workers who would choose the same occupation over again varies greatly. Whereas 89 percent of professionals, such as scientists, would choose the same type of work if they had their life to live over, only 41 percent of skilled steel-workers, 21 percent of unskilled steelworkers, and 43 percent of a cross section of white-collar workers would so choose.[7] These figures are in direct proportion to the prestige level of these occupations. Most of our sample rationalized their choice of career; however, their options were far more limited than those of their sons and daughters.

The Meaning of Work

To understand retirement, we must understand the meaning of the work course for an individual. Clearly, most of the retirees in our study have spent a considerable portion of their lives working at one sort of job for one employer. Thus, retirement must be examined directly in relation to what kind of work the person did and what rewards (and costs) were involved in that work. For individuals who have done many different jobs, the characteristics of what happened to be the last job probably have less of an influence on how they deal with retirement.

Before considering our interviewees' views in more detail, it might be good to delve a bit more deeply into the relationship of work and its satisfactions to retirement. People get many important needs fulfilled by working. These include money, prestige, something to do with one's time, service to others, pride (and shame if not working), accomplishment, power, and personal relationships. Obviously, different jobs are better or worse at fulfilling these needs. For example, being a medical doctor is likely to provide quite a bit of money and prestige, whereas driving a bus does neither of those. However, bus driving is very good for providing a fixed schedule, allowing one to interact with people without getting too intensely involved with them, and filling time. Being a factory worker gives at least money to live on and fills time, but it isn't likely to provide the same level of satisfaction or pride in one's product as being a skilled craftsman does, nor does it give as much prestige as, say, being a bank president (at least in some people's eyes).

We could go on, but the idea is clear: different jobs differentially fulfill a wide variety of needs, although working in and of itself usually gives at least some satisfaction. It is important that people have a good match between their particular sets of needs and values and those that their jobs can satisfy. Fortunately, most people do seem to have at least a reasonably good match, which can result from being in just the right job or from shifting what is important to oneself so that it matches with the job one happens to have. Remember that most of our respondents were very satisfied with their former jobs.

What this means for retirement can be summarized easily: What retirement clearly does is take away the positives that were found in a job that, more than likely, matched a person's needs and values very well. Insofar as one's work career has been satisfactory in fulfilling at least some important needs, retirement must either provide a way to fulfill the same needs to roughly the same degree or provide some extra compensations for the ones that cannot be satisfied. Again, fortunately, for most retirees, it appears that retirement can do exactly that. With health, adequate income, activities, and availability of choices, retirees may find in retirement at least as much self-satisfaction and satisfaction of important needs as they found in work. As in our study, equal satisfaction in both work and retirement can be found in a wide range of workers—blue-collar, white-collar, managerial, and clerical—because each is looking for different rewards—and finding them. Still, it is always important to place the meaning of retirement within its relationship to the meaning that work had for the individual retiree. Let us look at some of those meanings across the years of work as expressed by our participants.

Background and Realities

Our horizons are shaped by the timing of our birth or our arrival at adulthood. Think of the people who came of age during the Depression. Anyone graduating from high school or college in the early 1930s faced a bleak future. A young man who was fortunate to get on his feet before the end of that decade was likely to be called to military service in World War II. Most of our interviewees came along somewhat later, but several graduated from high school in the late 1930s and then did military service. Also, a few were hit by the Korean War, as was Arthur Ferraro: "At 18 I was urged by my uncle to get a job in a defense industry so I could escape the draft. I then started Muhlenberg College part time." All this stands out from the relatively peaceful and "safe" decades before and after the Vietnam War (except for the recent Persian Gulf involvement).

Another aspect of our sample was the lack of a college education. Nearly half were without a college degree. Until the late 1950s in the Northeast, possibly even more than in other parts of the country, a college education was regarded as elitist, and planning a career was not predicated on having a diploma. Unlike the remainder of the country, where education was more likely to be public than private, the generation represented by our sample could seek a technical or an upper white-collar career without a college degree. A typical case is Gerald Kenyon, who came out of high school in the 1930s and rose to a fairly high position in quality control in Bethlehem Steel. Both before and after retirement Gerald found much of his stimulation in his painting and became a noted artist in the Lehigh Valley. His counterpart today would presumably be a college graduate; however, the position, like many others, calls much more on a given intelligence level and effort than on specific college courses. Similarly, Roland Eisenhard recalls his struggles during the Depression: "I began as a clerk, then a bookkeeper, and did manage to get in two years at college, but soon ran out of money." This did not prevent him from becoming a successful accountant.

No less basic in career choice than the economic climate and accessibility of education is the individual choice of the direction in which one wants to go. Many know precisely what their occupational goal is, others are intrigued by more than one option, and in several instances, subtle or chance factors play a role. Matt Ewer remarks on his wavering between a teaching career and industry: "I was an engineer for two years at Lehigh, which has a tough program in electrical engineering, and I made the mistake of taking all the strenuous courses at one time. I should have spread them out with cupcake courses in between. . . . Finally I knew a change had to be made and I heard that the school district needed some science and math teachers." Later, however, he went to work at the Steel company.

Mark Cooper, a student counselor, regrets not having gotten a

Ph.D., as it would have meant a more secure and profitable road in his educational career, but realizes that the value of a degree depends on what year one gets it; that is, one must reckon with demographic cycles—high- and low-birthrate years and what that means eighteen or twenty years later. Also, economic cycles continue to shape the potential of each crop of graduates. Moreover, as implied above, the surplus of college graduates has in recent years meant an intense competition for white-collar and professional positions. Few areas are exempt. Lawyers, in particular, have become very competitive, as one complained: "When I came to Northampton County in the 1960s there were only a hundred lawyers, now there must be four times that number." A retired dentist said, "I would hate to be starting a practice now. I'm told that Allentown is way over in its quota of dentists."

Again, it is relevant to look at our sample in the context of the Lehigh Valley and its remoteness from the metropolises of New York and Philadelphia, where conditions such as large-scale unions and a bureaucratic indifference often permeate the labor arena. As railroad worker Jerry Peabody put it: "When I worked for the Reading in Philadelphia we sort of got the word from the boys up top: 'Why can't you work like the men in Bethlehem.' When I was transferred here I realized what they were talking about. Everyone did his work with no complaint, or almost none." Similarly, Arthur Ferraro spoke of the shift at Western Electric: "We were always known as the plant with steadiness. In fact, in those days there was a feeling of belongingness and security. Up to the early 1970s you sort of knew that your boss was there to stay. But increasingly it was sort of every man for himself. Then came the headhunters. A lot of men were looking for that spot that paid 10 percent more."

Another aspect was the somewhat unique character of the economic life of the community. In comparison to other areas, Bethlehem Steel dominated the Lehigh Valley, particularly the city of Bethlehem, and operated its empire, almost without a ripple from the outside world until disaster hit in the late 1970s with foreign competition and changes in American industry, especially the automotive.[8] When the cutback came it sent shock waves throughout the Lehigh Valley and beyond. No less than 2,500 employees were released by Bethlehem Steel on Black Friday in 1977, with similar explosions to follow throughout the early 1980s. As Alan Adams, a retired executive, said: "It seemed unbelievable that the nation's second most powerful steel company, which built the San Francisco bridges and the Empire State Building and made the largest guns of two world wars, was now about to fold. Not that I couldn't see signs of possible disaster when they built the Martin Tower—an enormous office building that had to be paid for and filled up with people doing something. Then, of course, there were the plush labor contracts, not that those at the top spared their own indulgences."

Further, the stability of the area's economic life was shattered when the textile industry was leaving in the 1960s, Western Electric was to become AT&T, and Mack Trucks joined the migration to the South. Although other communities had known a similar fate, it was a shock to many of the area's workers, who had had a fairly secure life since their coming into adulthood around World War II.

Inevitably, many of the changes these men and women were experiencing were happening elsewhere. Debbie Schulz witnessed the sad demise of the Philadelphia *Bulletin*: "Every few months you could see the curtain was closer to coming down. We tried different things but nothing really seemed to work." A number of the employees reflected on the increasing lack of loyalty the company showed to the employees or the employees to the company. Indeed, it was probably worse elsewhere. One engineer spent a year in the Silicon Valley in California: "Gee, out there the instability was that no one knew how long his job would last." He was only too happy to get back to the more predictable Lehigh Valley.

Patterns of Work and Career

For many men and women the occupational role consumes their waking hours. In any society, but especially a competitive one, it marks the individual and determines status and identity. Indeed, most persons seem to find no acceptable alternative to work. Further, work takes many forms, ranging from semislavery and subsistence to more creative outlets, extending into leisure pursuits as found in hobbies and "do-it-yourself" activities.[9]

The Nature of Work and Rewards

Work, then, takes on many shapes and shades. Moreover, workers move between intrinsic and extrinsic (or instrumental) rewards, the precise degree of each varying with the individual. Cliff Thomas, a supervisor at Steel, said: "I worked hard and they rewarded me. I left with some reluctance; I didn't want to go. I really enjoyed my work. If they called me back tomorrow I would go." Perhaps stability provided by employment is in itself a primary reward for most workers. Others like or accept change, occasionally encountering a very competitive order, as did Barbara Hunt, as she went from teacher–librarian to salesperson of cemetery lots: "They gave you $150 a week but then took it away in any sales you made.... After some battering around I gained a little more confidence.... In fact, I think all teachers should get out in the real world, because it is different."

Careers, Tracking, and Social Background

It is intriguing to ask how our work life was launched. For quite a few it was simply following the guidelines of peer group, family, or social class. Stewart Beers, a die maker at Steel, in looking back on his career comments: "I should have gone to college but all my friends were going to Steel." John Grossi was not alone in his remarks recalling his graduation from high school: "My dad said, 'I've been at the railroad at Steel. That's where you belong.'" But, unlike his immigrant father, John moved into a white-collar job and was not on track maintenance. On the other hand, Alan Adams, who came from the Main Line of Philadelphia with an engineering degree from an Ivy League institution, was slated for management at the Lackawanna plant of Bethlehem Steel. In World War II John became an enlisted man, whereas Alan found the right moment to leave Steel for officer candidate's school: "My boss wasn't enthusiastic about my leaving, but he knew it was hardly wise to stay and be drafted."

There are, of course, both smooth and uneven career tracks. Many work histories rest almost on happenstance. For instance, after receiving his engineering degree, James Foley joined the Sparrows Point division of Bethlehem Steel: "I couldn't stand the foul air in the plant so I went to law school nights and after four years I managed a shift into the research division." But a better example of how fortuitous developments can shape one's work is perhaps the case of Sara Timko:

"I grew up in the coal country. When I finished high school in 1940 I knew that area wasn't the world for me. I had seen too much of street fighting, vote buying, and everyone knowing your business. My mother was Polish and my father was Russian. It was wonderful to be in a family where members protected each other, but somehow it was a small world. So I went to Jersey City. It was still a bit of the same thing, where the Poles lived on First Street, the Italians on Second Street, and so on. But I did find work at Western Electric. War came and new chances came up. I had a chance to apply to get into a special section. I found out later that I had been checked out by the FBI and as it turned out we were making parts for a torpedo. Oddly enough, all our tools had been made in Germany!

"Anyway, I got married and my husband, Joe, a Slovak, was soon in uniform. When he was released from service we were both working, but his health was far from good and being near the river in Jersey City it was too damp, so we moved to the Lehigh Valley. He soon found work at the Reading Railroad. I was pretty much tied up with homemaking, especially as a new child came about every two years, plus taking care of my mother who was slowly dying of cancer. But rearing six children was expensive, since I wanted to see all those go to college who wanted to—and four did.

"It happens my only daughter had beautiful hair and I read up on hair care. So in 1967 I opened a small salon for permanents and the like. At the same time I got a chance to wait tables at the Lehigh Valley Club. Somehow the word got around that I had something of a beauty parlor, so business men were asking about appointments for manicures. Also, Wednesdays and Thursdays I would have their wives, whereas on Fridays and Saturdays I had mostly the women of the neighborhood and a different social cut. Saturdays I worked at the club and occasionally for a catering service. I enjoyed serving the public, and I soon got to know the lay of the land. There were clearly two kinds of patrons at the club—the old established families of Allentown and the ones who had just made it. I found the former a lot nicer. . . . I never let myself be taken advantage of. Once we had a foul-mouthed cook, and finally I couldn't take it anymore and I threw a platter of food at him.

"By 1979 my children were through college and I had had enough of being a waitress and hairdressing. Yet, even today, ten years after deciding to retire, I still do permanents for my old clients. Every Sunday I help out at the Shrine of Czestochawa down in Bucks County. I act as guide, do some selling and packing. I started doing this in 1952 after my mother couldn't do it any more. For one thing, it helps me to keep up on my Polish. . . . "

There are, of course, both smooth and uneven career tracks. Predicting a work course is something akin to forecasting the weather or the economy.[10] Many individuals have a trial-and-error period of finding their career path, as economic cycles, international events, and individual crises may intervene. For instance, Wolfgang Jung arrived in the USA at age twenty-six after fleeing Nazi Germany in 1935: "I was willing to take whatever came along. First it was a sporting goods store; then I was hired by a collection agency. I volunteered for service in World War II but was rejected. I found a job with Vultee Aircraft. After the war I finally settled in a textile plant.

Dual tracking and multitracking characterize many careers. After John Grossi began in the railroad office he pursued evening courses in business school and before long had an after-hours career in accounting, notably in helping prepare IRS tax forms: "I knew I could only go so far in the Steel-owned railroad, and I was determined to find a way of having a better standard of living. By opening this business in my fifties I have a Social Security account which supplements my railroad pension." As another example, Matt Ewer was torn between teaching and engineering, but finally opted for Steel as an electrical supervisor. At the same time, he stayed in the Naval Reserve after World War II: "I did it for financial reasons, and it pays off in lots of ways. I like to travel, and I can now fly on military planes both here and abroad."

Companies as well as individuals find a way of categorizing the pattern of a career. Aldo Carlucci had his first years at Steel as an hourly worker. His ad hoc employment was over when he was appointed as a salaried worker. Often traditions emerge in a company that may incorporate both community and individual needs and habit systems. John Grossi points to the ethnic patterns he found at Steel and its railroad: "It was clear that the men working on the track were mainly Italian and Polish. But the train crews were mostly Pennsylvania German. After all, they were here first. In the blast furnace it was nearly all Slovaks, who lived on the streets nearest the mill. Of course, nearly every street in south Bethlehem had and still has its ethnic group."

Ethnicity and religious affiliation could also play a role in management. Saul Goldman, an industrial engineer at Steel, recalls a conversation with one of its vice presidents a decade or so before he retired: "You're doing great, Saul, but there's no way I can promote you further unless you change your religion." Nor was Saul invited to join the Saucon Valley Country Club, a plush establishment underwritten by Bethlehem Steel until its fall in the 1980s.

Blue Collar and White Collar

The blue-collar workers in our sample were generally skilled, and a few might be described as craft workers. Research indicates that craft workers tend to be more stable and suffer from less alienation than routine blue- and white-collar workers.[11] Research also suggests that generally white collar is more stable than blue collar.[12] In reality, the distinction between blue and white tends to break down. In our sample, the passing of a worker from workbench to foreman placed many a plant worker at a higher status and income than many white-collar employees. It also permitted them other privileges, such as joining the Steel Club (as distinguished from the Saucon Valley Country Club, open only to the corporation upper staff). Even within the relatively open atmosphere of the company railroad, John Grossi discovered a cooling of the camaraderie as he moved up the ranks: "When I became Supervisor of Traffic, I no longer found the men chatting with me but simply saying 'good morning.'"

Even though studies show the white-collar employee feels more secure than the blue-collar, it was not apparent in our retirees. Kenneth Kline, who was at Sears and in banking, said, "There's always that uncertainty. You have a feeling in the back of your mind that something may happen because of the new generation coming in. You see this change coming, but you don't want to say it's going to happen to me." The older ones know that they are competing against the better-educated younger ones, though educational differences are not so relevant in the blue-collar universe.

Professionals and Semiprofessionals

The professionals have certain advantages and at the same time a few insecurities. As lawyer Herman Frankel put it: "It's great— you're a problem solver, it's clean work, you deal with the middle class, but the competition today is terrible." For the professional working in an industry, the role of scientist or lawyer can be ambiguous depending on whether it is *line*—that is, within the chain of command—or *staff*, where the role is advisory. Lawyer Greg Harrison at Steel said, "I found my recommendations ignored if they didn't suit the sales people or someone higher up. It didn't always sit well with my own sense of ethics. I just didn't like being in a marginal role." Engineer Walter Koch apparently was a threat to his superior by being more knowledgeable about a given process: "I would talk and I would show that his idea wasn't going to wash and we'd do something else. I didn't think about it at the time, but I believe I was taking away some of his authority or prestige."

In the corporation, especially in periods of expansion, the retention of engineers, for instance, could be a problem, especially as they easily could find work elsewhere. Arthur Ferraro reports that at Western Electric, "They began to create new titles like 'product engineers' or 'planning engineers' so we could have the same pay or status as managers, who were not necessarily professionally trained. This provided a double track, so becoming a manager was no longer the goal."

Several professionals, especially those in private practice, mentioned their own special problems, notably increasing pressures. Nathan O'Hara, an M.D., spoke not only of the long hours, but of "the need to keep up. When I first finished medical school it wasn't so bad, yet from the mid-fifties on you really had to read the journals. At the same time the emphasis was on specialization. Then in the mid-sixties came Medicare and other insurance programs with an infinite amount of paperwork. By the late seventies the fear of litigation made insurance rates bounce up to astronomic heights."

Scientific advances, along with the controversies that may surround them, can affect the professional, possibly more than other occupations. For example, the advent of fluoridation in the 1950s reduced cavities by more than half the former rate. George Davies gives us his account of that event: "It threw us dentists into a panic, even though we knew it was the right thing to do. The city of Easton did it first, then came Bethlehem. Allentown never did fluoridate its water, largely because of the opposition of Robert Rodale (a noted publisher on health-related issues). We watched dental schools cut their classes in half, and famous schools like Temple considered closing altogether."

Possibly the most pervasive of all the strains in the professional world is between the generalists and the specialists. The prestige and income remains on the side of the specialists. However, lawyer Jim Foley recalled that at Steel, "It was the generalists who were consulting with the vice presidents. We specialists who were in patents and licensing dealt more with the research department." But in the medical and dental professions the feeling persisted that the specialists were given extra privileges. Dr. O'Hara spoke of how the family physician comes up for more frequent relicensing than does the specialist. Dr. Bernard Horvath, an internist, despaired at what he called overspecialization: "Every year while in practice I heard of a new specialization. We used to think of ophthalmology as a genuine specialty; now it's a general field. There is now the retinal specialist, the cataract specialist, and so on. I guess it's one way of sharing the responsibility. Or I wonder if it's a way of passing the buck." To dentist George Davis, the specialties "like orthodontics almost border on a fad, or at least a fashion."

The boundary between professional and semiprofessional is an arbitrary one. However, semiprofessionals—teachers, librarians, social workers, and nurses—have a somewhat marginal or ambivalent role. They do not have the status, income, or level of education associated with the traditional professions. Most significant, they do not have the authority that professionals have. They are subordinate to administrative systems, such as a school board or other bureaucratic structures.[13] In other words, there is less security, even when they are protected by tenure or civil service. Curiously, semiprofessionals have tended to be female more often than male, even though a reversal of occupational sex typing has been evident over the last generation. For all of these reasons semiprofessionals do not find it easy to define their boundaries or assert their authority. An example is Flora Kenyon, who notes that in her years of public school teaching it was seldom easy to stand up to the principal or the superintendent:

"One of the things that bothers me is the way we are getting pressure to pass students along. The principal tells me that parents are unhappy when their kids fail. He says, 'After all they're paying the taxes and we have a lot less trouble passing the budget if they are satisfied.' I very much resent this as our students are not learning to think; in fact, many of my high school students don't really know how to read. It's true that not all of my colleagues really care about this problem, but most of us feel helpless in our desire to keep up standards."

In our sample, the most interesting profile of the semiprofessional—or professional—is found in nursing, as six nurses volunteered for interviews. It is well known that nurses are subject to considerable strain, receive only limited recognition, and must find various means of coping with their work pressures.[14] Since the nurses in our sample had been serving over a thirty-year period, their experiences are indicative of the changes in this profession. Obviously, as with any occupation, no stereotype is possible. For Alice Stratton the role was a tripartite one—nursing, administration, and teaching: "Each hospital was different, some very hierarchical, in others head nurses had some authority. Also, there was always a difference between the nursing school and the hospital. Naturally, at nursing schools that were in a collegiate setting, both the students and the teachers had more freedom than in the schools attached to a hospital."

Generally the nurses accepted and were happy with the service role they performed, but they also mentioned the changes they saw in the profession. Dorothy Schmidt reflected: "It's becoming more a paper chase than actual caring for the patient." Anna Haley was more incisive: "I simply had to get out of nursing. It was once practically my whole life. In the old days we were professionally trained. Now the girls have only a two-year program. There's no longer a code of behavior. Anything goes. Worse is that in many hospitals both the doctors and nurses are on drugs. It's such easy access. I don't mean it's true of most hospitals. . . . Worst of all, patient care has gone out the door. . . . I now find my satisfaction in volunteer work."

Entrepreneurs and Bureaucrats

One recalls from Economics 101 that the function of the entrepreneur is to take risks. Most of the sample were not businessmen or -women in the usual sense, yet all workers assume some degree of risk. The difference is the degree. First of all, work by the entrepreneur, even more than the professional, involves long hours, such as fifty to sixty hours a week for hardware store owner Oliver Burke, who said, "It got to me after I reached sixty."

But more to the point is the challenge. At age forty-eight Lew Fitzgerald was thinking of what to do with his life after his sudden departure from Steel. After a period of time, he developed his own consulting firm:

"I didn't want a gopher type of job where I would be getting into worse shape than I was before. I wanted a challenging job where I could improve myself. . . . I also felt that if somebody was going to invest their money in me I'd have to put on a strong effort in that end. . . . It's great to set our own hours and work with people who want to improve their income. . . . My business is Fitzgerald Associates; we're a network, of somewhere around a million businesses distributed throughout the world, that exchange information about and use a common supply system. . . . The steel salary didn't permit me to have a house like this, and now I dream about a condominium and a helicopter to take me down to the shore."

Several spoke of a dream that one day they might go into business but were sobered by statistics, as Tim Trueblood stated: "About 85 percent of the people who go into business for themselves fail the first year. That ended my thoughts of starting a financial consultancy."

All of us live among a variety of bureaucratic structures—our work, school, church, club or lodge, and perhaps most formidable of all, the government to which we owe allegiance and to which we pay taxes. The distress workers feel often emerges because of the large impersonal organization and its endless rules and regulations. Technological advances, notably the computer, have not lessened these feelings of remoteness in an inflexible world.[15] Aldo Carlucci spoke of his last days at Steel: "I felt that I was only a number."

But the bureaucracy is by no means an inflexible structure. Alan Adams remembers when he was climbing up in the corporation and was moved from his manager role at Lackawanna for a higher position in Bethlehem: "I went home and said: 'The axe has fallen!' My wife thought I had lost my job. But I simply couldn't think that we could live anyplace but Buffalo. Now we would never think of leaving Bethlehem." Another example of the possible escapes from the corporate labyrinth is the experience of Mike Ritter: "My first seven years at Steel I was in industrial engineering, with those endless time studies, evaluations, and the like, but I applied for personnel and finally an opening was available. From then on I had a much livelier job."

Let us turn to the report of Willard Schulz, who was in government, thus a bureaucrat by definition but one who could rise above the bureaucracy:

"Basically I was in local government. When I went to graduate school at Penn State, it was a program for local and state governmental administration in various capacities. Some of the people whom I went to school with went into the state government; I happened to go into city government, primarily because we had a family started at that time and I didn't like the idea of moving about. When I went down to the graduate school, my wife and I had two children. I had commuted back and forth to Philadelphia each week, but when I finished down there, I took an examination for one of the governmental jobs in the city of Philadelphia, and then I took the family down. We moved down in the summer of '52. I worked a little over thirty years. . . . We were responsible for a whole department's operation, both for preparing budgets and for the personnel work—processing people and anything to do with requisitioning, purchasing—that was part of the administrative work. You'll find that the typical city government is set up that way. They have administrative directors, so obviously the larger the department, the higher the salary. So I worked in one department from '56 to '65, and you get itchy after nine or ten years in the job when nothing is happening. I wanted to break out in different directions, and I've always had the attitude that sometimes if you get too good at a job they don't want you to leave, so you won't get a promotion. So I had to force myself out.

"I left the city and I went to the University of Pennsylvania for a position because I had friends up there who went there earlier from the management director's office. They were getting into a lot of new things. They were really in a growth program because the university and the hospitals were getting together and trying to get a lot of federal money. So I worked up there for about a year, and I finally decided that I probably wanted to go back because it was almost like starting over again. There was very little office space. You can take a starting existence for a little bit, but it was kind of indefinite about when things would begin to open up, when federal moneys would be coming, and that sort of thing. It was like any job of reorganizing, trying to centralize the whole treasury department with all these ten departments. It got to be a hassle with the various people and entities, so finally I decided to go back, as the city had been offering a fairly decent position at the time. . . . I finally wound up in the recreation division.

"It was the end of '68, so I worked there until about '83. During that time, I did the administrative director work and for a period of two to three years I became the director of recreation. When the political wind changed, a new director was appointed, and I went back to my civil service position as administrative director. It was a lesser position, but more money. That's a typical governmental kind of thing, when you have political appointees getting less than some of the civil service people. The civil service people are granted pay raises over a period of time, whereas not all the political appointees are granted pay raises because of the political climate and one thing or another. Actually, there must be thirty or forty people getting higher salaries than the mayor. That's a typical political situation.

"I realized then, in a sense, I had peaked early—I peaked when I was about forty-two, and then I kind of hung on knowing I was probably going to retire when I hit age fifty-five. As far as I was concerned, the political climate had changed completely. When I first got into city government, it was a different time. There was kind of a reclamation in the city of Philadelphia. . . . Really, by the way, to really cap the whole thing, a little before '82, there was a new administration. They were talking about changes again, and I wanted to serve out my time in recreation. Then they tried to offer me all kinds of things. They said, 'Why don't you consider going down here, we'd really like you in other departments.' So, finally, you get a sense at a certain age, especially with younger people, that they want to move you about. I knew my time was limited and I wasn't in anybody's long-range plan. So I said, 'Okay, if you want me to go there, I'll go.' I had a fairly decent reputation in terms of the city, and I think they kind of used me, in a sense, for cleaning up their situation that had deteriorated. So when I got into this department again it was even worse than the previous department I had been in—that is, in terms of the games that were played. Well, in the last situation, at least I knew everybody, and in this situation, I was dealing with a whole new set of circumstances. I literally felt isolated in the sense of figuring why am I knocking myself out to improve things; I'm not going to be here long, in terms of reaping the benefits, so I just did what I had to do and left it at that, but it was a funny situation to be in. Had I realized that it was going to turn out like this, I would have stayed in the other position and just have ridden out my time.

"As I said, the situation has become so political that it's very difficult for a person who is a professional administrator to maintain any sense of reasonableness. . . . After all, politics are politics. The reason that certain people get into politics is for power. Once you get in that power play, the whole idea is to get people elected and re-elected and to get positions of authority to take care of a few people for favors. Nobody's looking out for the general population. The problem is you're nobody's friend because the special interest groups are really in authority. It's the same old thing, to the victor belong the spoils. For civil service personnel it's kind of being a registered nonpartisan, the Republicans don't like you, the Democrats don't—you're kind of in limbo.... After a while, I began to realize that you can't satisfy anybody. You're not satisfying the people you're supposed to be serving, and you're not satisfying the special interest groups. It's a crazy position to be in, and after a while, you become philosophical about it.

"But then my wife and I were thinking in terms of retirement. We like to ski and enjoy the outdoor life, so we talked about maybe going to a different part of the country. In our travels through work and one thing or another, at first we thought of Colorado, exotic places. Well, we visited the places, we were disillusioned. It was nice to come back to the East. We used to go to recreation conventions practically every year, which took us to different parts of the country. So we were thinking of the idea of where we'd like to settle. Because of the size of the family we had, we really didn't want to get too far away from our family members. We even went up to the Adirondacks, that was like an eight-hour drive, and we were half serious about being up there. We were looking for something to do together, and one of the things we came down to was a motel operation. So we got ourselves a little experience with a motel chain, about two years ago. We worked with them for about three months, and I think that cured us of ever wanting to get into the motel business, because we really saw how demanding it was. We liked doing it for a time, and we knew we could do it. The question was whether we were suitable and whether we would mind the demand of twenty-four-hour work. We worked at various places in New England. Then you begin to look at these businesses from a real cold, economic point of view. You look at the economics, and the asking price, and you start to realize that the potential cash flow from these places is not worth it.

"The city of Philadelphia has an outstanding retirement system. I don't know that there were many retirement systems in the country that were as good. I think part of it was a guilt thing. They never paid a competitive rate with industry, so one of the things they had to attract people with and keep them was the decent pension system and other benefits. Of course, I look back and see the city versus corporations, and what's happening to corporations with some of their pension plans, and I feel I did a wise thing. . . . We liked the anonymity of a large town; you get into a small town and everybody knows everything about everybody and all their business. But I like Allentown; it's just large enough. We enjoy it thoroughly up here and we have been able to do a lot of our own pursuits, especially with the church and our family and friends. Well, we've become very active in the church now. We always liked singing and so do our kids, and a couple of them are very good. We've always been a singing group when we get together on holidays. We've been going to one of the local churches, where we always liked the sound of the choir. We joined the Church of St. Anne. We liked everything we saw there and got involved in the choir, and now we're getting involved in a whole series of things in that church. Yesterday we were tied up twice between a mass and singing at the First Presbyterian.

"Mainly, we like to see our children, who live in Ohio, New York, and New Jersey. I also would like to run, in theory everyday. Again, I haven't done that for two or three weeks because I just haven't had the time. I started about the same time we got into skiing, when I was thirty-nine. I began to realize that to save my sanity from cabin fever, especially when you have a growing family, I had to periodically leave the house and take long walks. The next thing I knew, I started jogging and I found that I felt much better. When you come back from this, you look at things differently. It's now part of my weekly activity. And, of course, I do a lot more reading. Actually, I still use my skills in writing. You use your skills all the time, whether you're dealing with communication like we are now in the church situation, or with my grown kids—I'm rediscovering my kids. There are different relationships that take place now. You finally get away from the 'parent' and the 'child.' You're trying to redefine that whole role in terms of being friends and advising, but not in a parental way."

Management and the Corporate World

It is instructive to look at the nature of the corporation, and for approximately a seventh of our sample, Bethlehem Steel was *the* corporation. Even more than other corporate structures, Steel, at least until its near collapse, represented a model of tight control. A retiree of its personnel office spoke of it as "rigid, authoritarian, and often doing the wrong thing in terms of what modern steel-making, personnel practices called for in the second half of the twentieth century." It may be added that during the late 1950s a turning point was reached, largely because of the illness and eventual death of Steel's president, Eugene Grace. After that at least three changes became apparent: (1) union demands were accepted with less negativism—the 1959 strike lasted nearly four months and no strike has occurred since[16]; (2) individual managers and supervisors were permitted more authority, and the team approach (democratically oriented work groups) became more acceptable; (3) research was now considered necessary if the company was to meet its competition. By the late 1970s, foreign competition along with the decreased need for steel because of the energy crisis and the production of smaller cars had catastrophic consequences. Indeed, in 1977 for the first time in its history, Bethlehem Steel went outside the corporation and imported accountant Donald Trautlein as president. A new desperate struggle for survival was at hand. Aldo Carlucci remembers, "On closed circuit TV throughout the plant was the face and voice of Trautlein urging us to greater productivity. But then within a few years half of us were gone."

However, many other companies were feeling the stress from national and international events. Harry Hemphill in airport traffic safety describes the effects of deregulation on airlines: "The financial situation was so critical that the bosses were making decisions on emotion and impulse rather than on whether they were going to hurt someone or not. In other words, they placed dollars above safety. . . . I have had to make decisions where for hours afterward, until the thing was resolved, I was scared to death."

But whether Bethlehem Steel, Mack Trucks, Air Products, Western Electric (which became AT&T in the Lehigh Valley), or an airline, industries are struggling to meet competition as well as to serve the public, all of which raises a number of policy decisions.[17] They also have certain characteristics. Inevitably, the search for profits is above other goals. Moreover, there must be a firm line of authority and decision making. We have already referred to the distinction of line and staff. In this connection, the company calls for total commitment. Alan Adams tells of his learning his obligations as he worked his way up the line at Steel, becoming manager of the Lackawanna plant, and finally occupying a high managerial position in the corporation: "I found out very early that you were expected to be on call night and day including weekends." This commitment became more demanding as financial crisis loomed. Arthur Ferraro refers to the change from the more permissive days of Western Electric to the period when AT&T had to begin thinking of endurance in a more hostile universe: "We were under some duress to put out the best possible product in the shortest time." Alan Adams notes, "It was very irritating to me to see how our standards of quality for steel became compromised in order to sell a product. The pressure came mainly from the sales staff, who seemed to say, 'We've got to meet the competition; so what if the steel bar doesn't last forty years. We won't be here to worry about it.'" In other words, commitment became more problematic as the battle for survival took shape.

Problems in the Workplace

Several kinds of situations or discontinuities are found in most levels of blue-collar and white-collar employment. These have surfaced in the preceding pages, but they are worth more specific comment.

Age

A number of employees felt pressure from younger colleagues that wanted their jobs. More often the situation was one of resentment on the part of the elder, who found the younger receiving higher status, income, and authority. Harry London, retired head teller from a large bank in Allentown, relates his experience: "They came in fresh from the university with a kind of contempt for the older people in the bank. Not only did they show no sensitivity or deference, but I had the feeling that they were very impatient to get ahead. As for the younger tellers and clerks, they didn't come in with adequate skills from high school or business school. And they seemed to be interested only in payday. I think that also applied to some of their bosses."

Gender

The rise of women in the work force belongs largely to this century—previously they were more or less chattel and employed only in menial work. The rise of the service industry as the manufacturing sector lost ground has been one facet of this change.

The evidence for discrimination against women—as with the aged and racial minorities—hardly needs documentation. In our own study the women had even more difficulty than the men did in securing a college education. Nor were women, even vigorous Evelyn Cohen or Sara Timko, encouraged to plunge into a full career in addition to rearing a family, although a few, like nurse–educator Alice Stratton or librarian Kathy Lowell, enjoyed rich careers.

There is little question of the conflict between a career and family responsibilities.[18] Concerning employment, the barrier most often mentioned was the motherhood role. In regard to her forty years of work in a supermarket, Edna Fisher remarked: "I was just a kid, fifteen years old at the time, and I started working during the war when there were no men around. After I was married and the first child came I worked part-time evenings. My husband would come home from work and I would take off for work. But I lost ten years seniority because when I had my children there was not even the thought of a maternity leave."

Dottie Fitzgerald had much the same reflection: "I make my own schedule to fit around Lew's schedule so that someone's here to watch the children. I don't really feel that I have a job. And there's no end of women who feel just as I do."

Personality and Networks

Naturally, each career depends on the abilities, needs, attitudes, and goals of each person. In our sample it is clear that Carmen Ricci had a strong need for recognition and/or sense of responsibility, running as she did for political office. Others have personal problems.

Also, society places a heavy demand on the individual. Was Arthur Zavecz unfairly treated when he was turned down by the Peace Corps because he was sufficiently honest to admit that he had had a prior but brief episode of alcoholism? These questions transcend the scope of this book.

At the same time, the retirees mention how interpersonal relationships can affect their work and the advance in a given company or organization. One's first and subsequent jobs are often the result of personal influence. The report of Evelyn Cohen is not atypical: "Through my medical technology courses at the community college I got a job working for an orthopedist. After a few months he said to me, 'I have a friend who is a dentist but is becoming a plastic surgeon.' I was to help him part time while he continued his courses in plastic surgery. He did become a surgeon, with hands of gold— absolutely phenomenal work—and I stayed with him for over twelve years."

It would be idle to think of pure technical or objective standards as the final arbiter of how decisions are made in any organization. Several of the retirees, from the executive to the workbench level, spoke of networks bordering on favoritism. Steve Kovacs was possibly the most articulate on the subject: "As I saw the heat on at AT&T and about a tenth of the work force being dropped each year, it certainly wasn't based on pure merit. Call it what you want, but it was politics. My own boss held up my promotion each time it came up for review. He had a problem accepting people who were in my ethnic group. He was Pennsylvania Dutch and I'm a Hungarian Slovak." Ethnic lines probably play a greater role in the Lehigh Valley than in large cities, but personal preferences taking precedence over other criteria would seem to be a universal process.

The Effect of Unions

Throughout Western society there has been considerable discussion over the pros and cons of unions. Two Harvard professors state this dilemma quite well: "The paradox of American unionism is that it is at one and the same time a plus on the overall social balance sheet (in most though not all circumstances) and a minus on the corporate balance sheet (again, in most though not all circumstances)."[19] In this connection, several of the retirees recalled how in their youth they were aware of fierce struggles in the automotive and steel industries for the right to bargain: "I remember how desperate it was for the coal miners, and it wasn't much better for the steelworkers." A number of the retirees of blue-collar background continued to feel positively about the unions and regretted their diminished power. Mario Moro spoke of what he saw at AT&T: "A weak union is better than no union at all." Although Matt Boyd had moved up at Steel, he felt frustrated at having to retire at age forty-six and was apparently voicing the sentiments of his former co-workers in saying: "If the Democrats ever get back in, then we'll have a strong labor movement again; security and working conditions will get better." But other voices were critical. Gerald Kenyon, who was up from the ranks, uttered his views: "By the 1960s it was sheer greed in the union at Steel. And the management simply caved in." Alan Adams was no less incisive: "How could the board not realize how labor costs plus our own extravagance at the top would drive American steel right out of the market?"

Ambivalence about unions came from other sources, for one, Arthur Ferraro, an engineer at Western Electric: "We in salaried positions were not unhappy to see the NLRB (National Labor Relations Board) insisting on the workers' right to vote on unionization. After all, whatever the union members get wouldn't hurt us. In fact, one year the engineers almost voted for a union. But on the whole we felt it would reduce our professional status. These elections acted as sort of a velvet hand." In this same framework a retired professor expressed his delight that the faculty at Muhlenberg College almost voted for collective bargaining in the mid-1970s: "This sent fear among the administrations of the other colleges, and we all profited from it in the next year's salary negotiations. Yet no one expressed any appreciation to the professors at Muhlenberg. I guess gratitude doesn't exist in the academic world, or maybe nowhere any more!"

In a few instances the reaction to unions was almost entirely negative. Teacher–counselor Mark Cooper recounts:

"I had harassment by the union. That's one reason I retired early. We had the New York State union moving down the river and the AFT coming up from Yonkers. One day in the faculty room I was having coffee when two of my colleagues were putting pressure on me. I had planned to join anyway, but when they said that we psychologists would lose our differential if I didn't join. . . . Later there was a strike and I was in an administrator's office and they were outside picketing. The superintendent asked them to come in and have some coffee. Well, they didn't. Anyway the whole thing was not the way I visualized my profession."

This opposition is found less among the plant workers than professionals and semiprofessionals. Yet opinion among the older workers seemed to question the achievement of unions in today's world. This general attitude is reflected by analysts who think of unions as "irrelevant to the concerns of a new generation of workers and the issues of a new kind of workplace; at worst, a serious obstacle to technological change and economic competitiveness."[20]

Related Factors

Inevitably, one thinks of other situations that shape our experience and reactions to our work history. For one, *health* can affect one's work, and the reverse can occur, as Robard Young can testify: "I was a planner. I planned how to get products through the machine shop in the most economical way, and I was pretty much on my own. I'm the kind of guy that had to have it perfect. I had to get it through the shop in the cheapest way in the quickest time. That's why I say the stress that caused the angina was of my own making."

Another quite different variable is *technology*. Our sample had seen more or less of four decades of changes in industrial development. They saw automation, computerization, and dozens of other breakthroughs. Jerry Peabody, who inspected the equipment for the Reading Railroad, found his maintenance duties more feasible because of new devices: "The men can now do what was awfully hard for us, especially in winter; getting to all those switches, brakes, and so on is a different story today." On the other hand, many of the

industrial workers were encouraged or forced into retirement because of the elimination of older processes, because a competitor,
either domestic or foreign, had found the secret of doing it more
efficiently: "The Japanese have this secret now. And they can put in
the latest equipment."

We have seen some of the thoughts the retirees had about their
work years—often two-thirds or more of their lives. Choice of and
socialization into the career was found to vary with the individual
and the setting. Children of the Great Depression—most of the sample—had not found so easy a route as did their sons and daughters.
Yet, one of the more salient aspects of their careers was how they
came to an end. Over a third found the threatened breakup or takeover of a company a major reason for their entering into retirement.

There is little question that for most of the sample a major
meaning of life was their work. Nearly all of them enjoyed or at least
rationalized their work. This work ethic probably is in large part
responsible for the devotion with which they throw themselves into
volunteering, for instance. Again, individual personalities explain
the reactions they had not only to the workplace but to how they treat
leisure.

All these generalizations are to be modified by the kind of career
they had—blue-collar, white-collar, professional, managerial, or en-
trepreneurial. What is illuminating is the resilience with which some
moved from one kind of work activity to another, often at retirement.

References

1. Studs Terkel, *Working* (New York: Pantheon Books, 1972).
2. Karyn A. Loscocco, "The Instrumentally Oriented Factory Worker,"
   Work and Occupations, 16 (February 1989), pp. 3–25.
3. Joel O. Raynor, "A Theory of Personality Functioning and Change," in
   Joel O. Raynor and Elliot E. Entin (eds.), *Careers, Motivation, and Aging*
   (Washington, DC: Hemisphere Publishing, 1982), pp. 249–302.
4. *Ibid.*, p. 286.
5. Michael L. Schwalbe, "Sources of Self-Esteem in Work: What's Important for Whom?" *Work and Occupations, 15* (February 1988), pp. 24–35.
6. Jeanne S. Hurlbert, "Social Networks, Social Circles, and Job Satisfaction," *Work and Occupations, 18* (November 1991), pp. 415–430.

7. Bernard J. Gallagher III and Charles S. Palazzolo, *The Social World of Occupations* (Dubuque, IA: Kendall/Hunt, 1977), p. 25.
8. John Strohmeyer, *Crisis in Bethlehem* (Bethesda, MD: Adler & Adler, 1986).
9. William F. Roth, *Work and Rewards* (New York: Praeger, 1989), pp. 27–28.
10. Nigel Nicholson and Michael West, "Transitions, Work Histories, and Careers," in Michael B. Arthur, Douglas T. Hall, and Barbara S. Lawrence (eds.), *Handbook of Career Theory* (Cambridge: Cambridge University Press, 1989), pp. 181–201.
11. Edward B. Harvey, *Industrial Society: Structure, Roles, and Relations* (Homewood, IL: Dorsey Press, 1975), pp. 224–227.
12. David Dunkerley, *Occupations and Society* (London: Routledge & Kegan Paul, 1975), Chap. 4.
13. Richard H. Hall, *Dimensions of Work* (Beverly Hills, CA: Sage Publications, 1986), p. 50.
14. Saroj Parasuraman and Donna Hansen, "Coping with Work Stressors in Nursing," *Work and Occupations, 14* (February 1987), pp. 88–105.
15. André Danzin, "The Nature of New Office Technology," in Harry J. Otway and Malcolm Peltu (eds.), *New Office Technology: Human and Organizational Aspects* (Norwood, NJ: Ablex Publishing, 1983), pp. 19–36.
16. Strohmeyer, *Crisis in Bethlehem,* Chap. 6.
17. Walter Adams, *The Structure of American Industry,* 7th ed. (New York: Macmillan, 1986).
18. Kathleen Gerson, "How Women Choose Between Employment and Family: A Developmental Perspective," in Naomi Gerstel and Harriet Engel Gross (eds.), *Families and Work* (Philadelphia: Temple University Press, 1987), pp. 270–283.
19. Richard B. Freeman and James L. Medoff, *What Do Unions Do?* (New York: Basic Books, 1984), p. 248.
20. Robert Howard, *Brave New Workplace* (New York: Penguin Books, 1985), pp. 174–175.

Part III

Retirement as a Way of Life

Chapter 6

Challenge and Activities

"Officially, I [Evelyn Cohen] retired as of last year. I was an office manager here in Allentown for three years, and then prior to that I was a medical secretary. I took a medical assistant's course after I got out of New Jersey State Teaching College. I never wanted to be a teacher. I always wanted to be a doctor. My friend at the time said it's no profession for a woman. I also talked to my mother and dad, and even my granddad said, 'That's right, it's no profession for a woman. You just go to school and be a teacher.' I wasn't happy.

"In 1942, I got married. I met my husband through a mutual friend. Of course, it was wartime. From then on I decided that I was going to go to business school. I went to a school in New York City, and then got a job. My husband then went into the service. I followed him and worked in an army hospital for two years. . . . That was my first taste of medicine. I guess it left a long-lasting taste in my mouth. Not a negative taste. I wanted to continue in medicine. Then my husband went overseas, and again I went into the office-managing field. When my kids grew up to the point where they were on their own and the youngest one was in about eighth grade, I decided to go back to college and take some medical assistant courses.

"Around the time that I retired, my husband didn't feel well, and he got to the point where he didn't care. He used to sit on the corner of the couch constantly and read. Little things began to irritate me, and I felt it best that I wasn't there to start any arguments with him. But after a while, we straightened things out.

"After my husband's death, I came back here to start working for my son. He had just gone into business shortly before we came down, and one day I went in and said, 'Gee, you look as if you could use some help in here.' His secretary agreed. I didn't mind—I was going crazy already not doing anything—and it turned out to be a full-time position. Well, that was my last employment. I was becoming too involved in the business. It was his business and he had to run it the way he wanted to, even though there were a lot of things I didn't agree with. I just felt that I was becoming too involved because I wanted to do more things. But before quitting, I used to not sleep nights. I used to stay up thinking about little odds and ends. I think it was at times affecting my health. I know I used to go to the doctor. I don't know when it came on, whether it was while I was working for my son; I had a blood pressure problem, which is under control now.

"Once I quit my job—the first time I retired—I wanted to go to Israel. Actually, it wasn't a longtime dream. I had wanted to see the United States more than Israel, but I have very dear friends in New York whose daughter was being married in Israel. They called me up to tell me, and without blinking an eyelash I said, 'Myra, you want company?' Then when I got off the phone I thought, 'What did I do?' I hadn't spoken to the kids or anything. But I went and had a terrific time.

"I've also become involved in volunteer work again, as I was once before while the children were growing up in Rockland County. I'm with SCORE, the Senior Corps of Retired Executives. We help people who are interested in going into business by giving them advice. It's what they now call the Small Business Center. My particular position is to help anybody who wants to go into a typing service or an office service. Most of my work is done on the phone. I am also a member of the Seniors Helping Seniors, which is the elder law project in Allentown for simple legal services. It's for senior citizens who don't have the high incomes for regular lawyers. I'm also on the board of landscape architects. I also joined a synagogue. I'm on the Situd Board, along with my involvement with the Governor's Commission. I guess that's it. Oh yes, one more thing, I read to the blind on Monday nights at the radio station.

"All my life I always had a desire to help people. That's the way my mother was. She would go out of her way to help somebody and I guess I follow through on it. Of course, now that I'm alone, as I said to somebody the other day, it helps me keep my sanity. It's uplifting.

"The best thing about retirement is being on my own, being able to do what I want to do. And the worst thing about it, I guess, is eating alone or waiting for a telephone call. It's lonesome, especially in my particular situation.

"In any case, I'm an avid letter writer and have friends all over the United States. I keep contact by mail, so it keeps me busy. Also, I do a lot of reading. In most cases, now with the holiday coming up, I write a big family newsletter and send it to everybody. I also like to travel. I went to Indiana to visit my daughter.

"One thing about retirement that surprised me was how many people are so lax and unknowing about things. They read newspapers, and they don't even know what they're reading. Their lack of interest in things bothers me. Some retired people have no interest in anything except, to put it plain and simple, watching the boob tube. There's a man downstairs from me who is not a senior citizen but is disabled. He does volunteer work. The other two people in the building don't. They watch their television and that's it. I have to be honest with you, I know that I'm going to sound like a snob, but I would be surprised if there are sixteen families here, well ten out of the sixteen, who finished high school. That might account for it. Like the woman next door, or the one downstairs—they come from poor families, and did housework until they were about sixty or so. I think it is their upbringing, their backgrounds, that is part of the problem. Another part of the problem is the lack of stimulation in the community. By contrast, my aunt lives in the Bronx, in a housing development in Port Chester, and every week the library comes to her with a book delivery."

* * *

Evelyn Cohen is one of those determined, well-adjusted, high-energy people who know where they are going. In our sample, reactions to retirement ranged from the few who became morose and alcoholic to the majority who felt immediate enjoyment and few regrets. Many said they did not feel the need to take conscious steps toward adjustment and were just letting events take place. Yet, most felt that they were aided in their transition into retirement by several means: their own psychological and mental self-preparation and attitude, involvement in new work, increased activities, religious faith, and support from family and friends. Several said they were helped by reading articles and books like the AARP's *Planning Your Retirement*.[1] Finally, some sought advice from their physician, minister, or in a few cases a psychologist or similar professional.

Springboards to Action

The process of adjustment to retirement begins in most cases even before the decision to retire. While still employed we imagine and try to prepare for what it will be like not to go to work. What shall I do with my time? Will my money hold out? How will my life style change? How will it feel to be outside the work stream of daily colleagues and responsibilities? In facing retirement, as in making any adjustment to change, the best aid is one's own attitude. In our study, those fortunate enough to have longer lead time in which to prepare themselves found adjustment easier than did those forced suddenly into retirement by their employer or by their health. We have already shared their fears and hopes, the indecisiveness about when and whether to retire, and the inevitable anxieties of the unknown in the future for self and family.

An example of this can be seen in the following excerpt from the interview with Esther Mueller, a public school teacher who had decided she would retire voluntarily in a few months at the end of that school year. Her adjustment had already begun.

"I always dreaded retirement; I didn't want to retire. My best friend at school did and that started me thinking. But I always dreaded it. . . . Yet, I won't have to change my life style all that much. I don't have many needs for myself. But my family—I love to do for them, especially my grandchildren. . . . I want to get out and do things. There are so many things to do. I just love the smell of that earth, working with your hands in the earth and watching little green things. You feel so close to God. I feel great when in that garden. I will also probably continue to work with the top students interested in the statewide history essay competition, in which three of my students have won."

The New Leisure: What to Do?

Whether in voluntary or compulsory retirement, a fundamental issue is the potential of the individual to find a meaningful life in a range of activities—work, volunteering, and a variety of leisure pursuits. Perhaps even more important is the support system he or she can rely on in the setting of family, friends, and organizations. One can plan in the years before retirement for this increase in leisure time, but most retirees simply improvise in the days and weeks after retirement. Others never quite accommodate to this unfilled space in their lives. Generally, studies have shown that white-collar workers and professionals have done better than the blue-collar manual laborers in accommodating to this large vacuum in their lives.[2] In our study, one blue-collar worker said, "I lost my incentive to work after I was laid off. Now I can't even seem to get up in the morning. I just lie there." Another said, "Because you've been doing something for so long, you just don't know how you'll react. You get up the next day and you know you're not going to work, and what are you going to do with your time? You go through a lot of soul-searching until things iron out." The need for a schedule is important for most individuals, but seems to be especially necessary for blue-collar workers, who are accustomed to a routine on the assembly line or at the workbench.

The Option of Work

Most retirees ask themselves whether they can, should, or want to seek employment. Although the United States institutionalized retirement in the Social Security Act of 1935 and in a great deal of subsequent legislation, the general ambivalence toward the retired, which allows age discrimination in employment, still acts as a deterrent to a meaningful occupational role for many retirees.[3] One problem is the lack of a coherent national policy on the status of the upper-age population.[4] Our society does not seem to be comfortable with the idea that the elderly should be productive (or totally "unproductive," for that matter!).[5] We want older people to be productive, but it is difficult for them to work when their Social Security benefits are reduced after a very limited amount of earned income. However, the Social Security system has become more accommodating to those retirees who wish to continue working either full or part time. Research reveals that those who have Social Security benefits are more likely to work than those who have employer pension plans.[6]

Most studies show that between a quarter and a half of retirees find work after retirement, and more often this work is of lower status than their former employment.[7] In our sample, well over a third (42 percent) reported they had found postretirement work. Only five of forty-eight of them worked full time, and by the time of the interview, some no longer continued postretirement work. The work was usually in a different setting from their earlier employment; 42 percent of those who took postretirement employment worked for a different employer, 21 percent were self-employed, and 25 percent acted as consultants, with the remainder not fitting any of these categories. Twenty-one percent described their postretirement work as "very similar" to their former position, 38 percent as "somewhat similar," but 25 percent indicated it was quite different, and 17 percent "extremely different." Thus, a wide range of opportunities was available—and used.

As compared to their former employment, generally the retirees found their new work equally or more rather than less satisfying:

Much more satisfying	6%
More satisfying	23%
About the same	44%
Less satisfying	25%
Much less satisfying	2%

This apparent enthusiasm is not surprising, as they may not have the same level of aspiration in their new employment as they had during their earlier career. The change of setting, the realization that they were lucky to find a job, or the stimulus of new colleagues are other possible factors. For some, it may have been a matter of "any port in the storm." Still others clearly found positions that paid them to explore sides of themselves not afforded by their former employment.

The Careerists. A number of the men retired with the idea of starting a new career. A typical case is John Worth, a salaried employee, who at age fifty-six voluntarily chose to accept a lump sum retirement enticement from Steel, for whom he had worked thirty-four years, ever since college, first in fabrication, later in sales engineering. Apparently he did so with the full intention to seek other employment at once. He formed his own corporation and within five months after turning down several offers accepted a position with a manufacturer in New York City. He works forty hours a week out of an office in his home, nearly 100 miles from New York City, traveling when necessary:

"The best thing about retirement for me is that I've been able to get this new association going. I thoroughly enjoy what I'm doing. The real satisfaction is I'm more on my own. I'm doing something I like doing. My self-confidence has probably increased 100 percent. When I worked for Big Brother, sixteen people had to say 'yes' to everything. Now I work for a small guy who's got *his* money at stake, but he has faith in you and you're told to do 'whatever you think best.' For myself, I would have distinctly suffered a loss of personal self-image if I hadn't found work. I have a pretty strong work ethic; yet I know others whom it wouldn't bother. I'm using skills I developed in the other job in the Fabricating Division. I'm estimating and selling structural steel and managing the projects after they're sold. . . . I've never regretted my decision—not one day."

Chester Smith, a chemist with Air Products, was, along with all employees over age fifty, offered an attractive package at age fifty-seven, after only nineteen years with the company (prior to that he had been a college professor). He describes his decision and his current work this way:

"I intended to find employment of some kind. We knew we could have survived financially even if I didn't find other work. I squeezed a bit more out of my employer by getting a fixed number of consulting days with them. That kept me working pretty much full time, but when those days were used up, then I was retired for three days! Then I started to work with a polymer company. The week before I started that I had the most difficult decision of my life because in that one week I got three job offers. I think I'm happier now, just for the change in environment. Also I have the potential to make a great deal more money; as I told you, I was motivated by greed. I've been here in this lab a month. If things work out, well, I might earn part ownership. . . . I'm working much harder but I don't mind it. It's more fun; there's a reward in that."

Finally, there's the case of Edward Volpe, who retired in 1981 at age fifty-nine from assistant superintendent of a vocational high school—largely because of declining student quality and the tendency of a number of school districts "to dump their problem cases into a school that had once known fairly high standards." After retirement he continued his previous pattern of summer work, with nearly full-time consulting, structural detailing and estimating, and mechanical drawing. In addition he served on no less than ten civic committees, ranging from the school board to the redevelopment authority, often ending up as chairman. He comments, "I guess some people would call me manic, but I'm not one to remain idle. But the last year or two I'm now taking time off for travel a few times a year."

The Explorers. More often, entering the job market is a struggle, and for both professionals and technicians a lengthy period of trial and error, fortuitous leads, and occasional frustration become the reality.

Arthur Ferraro found enjoyable work as a lab instructor at a nearby college after retiring at age fifty-two from a position as senior engineer in Western Electric (AT&T), where he had worked thirty-four years. He had gone to work right out of high school, went to night classes for twelve years, and earned a B.S. degree in physics while he worked his way up in the company: "I couldn't have gone to work teaching as a lab instructor as a career because financially it wouldn't have given me enough money. Now it's just a supplement. You can subsidize a second career with savings from the first career and a pension. And it allows you to do something you really would like to do and couldn't afford before."

The stimulus and challenge of work motivated several men. For instance, within six months after retiring with a lump sum and pension from a very large manufacturing industry as senior staff accountant with thirty years of service, Tim Trueblood was offered a job teaching the use of accounting on computers. He said he did not start the work for need of the money, but rather: "You can only do so much painting and plastering (in several apartments he owns) without getting somewhat bored. I was only fifty-three, and your work-life is supposed to add at least eight years to that. I wasn't using my mind. My son says I seem happier since going back to work, though my wife thinks I'm spending too much time on it."

Aldo Carlucci struggled desperately to find work, but in the end found his niche: "I didn't start job hunting, because I thought at my age the prospects were not good. But I finally heard of a part-time job at the state liquor store at $4 an hour. At least it keeps me busy, you know. At first it was just two days a week. Now it's up to four days a week."

Women, too, might encounter a rough road in the job market. Barbara Hunt was a school librarian, but got tired of her colleagues using the library as a "dumping ground" for wayward children. When the administration "changed for the worse" and health problems surfaced, she decided it was time to retire. Feeling better, she looked for employment but found she was "overqualified": "So, kind of out of desperation and because I wanted to do something, I went over to Valhalla and sold cemetery lots. I only did it for ten months. Who would think I would benefit from that? But there was a man there who would teach you how to do sales." Then after six years of sales with Avon Products—and somewhat weary of the uncertainty of commissions rather than a salary—Barbara decided it was time for a change. She worked for a business school, where she found relative chaos in the treatment of personnel:

"None of us was really business trained, so it was like cutting off your nose, and I started seeing the wrong people being fired for the wrong reasons. It's not like teaching. When you're in business and you're not in the union, you're really not there. . . . Finally I went over to High Top Manor, a nursing home. It seemed a little better, then I saw them doing the same antics as the business school did. They taped your phone conversations to make sure you said the right things. That's pretty easy to do; you just get to Radio Shack and buy the right attachment."

The Contented. Partial or intermittent work provided a portion of the sample with a certain degree of interest as well as additional income. For example, Neal Rossi, a widowed retired teacher, tutors a few hours a week at $12 an hour and also delivers for a flower shop for twenty hours a week. Matt Ewer, another ex-teacher, remains in the military reserve, mostly, he said, to improve his standard of living. Ex-insurance agent Norm Reinert, who hardly needs to supplement his income, chooses to work with his brother, a psychiatrist, in raising Christmas trees: "We have about forty thousand trees, and that's a specialty crop—they get diseases, you have to trim, you have to weed. My brother is getting his son started in that, is picking up big money, and taking a tax deduction because it's on his land. For both my brother and me it's a kind of relaxation. I'd work there a lot more if I had the time."

Then there is Steve Kovacs, who did not have an easy adjustment following his departure from AT&T in 1985 at age fifty-nine. He began driving a school bus, but by 1990 had worked out a dual career in offering maintenance to a pharmaceutical and medical supply firm in addition to establishing computer repair and related service to his local community, not to mention his diverse hobbies and volunteering.

The Struggling. Almost one-fifth of our sample would like to work but have not had the opportunity or the determination to move successfully in that direction. Some of them made specific attempts to launch a second career. Sally Brown, a former training associate with Bell Laboratories, notes:

"The work ethic is very strong in me, and pay is not too important. I thought I'd like to do some driving for the senior citizens for a fee. My husband does that for Catholic Charities, for free. I went to a seminar that was offered to all of us on how to work in a consulting capacity. I thought of being a transportation consultant—an escort for older people or driving senior citizens to and from the airport. I talked to the Better Business Bureau, but then I ran into insurance problems. . . . My newest idea is operating a bed and breakfast. We have the extra room and I'm good at interacting with people."

Motives and Methods

When asked on the questionnaire why they went to work again, the 42 percent of retirees who chose work checked the following items (many obviously checking more than one): "to use my skills" (69 percent), "to have contact with people" (43 percent), "financial reasons" (42 percent), and "not working gave me too much free time" (33 percent). Among less frequent reasons was the belief that not working could cause either family or health problems. At least one retiree felt he was reducing his nervousness by getting a half-time job. According to a study in England, the lack of social contacts drives many retirees back to the workplace,[8] and, as noted in Chapter 4, a fourth of our subjects said they felt more lonely after retirement.

More often than not, retirees who work appear to emerge from two extremes: the lower blue-collar because of their economic need, and the upper white-collar because they find a stimulus in work.[9] Studies on both sides of the Atlantic confirm these findings.[10] Of the 58 percent of our sample who did not work, 17 percent would like to be working, 64 percent would not, and 20 percent were not sure. The most frequently given reason for not working, if one wanted to, was a lack of appropriate job offers. Health reasons and family obligations also played a role. From the interviews one can quickly gather that many of this 58 percent are so enjoying their freedom—the leisure to do what they want to do, the flexibility or absence of schedule, on top of an adequate income—that they do not consider a second career. Perhaps most important, about 50 percent of retired persons and 40 percent of retired households across the United States in the early 1980s were judged to be "economically advantaged." Moreover, approximately 90 percent of all retired persons receive Social Security, and well over half of these have private pensions or other assets.[11] Finally, for "a large proportion of retirees, the best thing about retirement, in fact, is not working."[12] It is time to find a new meaning in their lives.

Activities

Though a number of the retirees found a vacuum when confronted with free time, most plunged enthusiastically into all kinds of activities, either for the first time or increasing the time from what it was before. These activities include work around the house, socializing with family and friends, reading, travel, sports, hobbies, and volunteer services.

On the questionnaire the subjects were asked to indicate what activities increased (or decreased) in their retirement. Over half of the sample indicated a dramatic increase for at least five different pursuits:

Working around the house	70%
Reading	67%
Travel	59%
Time spent with family	57%
Sports activities	57%
Volunteer service	45%
Activity in social organizations	33%
Watching television	32%
Going out	27%
Other	11%

Most retirees had engaged in these activities during their work years, increasing their commitment after retirement. The opportunity to expand these pursuits was one of the positive aspects of retirement. (Since, during the interviews, so many spoke of church work, we assume they tallied it under "volunteer service" or "activity in social organizations.")

Volunteering

Most of us fail to realize the enormous social and economic contribution that volunteers, both the retired and nonretired, make to our culture. Increasingly, this kind of service has fallen on the upper-aged, as women—formerly the pool for this activity—have sought employment outside the home. A national survey of volunteers underlines the social motivation: nearly half said they wanted to "do something useful, help others," and "have a child, relative, or friend who was involved in the activity or would benefit from it." Religious convictions were also a factor.[13] According to a Minnesota study, volunteering in organizations was most influenced by educational level. Older persons who had been to college were over 50 percent more likely to volunteer than those who had not completed high school.[14]

In broad categories, the type of volunteering noted on the questionnaires seemed almost equally divided between health, educational, civic, and welfare needs. Service activities ranged from reading to the blind to being a guide in a game reserve, from teaching senior citizens to drive more safely to chairing a committee on urban renewal. Table 6-1 outlines the categories of volunteering as reported in the interviews. A detailed listing is found in Appendix B.

Volunteer service work, which averaged some four hours per week, was a major source of satisfaction for many of our retirees. Lorraine Dorfman and Mildred Moffett[15] corroborate this finding by reporting a positive correlation between satisfaction in retirement and volunteer participation, especially for widows, even though we didn't find such a correlation. They believe that volunteer service compensates for loss of the work role and contributes to the community. One man in our study spoke of his and his wife's service in the county nursing home for the aged: "It has given us a feeling of usefulness. Each of us works there over ten hours a week." Several listed six to twelve different community activities in which they now participate, while perhaps the majority concentrate their help in only one or two organizations. For example, Wolfgang Jung reportedly spent eighteen hundred hours over a three-year period as a coordinator at a blood bank.

A few of both men and women said they had not taken on any volunteer activities because of their strong desire to be free from a schedule at last. Dr. Nathan O'Hara explains, "After retiring at seventy-seven, and being in civic activities in addition to a sixty-hour work week, I've been just too tired, and so both of us are taking a long rest." Others have their own reasons: "A friend of mine was deliver-

Table 6-1. Volunteer Services in Organizations

Number reporting participation	Activity
49	Church or temple related, including food banks, educational roles, and offices held in the organization
12	Hospitals and related services (including blood banks)
17	Fraternal organizations (Elks, Lions, Masons, Rotary)
13	General community development (musical festivals, Historic Bethlehem, Burnside Plantation, library commission, and related)
8	College or school services (alumni committees, consultants)
8	Veterans' organizations
10	AARP (American Association of Retired Persons)
9	MORA (Men of Retirement Age)
10	Medically oriented societies (American Cancer Society, Heart Association, Lung Association, etc.)
9	YMCA, YWCA, and related service groups
7	Self- and other-oriented welfare activities (Alcoholics Anonymous, Rescue Mission, Visiting Nurse Association, etc.)
9	Company-based service groups (SCORE—Senior Corps of Retired Executives, REBCO—Retired Employees Benefit Corporation)
8	Meals on Wheels
36	Other

ing Meals on Wheels and found a woman dead. No, I guess I'm not ready yet."

The following excerpts from some of the busiest retirees demonstrate the variety of activities and volunteer services. For example, Arthur Zavecz, a high school teacher for twenty-five years, retired four years ago at age fifty-five, was volunteering in the operating room of the hospital two times a week, part-time teaching at the community college, directing a choir in a major church, singing in the Bach Choir, acting in community theater, and doing flower gardening. No less driven is John Grossi, who is deeply involved in MORA (Men of Retirement Age), AARP, UNICO (an Italian-American social organization), the American Lung Association, YMCA, and Lions Club, serving as an officer in most of these organizations—"I just got so involved that I stopped playing golf as I used to do when I worked for the railroad. I don't need that release from tension any more."

Or take the case of Carl Hoffman. He's still working as a part-time consultant to his former employer:

"Once a month my wife and I volunteer to help the Food Fund at our church, shopping for people who cannot. I was president of our company's Quarter Century Club my first year in retirement. Also, we work on our Lutheran church's food bank distributing surplus food. I'm president of our congregation. . . . We traveled to Europe and the Rockies with friends who are also retired. I'm now running another trip to Europe—the fourth one. I serve as collegial adviser to our minister. For two years I have been president of a local civic association, which sponsors a crime watch for our neighborhood, and I now serve on their board of directors and put out their newsletter."

Among the women retirees, some of the registered nurses seemed to be involved with the most volunteer services. For instance, Adelaide Williams, a former nurse, retired only eight months, enjoys a world far beyond her trailer park:

"I thought I would miss my work and the people I worked with because it was like a part of me and they are my friends. And I might have, if my life weren't so full. I'm very, very active at our Wesleyan church, as director of community missions for the Women's Missionary Society and as Assistant Sunday School Superintendent and expect to be president within the year. I also serve as a trustee on two church committees, sing in the choir, and started a cradle roll department at the request of the pastor. Then, one day a week I volunteer at the county nursing home. . . . Our income was cut 40–50 percent when I stopped work, so I started a little cottage business making purses; I knit, crochet collector's dolls, do quilting and trapunto art."

One has the impression that volunteering assumes different styles. Some prefer or often find themselves in a leadership role as did Carl Hoffman. Others, like Adelaide Williams, move between the service and the leadership role—in many organizations only a thin line separates these roles. One may ask whether these volunteering styles reflect the way the individual approaches other choices in life, both before and after retirement, or is it simply the outcome of the situation.

Alice Stratton is another admirable example of volunteering in retirement, retired eight months ago at age sixty-seven from a college staff where she was chairman of the degree nursing program:

"I didn't have any strong feelings of uselessness. I had so many things to do here at home plus my volunteer activities that I didn't miss my work. That surprised me. I am a quasi-consultant to the new chairman of the nursing program. Two times a month I go back for a committee on gerontology at the college and I've continued as chairman of several other committees there. I'm still chairman of the Clinical Coordinating Committee for the several local colleges that have nurse education programs. I am and always have been involved as a volunteer on the board of directors of the Cancer Society and with the Heart Association on the local, regional, and state levels. Since retirement I've become chairman-elect for the regional office of the Heart Association and added the YWCA board of directors; the latter involves serving on two committees plus the board and involvement in a lot of projects."

Leisure and the Pursuit of Enjoyment

Travel, time with the family, and physical activity all increased for over half of our retirees and their spouses, as noted on p. 158. Leisure pursuits, of course, took a number of directions. Perhaps among the most fulfilling were hobbies. These ran the gamut from gourmet cooking to playing chess on the computer, which Jim Zimmerman did for two hours a day. He also kept horses for his daughters, displayed his mechanical skills in his workshop, read voluminously, and entertained himself with his video equipment most evenings. No less diverse were the interests of Gerald Kenyon, who simply expanded his hobbies of preretirement years—painting, flying, and coin and stamp collecting: "I started when I was young. By the way, stamp collecting lost its genuineness after FDR kept having new stamps issued." Retired manager Michael Ritter says, "I move between tennis, motorcycling, cooking, and reading spy novels. I always did enjoy these, but now, out of the clutches of Steel, I get to do a lot more."

In several instances the hobbies of our retirees were carried on in a highly organized manner. For instance, the usually casual Jim Dowd, who was famous among his friends for his rich harvest of vegetables and flowers, had a filing system on what was growing where. He also had a means of combining fun with work, as when he was social director at a church conference center on the Maine coast in summer. Several hobbies bordered on the exotic. Daisy McLean had the distinction of not only concentrating on dyes and herbs in her own garden, but was director of the dye gardens for the local historical society.

Sports were another major pursuit. Golf was the favorite, cross-country skiing was possibly next, and walking provided relaxation for others. Homer Evans, who lived in the hills, joined the Sportsman Club after he retired, but confined himself to fishing; hunting was out: "I don't care for killing deer even if they are eating my rhododendron every winter."

Most interviewees mentioned increasing their time for television and reading, especially the latter. Several commented that only in retirement were they able to read the daily paper at leisure. Norm Reinhert said he finally got to read *Gone with the Wind* after he retired. Reading tastes varied from mysteries to travel books and articles, from biography to current events and science. There was no strong correlation with educational level. Dorothy Schmidt found her escape from her heavy work load as a committed nurse and caretaker of an alcoholic husband by reading Alvin Toffler's books on anticipated social change: "I just read *The Third Wave*. It's much more optimistic than *Future Shock*." With the relatively high number of college-educated in our sample, it is not surprising that TV programs like Nova, Frontline, and National Geographic were more often mentioned than sitcoms. However, there may be less than an accurate recall of TV exposure. When asked what their TV viewing time might be, several respondents said "a few hours in the evening." Yet the TV was somehow on at midday! Perhaps it is one more indication of self-consciousness when violating the work ethic. Then there were those who referred to TV as the "boob tube." Even they had their favorite programs, but more often on the public channel than on the commercial networks.

Several retirees are not so drawn to volunteer service, but rather to the enjoyment of leisure activities for which they did not have enough time while employed. Here is what preoccupies Lois Bennent, a widowed registered nurse, who had to retire early because of a fall that injured her back (for which she is still under therapy). Besides the care of an eighty-eight-year-old mother, she goes to New York City for the ballet and opera, theater at two or three local colleges, the Community Concert series, and the symphony.

Neil Rossi, a teacher, who retired at age fifty-two because his wife was fatally ill, finds his outlet going to a racquetball club and doing aerobics three to four times a week, besides tutoring two or three students and driving a florist's delivery truck three days a week for a little money.

Roland and Linda Eisenhard retired at ages sixty-two and sixty, respectively—he as treasurer of a motor club, she as proofreader for a printer/bindery company. Together they took three trips in the first year that both were retired. She said that despite a fall that laid her up for six months and despite arthritis and bursitis, she goes out to lunch or breakfast with friends (mostly widows); does handwork with felt, sequins, and beads; and helps at the church with surplus food distribution. Both do a lot of reading, using the public library. They spend ten weeks in Florida each winter because of her arthritis, and they go on senior citizens trips. Like many others he belongs to AARP and similar groups.

The Davises are another couple plunging into a variety of activities in retirement. George notes: "I was never even in a tent and we went out and bought a pop-up camper!" Then they went to Europe and later bought a vacation home in the Pocono Mountains, giving him plenty of yardwork and upkeep chores. His wife also was enthusiastic about his retirement: "We are doing a lot of crazy things now that we never did before—like camping. I'm fortunate to have a good marriage; I have friends who do not. Their husbands do not care to go shopping with them, or eat out, or socialize. How many other men do you think would go out and spend the whole day in Flemington or New Hope at the discount centers to shop?"

One has the impression that our sample does not relish long-range travel as compared to, say, Californians. Most of them prefer trips along the Eastern region—the Jersey Shore, New England, and of course, Florida. This preference for intraregional travel and migration has been documented for a sample of New Englanders. The proximity to kin and familiar settings appears to provide a kind of stability.[16] As another variant, the Carluccis alternate between the Poconos and the shore, but splurge once in a while with a weekend in the Vista Hotel in New York. On the other hand, the Volpes, who live in a modest home in Bethlehem's South Side, now take at least three major trips a year—in the last twelve months to Portugal, New Zealand, and Venezuela, no less!

Happily, there's no consistent pattern on how one chooses to use one's leisure time. Individual preferences, chance factors, success and failure, time, and income are among the determinants.

The Role of Religious Faith

A fundamentalist religious faith is clearly a source of aid and comfort in adjusting to retirement for one segment of the interviewees. Nearly all of them had grown up in a world that revered religious values, which were important for the vicissitudes of their younger years, as Stella Zimmerman explains:

"We had a rough time in the Depression. But my mother was very dedicated to the church. All of us sang in the choir. No missing church or Sunday school. If you missed you didn't go out the rest of the day. That was the kind of family I came from. We learned. Lew and I lost a lot of this regime because of our work and moving so much. But when we got back here I started the kids on their catechism class and Sunday school. . . . Once they got married it was their decision whether they went on or not. . . . I was raised Protestant. My mother was brought up Catholic but she changed at marriage. We certainly needed the church through the Depression. Without the church we probably wouldn't have eaten right."

For many of our retirees the ability to rely on the belief that God determines, directs, or at least watches over one's decisions and their outcome surely provides not only comfort but confidence that "God will see us through." As one woman put it, "God does not make mistakes." To these persons the belief that retirement and what one goes through in adjusting are being guided by the Deity provides the assurance that all will work out. Thus the burden of worry or fear about the future is lifted, for God will protect them.

With the burden of her alcoholic husband, Dorothy Schmidt said, "If I didn't have a deep abiding faith, I couldn't go on, but I know that the Lord gives me what I need every day." And another retired nurse spoke of seeking aid through prayer: "I pray a lot for my husband to take a more positive attitude toward his retirement. I have faith. I think something good will happen if it's supposed to. I feel God has a plan for you, no matter what."

Adelaide Williams once more expresses her humility: "There's a place in the Bible saying 'consider the lilies of the soil, they toil not, neither do they spin, and the Lord takes care of them.' We have that kind of faith, and I believe, really and truly, that we will go on to be productive people until the end of our lives here."

Cliff Wellman, asked to consider retiring at age sixty as vice president of finance for a city hospital, now in financial planning as a second career, spoke of the power of religion at the time of his retirement:

"When it came I felt perfectly at peace. I have a close relationship with the Lord. I'm a born-again Christian believer, and I have drawn upon that particular strength to assist me in the transitional period, with concern for keeping my health and for help with my attitude toward my boss, with whom I did not see eye to eye. I was able to have peace of heart and mind, so that even when he broached the subject of my retirement I was completely at ease. I could absorb this and not become devastated. I don't even think my blood pressure went up."

Religious devotion seemed to cut across both age and educational level. Lew Fitzgerald saw an efficacy in his religious faith: "I believe in Jesus Christ and God, and I think that He's up there watching out for the clan. If in working my business I find somebody to offer a business opportunity to and maybe answer his prayer, I help, and that might be helping me too at the same time. . . . Some of these threads we're hanging by and the reasons we're here and there are hard to figure out sometimes. What puts these opportunities together at this particular instance in time? . . . A lot of it is trust and a lot of it's faith."

Variations of the Religious Theme

The religious experience expresses itself in different ways. As we shall see in Chapter 8, Harry Hemphill's involvement in Alcoholics Anonymous—possibly along with his political conservatism—might be interpreted as a form of religion: "I am still out three nights a week at a meeting. Helping others to save themselves as it happened to me once is really thrilling to me. It's total involvement for me these last several years."

For others, volunteering and organizational involvement may be an extension or a substitute for religion. Yet a small number of retirees mentioned their problems with religion. Neal Rossi, for example, left his church, as he found little of what he called the Christian spirit in the clergy or the parishioners. Moreover, he could not resolve the problem of suffering: "If there is a God why did my father have the years of pain he did?" But for many of the sample, religion was a refuge and a guide.

In looking over our retirees we have to realize that their gung ho attitudes toward work and activities may be a product of the volunteer sample. As pointed out in Chapter 1, the individuals who said "yes" to submitting to a survey are those who are more engaged in life. At the same time, the diversity of feelings toward the use of a new leisure reveals a lack of stereotype in their approach to retirement. Specifically, their general warmth toward religion points to their position in their life cycle and once again to the fairly conservative social climate of the Lehigh Valley.

References

1. American Association of Retired Persons, *Planning Your Retirement* (Washington, DC: AARP, 1989).
2. Dean W. Morse, Anna B. Durka, and Susan H. Gray, *Life After Early Retirement* (Totowa, NJ: Rowman & Allanhead, 1983); Erdman B. Palmore *et al.*, *Retirement: Causes and Consequences* (New York: Springer Publishing, 1985).
3. Ruth Crary Blank, "A Changing Worklife and Retirement Pattern: An Historical Perspective," in Malcolm H. Morrison (ed.), *Economics of Aging: The Future of Retirement* (Van Nostrand Reinhold, 1982), pp. 1–60.
4. Alan Pifer, "The Public Policy Response," in Alan Pifer and Lydia Bronte (eds.), *Our Aging Society: Paradox and Promise* (New York: Norton, 1986), pp. 391–413.
5. Malcolm H. Morrison, "Work and Retirement in an Older Society," in Pifer and Bronte (eds.), *Our Aging Society*, pp. 341–365.
6. Daniel A. Meyers, "Work After Cessation of a Career Job," *Journal of Gerontology, 46*, S93–102, 1991.
7. Palmore *et al.*, *Retirement*, p. 169.
8. John Tunstall, *Old and Alone* (London: Routledge & Kegan Paul, 1966).
9. Palmore *et al.*, *Retirement*, pp. 169–170.
10. Stanley Parker, *Retirement and Work* (London: Allen and Unwin, 1982), pp. 123–126.
11. Christopher J. Ruhm, "Why Older Americans Stop Working," *Gerontologist, 29*, 294–306, 1989.
12. John E. Crowley, "Longitudinal Effects of Retirement on Men's Psychological and Physical Well-Being," in Herbert S. Parnes *et al.* (eds.), *Retirement among American Men* (Lexington, MA: Lexington Books, 1985), pp. 145–173.
13. Carol Jusenius Romero, "The Economics of Volunteerism: A Review," in Committee on Aging Society, *America's Aging: Productive Roles in an Older Society* (Washington, DC: National Academy Press, 1986), pp. 23–50.
14. Lucy Rose Fischer, Daniel P. Mueller, and Phillip W. Cooper, "Older Volunteers: A Discussion of the Minnesota Senior Study," *Gerontologist, 31*, 183–195, 1991.

15. Lorraine T. Dorfman and Mildred M. Moffett, "Retirement Satisfaction in Married and Widowed Rural Women," *Gerontologist, 27,* 215–221, 1987.
16. Lee Cuba and Charles F. Longino, Jr., "Regional Retirement Migration: The Case of Cape Cod," *Journal of Gerontology, 46,* S33–42, 1991.

Chapter 7

The Individual, Family, and Social Networks

Retirement, as we have discussed, is one more episode in the life cycle. It occurs along with other changes and complications, as it did with Kathy Lowell—a second marriage, the absence or presence of children, intellectual interests that may make her different from those around her. Fortunately she entered retirement with a degree of insight on how to adjust to changes that she knew would come to her.

"I suppose I started thinking about my retirement when my husband Ed, who is three years older than myself, started talking about his. I was the circulation librarian at Chatham College, and I also had charge of student assistants taking training in the library. In retrospect, I can say the field of librarianship was very satisfying. I had planned to retire before. I was going to do it when I became sixty-two. I felt that it was time to relax. I was actually sixty when I retired. My husband took early retirement from the railroad. I thought he was going to retire all by himself. That was a selfish attitude. He offered to drive me to work every day, but I thought about why he could just go off and do whatever. Maybe I was envious of him, but when things started to change over at the college, I wanted to live as he could. Things at the library were different; time was catching up, they were striving to automate, and they brought in computers.

"We moved into the Lehigh Valley right after our marriage, twelve years ago. I had just gotten my degree. I was married before, but my husband died in 1972 and I wanted to make myself economically independent. I did not want to join a card-playing group. I had worked on a nonprofessional basis as librarian in Quakertown for a number of years.

"I went to library school at age fifty, and I sublet an apartment. When I look back on it now, I tremble. It was a fascinating phase of my life because I packed up things to start a new life. I had beautiful memories, but I wanted something new. I had to get out; I just had to be a different person. I had no children, so I was pretty much alone. Not too many relatives either. I chose to go to graduate school at Syracuse, but it was a struggle to get in at my age. They really discouraged me. The last time I went to school was when I got my degree in 1944 from Wilson College.

"I was a little frightened to go back to school after being out for so long. I had tidied up my affairs in Quakertown and sublet my apartment to a friend who said he'd care for my dear dogs. I simply marched out of the house one day and opted for graduate housing at the university. I roomed with three young ladies, all in their twenties, and I was fifty. But I dressed young. I never had many older friends; my friends were always young. I'm going on sixty-five now. It was a marvelous year, but it was a struggle for me. I had to work twice as hard, maybe three times as hard. I had to restructure my act of concentrating on things, meetings, and deadlines on courses. I didn't cut one class. The other kids would have a lark cutting class, you know the usual thing.

"I kept myself in excellent shape. I must have walked about ten or twelve miles every day, then I walked back and forth to campus. I was motivated and I survived. In fact, I got a 3.5 grade point average. I had no one, so I had to make it. It just drove me. To this day, I am still in contact with some of the people I lived with.

"I must say I enjoyed my years at Quakertown on a professional basis because I had trained for public library work. Then I worked about a year and my husband came on the scene. A couple weeks later, he came into town and called. We went out for dinner and began renewing a friendship. A couple of months later we decided to marry. He was transferred over here, so I came to the Lehigh Valley. I didn't want to do public library work at that point. I thought I'd like to do library work in colleges. I love the college atmosphere; it's one of the things I miss. I miss having colleagues around; I could always find someone to discuss things with. There were enough people with challenging ideas. Now I'm in a different community, so I find nothing that is challenging here. I find I have to go to academe to get this.

"I am a member of AAUW. I still have not become active in it because I haven't found a need for it. I don't have enough time, and what I also want to do is get away from structured things. I want to live life on my own terms now. But we can't live entirely unstructured, of course. I was in the AAUW for fifteen or twenty years back in Quakertown, was vice president, worked my way up. I enjoyed it, but things were different then. I don't want the same things now.

"I feel very fortunate that I'm able to do things that I was never able to do. I'm interested in my house. I have moved every piece of furniture in every possible combination, so that's becoming boring too. I enjoy doing things with Ed. I enjoy cooking. In fact, I still go to gourmet classes. I do go hiking. I love flowers and I fiddle around with our little garden. I do needlepoint, but that was always a source that would calm me down; it's very soothing. In fact, I made pillows for my late husband while he was ill. Back in the sixties, he had open heart surgery and all kinds of things. So the last four years we lived together were very traumatic. They were also some of the most beautiful years that I had. You learn how to live when you're facing death.

"Now there's a lot to do. We don't travel much. Ed would like to travel more. I traveled all my life with my first husband. We used to spend all February in Maryland . . . did that for about ten years. It got boring after awhile. Then I think the traveling to end all traveling was after I got out of graduate school. I treated myself to a trip. I took six weeks to go to Pakistan and Afghanistan with the Smithsonian Institute. It was a fabulous study trip. I had made friends at school who were Pakistanis. That was a debilitating trip, though, because it was a study. Thank God I was single. It took my intestinal tract six months to recover after I came back home. We do take a trip now and then, but Ed would like to go across country on a train, going through Canada. We will get there someday. After my first husband died, I took up skiing.

"Sometimes I feel I'm a snob. My husband does not have a college education. Sometimes I think it upsets him that he doesn't. I

become frustrated with people of the world—the younger generation. The younger people who go to college now just don't know how
to study.

"I'm happy in my new marriage, but my husband isn't very
dynamic. We have the added complication of his two boys. They're
both married now, but when we married, one was just going to start
college. It was a challenge. I never had any children.

"It bothers me that we don't have a family around sometimes.
I'm afraid I may have a stroke sometime and be helpless. I don't want
to be stuck in a hospice or an old folks home. When we chose this
community out here, we chose it because it's a mixed community.
We didn't want a retirement place, so there's a lot of young people
here. It's got vitality in it. I'm glad we're here.

"I feel uncomfortable with the future since my mother was an
invalid. She was a very fabulous, very vital woman. She had rheu-
matoid arthritis. Fortunately, my family was well off enough that we
had a housekeeper. She was a vital, domineering woman and never
left her wheelchair, but she'd whip around in it. She died when she
was eighty-three. My mother never knew a well day. We were away,
and since we were in Virginia, she did spend some time in a home.
Fortunately, she wasn't aware of the stark reality of her situation. She
was in and out of it, so we had her at home at times. But then it got
to the point where we could not cope. I think that's what bothers me.
I see callousness today. What you have can be simply wiped away
when you go into this type of residence. I find it terrifying."

* * *

Retirement occurs within a given sociocultural setting—usually
to those individuals who reach the sixties, or occasionally before—
who more often than not are married and have ties to other relatives,
especially their children and upper-age parents. We are socialized to
accept the end of our work career, partly through the cues from
others, but mostly from our inner motivational system—which may
be favorably or unfavorably disposed to this fairly momentous shift
in the life cycle. With our emphasis on youth and its culture, retirement is seen by many as one more symptom of getting old and
useless.

Retirement also involves a change in our social networks. In this chapter we are concerned with how the individual perceives and interacts in the marriage as well as with others, both within and outside the home, in the context of the past, present, and future.

Men and Women

Our culture has long been identified with highly divergent statuses and roles for men and women. Indeed, even research on retirement has largely focused on the male experience, and little attention has been given to the financial and other difficulties of women.[1]

Even though this century has seen some rapprochement between the sexes, few women, including our interviewees, could fail to be aware of the differentiation in the labor scene. Jennie Fisher, a former inspector on the line at General Electric, comments:

"We're in a competitive market, and you can't go around wasting a box of screws or anything else. That plant was strictly for women. . . . In fact, I had a foreman say to me: 'Well, you know, Jim's having back problems today; I'll put Shirley on the job.' And it was unionized. Any women who went out of there knew how to work. Boy, did they work the women. The men would stand and talk for an hour and nobody said anything. If a woman did that they'd say, 'Don't you have anything better to do?' Somehow that was never asked about the men."

Nor is it a secret that the two genders respond to events with somewhat different approaches. In part, this difference is biological and demographic. Women live on the average nearly six years longer than men. This difference is compounded by the disparity in the age at marriage; the bride is some two to three years younger on the average. Consequently, if the two retirements are to be of equal length, the women must retire younger. At least until recently, the occupational role has been thought to have less importance for the woman than for the man. Thus, women who feel a low identification with their occupations have more positive attitudes toward retirement than do those with strong identification with their careers.[2] However, most women who belong to a pension plan postpone retirement until the maximum eligibility and therefore retire later than their husbands.[3]

In our study we anticipated a number of gender differences, but few appeared. However, women found retirement to be easier than they had anticipated, whereas men found it to be about what they expected. Women were less concerned with the loss of status after retirement than were men, but this was not very much of a frustration for either gender as compared to, say, missing their friends, which was especially cited by the men. Women may not need this kind of social support, as they appear to be more self-reliant or have maintained a network of friends outside the workplace.

Another problem that women face in their longevity is the inflationary cycle. Even though Social Security benefits are adjusted for cost of living increases, most private pensions are not. Furthermore, most pensions, being based on last salary, leave working women with smaller pensions. Indeed, it is well documented that women, along with minorities, suffer more financially in upper age than the middle-class married white male.

One intriguing aspect of the gender relationship is how occupational roles have tended to keep the two sexes apart.[4] Although many work settings may bring the genders together, as with the boss–secretary, doctor–nurse, it often includes a subordinate role for the female. Most work areas have traditionally found a clustering of men, as in a steel factory, or women, as in the textile mill. Although recent employment practices have tended to bring the two sexes together, our own sample spent much of their lives in the traditional separatist style.

Husbands and Wives

It is in attitudes and role structure that gender differences become intriguing, particularly in marriage. Men are usually associated with *instrumental* roles (work, power, decision making) and women with the *expressive* (socializing, emotional, and supportive). In this century these roles have increasingly begun to merge, but society still encourages the more directive status for the male, and a submissive one for the female, even if the relationship of these roles has become rather subtle. Research studies show that this division is less acute in later life, notably in personality traits.[5] The interviews sometimes showed one of the spouses as dominant over the other, but there seemed to be a blending of personalities or at least of roles for many couples. As most people tend to present a favorable image in public, interviews often indirectly encourage this kind of facade. Yet, in several instances conflict was apparent. Several marriages represented what has been labeled the *complementary needs* type of marriage. That is, the husband and the wife seem to have different deep-seated needs and value systems, which indirectly complement or support each other. Bill and Martha Flynn had something of this. As he said, "With an Irish background and many years in Puerto Rico I'm a bit of a dreamer. Martha is *still* Pennsylvania Dutch, terribly practical." In this instance, the difference may be more cultural, but in other instances it is a question of personality orientation or habit systems. Retired mailman Bruce Shoemaker is a case in point: "I get up every morning at five o'clock. I'll go out and go downtown and have breakfast. She sleeps. I wake up before the alarm most of the time. She likes to watch different programs on TV and to read well into night. Half the time I don't know what time she comes to bed."

Research studies have shown that the wife generally makes a greater adjustment in marriage than does the husband.[6] This is not surprising in view of the dominance that Western culture has conferred on the male. The interviews with single women and widows somehow gave the impression of stronger personalities or possibly more vibrant lives than what seemed to be the situation with the married women. Or, at least, single women have greater freedom in decision making, while the married appear to live more in the shadow of their husbands. At the same time, it seems that for centuries women have learned to develop their antennae in order to pick up cues from men, if for no other reason than assuring their own survival. This greater sensitivity of the wife came through in our interviews. A retired librarian reflects: "Somehow Jim changes his attitude when I'm not employed. If I see a pair of pink shoes he's not going to let me buy them if I can't produce my own money. Now that I'm no longer working I'm supposed to do all the chores around the house, where before, he would pitch in once in a while."

Some husbands, however, at least recognize the needs of the wife, as reflected in the remarks of Harry Hemphill regarding his past employment as an air inspector with long hours and extensive travel: "Too often an employer forces people to do things that their wives or children don't want to happen. They end up with an employee in the job, but not necessarily a good employee because he has problems at home, problems with his wife."

In other instances, husband and wife become so intertwined that they even look alike. This strong identity between the spouses was illustrated by the case of John and Esther Mueller. They share deeply in their various experiences, not least his forced retirement from the college: "We were both hurt. He didn't show it but I could see he was hurt." Like many other couples, they are held together by decades of common experiences, interests, and a shared value system, deeply rooted in their Protestant religion. And in this instance, they both had been teachers.

In the conservative life style of the Lehigh Valley, traditional gender roles are the rule. The man exhibits his decisiveness and usually sets the style of the marriage; the woman defers to his judgment. Exceptions are found: the wife could mold the personality of the husband. Men could be resourceful, too. After he was widowed, Barry Lichtenweiner responded to his loss by getting very involved with the Visiting Nurse Association as both recipient of aid—participation in the bereavement program—and a volunteer who provides similar assistance. In other words, a major crisis, such as death of the spouse, can lead to gender role reversals, or at least a deeper identification with the opposite sex.

This close identification between the spouses is shown in the reaction of Betty Carlucci to her husband's retirement: "I was more worried about him than anything else, that he'd be able to cope with it, because I knew that he liked to work and be on a schedule. I just prayed that he'd come through okay."

In at least one case the dependency was especially acute: "We haven't been separated from each other even for one night in these last ten years or so." In retirement an almost identical pattern remained: shopping together, looking at the same TV programs, even sports.

Emotional Reactions and Dependency

One aspect of the instrumental-expressive axis is the different ways the two spouses react to changes in the life cycle, whether the arrival or departure of a child, a change in residence, death, or retirement. In the upper years, at the twilight of earning and child-rearing tasks, expressive roles are probably more acute than the instrumental roles. In Chapter 4 we spoke of the greater impact that forced retirement, notably the perceived unfairness in company policy, had on the wife as opposed to the husband. We return to the case of Walter and Irene Koch as illustrative. As a researcher and chief engineer for pneumatic conveyor belts, he was forced to retire because of his refusal of a work overload beyond the seventy hours he was already putting in. His company did allow him to continue a few more months in order to be eligible for their early retirement compensation plan—"not enough to live on, by any stretch of the imagination." Now two years after retirement and enjoying a consultancy equal to his highest pay period, he reflects: "Retirement was the best thing that ever happened to me. Yet my wife went through a lot more anger than I did." His wife: "It hit us both awfully hard. He pretended it didn't but I knew different. The point is that after he'd given so much of himself—he had so many inventions for the benefit of the company—the way it was done was very cruel. . . . But now being a consultant on his own is marvelous!"

How Does Retirement Affect the Marital Relationship?

Studies have shown that married couples move through three periods of differential satisfaction: (1) couples are more satisfied with the marriage in the early years before the arrival of children; (2) satisfaction scores decline with the arrival and rearing of a child, as these years are surrounded with pressure and anxiety, whatever compensations this role brings; and (3) marital satisfaction scores generally rise somewhat as the children move out of the home—which in most cases occurs before retirement. Consequently, the couple is fairly stabilized in the years approaching the cessation of work.[7] Research studies do not show any major dislocation in marital happiness following retirement.[8]

In an intensive analysis of twenty couples at midlife, three major shifts were identified: (1) an increase in the wife's power and autonomy, (2) the wife's support in bolstering the husband's "defensive mythologies about themselves," and (3) the formation of a habit system in supporting each other in feelings and attitudes, each requiring the other to provide the emotional qualities that they feel they lack or choose not to exercise."[9] Any major event can hardly fail to have an effect on marriage dynamics. Many industries recognize that retirement has far-reaching consequences. For example, at AT&T and Bethlehem Steel, wives are invited to participate in a two-day seminar after the husband is called up for termination.

A major change in the life cycle has varying impact on the person or the marriage, and spousal reactions can assume a variety of forms. In fact, a few of the men, referring to the trauma of a sudden retirement (especially at Steel), said "I didn't want to take it out on her." There were several men who fell into a depression after retirement. At least three husbands and one wife began to drink more heavily than before and on some days never got out of bed. More often than not, the wife defers to the needs of the husband. For instance, Adelaide Williams's husband was ten years younger and had six years less education. She began to feel physical strain and was also conscious of the need to protect her husband's self-image. Reluctantly, after two decades of nursing, she retired "because of my knees and my husband!"

Tensions can occur between the spouses as the period of retirement approaches. One study revealed some conflicts when the wife continues to work beyond the retirement of the husband. The universal problem of the husband's failure to meet the domestic needs of the household is a point of contention.[10]

As one interviewee said, "Retirement is just one more adjustment we have to make in life." Yet, as we have seen, retirement can create disruption, including the marital bond. For some couples the sexual relationship was disturbed. Others volunteered that sex was "as good as ever." Habits tend to change; she watches more TV, he spends more time on hobbies or is off to bowling more often. One engineer mentioned that "she is terribly jealous of my love affair with my computer." For Cliff and Leona Wellman retirement provides a new horizon: "It's great fun to have him around, we go biking almost every day, but we still have our separate interests. He's deep into sports, and I'm very much with my piano." Richard and Lois Lucas also see retirement as a new level of sharing: "We've been on two Elderhostel programs—one out West on ecology and one this summer at Penn State on word processing. Also, we now have more time for local concerts and lectures."

Although marital bliss characterizes some couples, others are not so certain. Harriet Goldman reflects:

"It was only a few weeks after Black Friday (the day the bell rang at Bethlehem Steel) that I realized that we could easily get in each other's way. I've about stopped going to my bridge set because I'm so sick of hearing my friends talk about how the husband comes around the kitchen leaning over their shoulders, lifting the lids off the pots. Dan has been pretty good, but it irritates me how he will use my calendar for his own appointments. I don't know how many calendars I've bought for him, but he uses mine. . . . As one of my friends said, 'I married for better or worse, but not for lunch every day together.'

Another put it this way: "If only he'd leave town for a night or two." Or as Janice Ewer, an ex-teacher married to an electrical engineer at Steel, remarked: "I'm so glad I retired first. Then I could get used to being home before he was under my feet."

One retiree said that a number of his friends kept postponing retirement because of the potential negative effect it might have on their marriage: "I kind of know it isn't going to set well with her. I just feel it's better to let sleeping dogs lie." Harry Hemphill spoke of one acquaintance who had been fairly domineering over his colleagues and in his bitterness on being required to retire brought so much grief to his wife that they nearly landed in the divorce court. The stand-off was somewhat relieved when he developed a career as a consultant. Kathy Lowell comments: "Why do you think we bought this townhouse? We wanted a place that had enough room so we could each have our space. We both recognize that. We don't share a lot. I really don't care about sports at all."

Several pointed to the need for each spouse to develop separate interests and hobbies "so as not to get into each other's hair"; "It's not a bad idea to take a separate vacation." Evidence suggests that the husband has to make a greater adjustment on retirement than does the wife, as our culture has traditionally placed her into a domestic role, which she continues after leaving her employment. As one perceptive interviewee remarked, "Retirement takes the man out of a man's world." This greater need for adjustment is often expressed by a husband being affected more by his own retirement than his wife's. But the wife's feelings are more affected by her spouse's retirement than by her own.[11] These observations may become less pertinent, as women are now assuming careers, but most of our sample belongs to a less egalitarian tradition.

The Eye of the Beholder

As implied above, nearly all our couples seemed to have accepted their marital union as a satisfying one. When asked "Who has been most helpful in your adjustment to retirement," 69 percent said it was their spouse (their children and friends followed next in importance). The strong affinity of husband and wife is not surprising. After all, the unsuccessful marriages have largely ended in divorce, and most of our respondents had been married well over twenty years. Also, we are again reminded that most volunteer samples represent the more contented members of our society. Or as individuals we mask our frustrations either to others or even to ourselves. A few wives prided themselves on a better situation than what they saw elsewhere: "I have friends who do not have good marriages. Their husbands don't care to go out shopping with them or for dinner; they don't like to socialize or they might have a drinking problem or they don't have a happy marriage. So, the wives have to find their own outlets. So, I think I'm very fortunate."

As one example of a husband and wife relationship we turn to the story of a retired student counselor Grace Shoemaker. She seems to integrate her husband and other kin, as well as other activities, into her life with minimum crisis:

"Let me start by saying that my husband retired before I did. He's a big help to me. . . . I didn't mind at all. . . . He helps with the housework and does all the grocery shopping. My husband is retired from the post office because if you worked for twenty years and were sixty years of age then you get your pension. Or then you can retire after thirty years at sixty-five. So, while I was working, he would do most of the housework, the cleaning, the laundry. . . . We've been paying 7.2 percent toward our retirement. We didn't pay Social Security; we paid into our own pension plan, which provides a half-way decent pension. My husband assigned a percentage. The reason he did that was for me to receive his medical insurance. I would get widow's pension from there, and I have their medical coverage, which is a lot better than Blue Cross–Blue Shield. They take that right out of your pension.

"I began to feel that there was too big a gap between me and the children in the Middle School. I sent in for a statement of what my pension would be, and I was surprised because it was more than I thought it would be—so I decided to retire when I turned sixty. I talked to my principal about it so he could secure a replacement for me. He suggested that I take a half-year sabbatical leave, since I'd been there twenty-five years and never took one. So in the fall of '84 I took leave, and when I returned I had an intern to learn from me what I did. It was like returning and having a private secretary; it was wonderful and it made my last semester a very pleasant one.

"My former colleagues have to get a drug prevention program off the ground, and they're getting parents involved with suicide prevention. These are the things that I would have had to get involved in and, quite frankly, I'm at the age where I no longer want to get into that kind of thing. . . . My psychiatrist sees people who have all kinds of problems about retirement and she said I was an unusual case. Sometimes I thought that people who have problems when they retire had problems before they retired. My husband and I know quite a few people who are retired, and I don't know of anybody who is not completely satisfied.

"Another important thing is that we don't have financial problems. We only have one daughter, and she has a Ph.D. in chemistry and is married to a man with a very good job, so we don't think we have to help her. We have enough money to do what we want to do, . . . we're not tremendously wealthy but we're comfortable. The people whom I have heard about who do have problems with retirement do have financial problems a lot of the times. We went to Ireland a few years ago and one of my husband's friends said to him, 'What are you spending all your money for? You won't have any left for your daughter.' My husband told him that our daughter probably has more money than we do right now. We gave her a good education and we are going to use our money to enjoy ourselves. One of my friends has three grown children and she said to me, 'You know, you never think that they can grow up and can handle their own problems—you always think of them as being about eighteen.'

"My daughter and son-in-law don't intend to have children. It doesn't bother me not to have grandchildren. I think my husband would like them because he is fonder of young children than I am. I didn't like the age of diapers and bottles; I liked it when she reached the age of talking. . . . Before they got married, my son-in-law asked me how I felt about their not having children. I told him that if he didn't want them I would be the last person in the world to tell him to have children after what I've seen in school and heard from children who felt that they were at the root of their parents' divorce— they felt responsible for it. I knew many of these parents, and in some cases the divorce was caused by the problems of their children. In a lot of cases, if the parents did not have the children, they would have gotten along better. Now my son-in-law travels a lot, and my daughter doesn't mind because she does a lot of crafts, and when they want to go somewhere they simply 'put the dog in the kennel,' and you can't do that with a child.

"I'm just so happy to be retired! I don't miss my friends. I had a group of friends in school and they still come to see me. I thought these friendships would end, but they have continued. They often tell me more about what's going on at school than I care to know. I'm not interested in it anymore, but they come to me with their problems, for help. . . . I have been meaning to volunteer since I retired, but I just haven't gotten around to it. There always seems to be something to do. I read a lot. I haven't felt that I needed something to fill my time. When my time comes, then I will volunteer. Some people will volunteer even to meet people. I've been asked to join my friend's bowling league and I told my friend, 'I've worked for twenty-five years so that

I could do what I want to do, and when I wanted to do it. I'm enjoying this, and I don't want to be tied down to Wednesday morning at nine o'clock to have to be at the bowling alley.' I just don't want to do that. . . . I've reached a point in my life where I can say 'No.' Once I was making an excuse to a lady asking me to collect for the Heart Fund and when I hung up the phone my daughter said to me, 'Mother, why didn't you tell her the truth?' The truth was that I had done this in the past and I was treated rudely by the people in this area. So I decided that the very next person who called me for something I didn't want to do, I would tell them the truth. I don't make excuses anymore. I tell them this is the way it is and this is how I feel. . . . What I would like to do sometime is maybe go into the hospital and read to the children and maybe tutor those who are in for a long time, read to the elderly, write for the elderly, things like that."

Conflict and Resolution

Few couples found retirement to be a threat to their marriage. In fact, interestingly, most feel there was no difference in their already positive marital relationship after retirement. Even this major life event seems to be assimilated into the existing feelings and affection. Yet the departure from the workplace can mean that the "tremendous trifles"—choice of TV program, who does the marketing—become more blatant, as there is now more time and less space in which to concentrate on the differences with the spouse. There may be new problems to resolve—domestic chores (especially if the husband retires before the wife), how to spend the new leisure, or the problem of reduced income. One couple found the choice of a burial site a major source of conflict—he could be buried at no cost in a veteran's cemetery; she spoke of the two plots her parents had left specifically for them.

For Betty Carlucci, a number of tensions came between her and Aldo:

"As long as I know we have the money we can spend it. I don't feel guilty about spending on a vacation as he does. He says, 'as long as

I don't have to touch any of that green stuff,' but why keep putting
and putting away and not enjoy life a little? . . . I know I smoke too
much but I could've been drinking, or a lot of other things. . . .
Anyway, it bothers him, because he smoked and then quit fifteen or
eighteen years ago. They say someone's smoking bothers you more
when you quit."

However, emotional identification was stronger for the Carluccis—as it seemed to be for most interviewees—than was their
conflict. When the dreaded day arrived at Steel, and he came home
in agony, she said, "We both cried. We knew it was coming but we
didn't know when." She tried to lessen his depression, and eventually he took courses at the local community college, which helped.

Conflict between the spouses at midlife is often the result of
interwoven causes. Matt Boyd tells of how the combination of his
being laid off at age forty-six from Steel, the children leaving home
for college and marriage, and other pressures aggravated his wife's
drinking problem. A divorce followed, and after some inner upheaval he established a successful consultancy in insurance and
health plans.

Occasionally the impasse is caused by a health crisis. We return
to the case of Robard Young, who at age thirty-nine had a triple
bypass. Continued heart trouble led to his retirement from Steel at
fifty-one. At that time his wife Ruth was at menopause, and the strain
of finances with one of their sons still in school brought them to
despair. Yet both realized that they still had their "inner resources."
She found work in a day-care center, and the medical package from
Steel staved off disaster. Still, they realized that their Social Security
would be reduced once their son reached eighteen. "It's our commitment to each other that keeps us going. Our belief in God also helps,
even though we don't go too often to church."

A few couples felt that their conflicts became more acute at
retirement as the loss of their occupational pursuits left more time to
focus on their differences. Evelyn Cohen comments on her reluctance
about retirement: "I was concerned. What was I going to do, how was
I going to occupy my time? And what made it more difficult was the
fact that my husband was home and was not well and a lot of the
things he did irritated me. I didn't want to be there to see them." The

case of the Fitzgeralds, age forty-eight and thirty-three, well represents the themes of both complementary needs and conflict. With his forced retirement from industrial middle management and shift to another career, and her employment as a part-time nurse in radiology, they became aware that pressures of one kind or another—children to raise, finances, community involvements—moved them to drive their differences underground, and at the time of the interview they were working out their marital problems. He saw the marriage as the two roles complementing each other, but in a traditional fashion:

"Before retirement we never paid enough attention to our personal needs, what with the job and the children. I think a lot of that adjustment and blending has to happen early in a marriage. But we were both so busy we pushed it back and never confronted the problem. I think a lot of people say, 'Well, he's off to work and I have my world, he's got his, and we're going our separate ways.' But I think the husband and wife should complement each other. She can do lots of things I can't do, and vice versa. I have the foresight and the logic; she has the intuition and sensitivity. They have to complement each other. We're now trying to get our family, our finances, and our social, religious, and community life all in good balance."

As a very young wife of a retiree, Dorothy Fitzgerald expressed what in popular opinion is true for many wives of retirees: "His retirement definitely changed my life. No doubt about that. I can't do things about the house the way I did when there wasn't a man around. I can't keep the home the way I used to, because now, instead of just my seven- and five-year-old, it's now like having three children at home, with things all over the house. He'll eat at one time, the children at another. Somehow he gets less done around the house now than when he had a fixed schedule."

How Do We Relate to Our Children?

Despite the rumors and laments about the "death of the American family," it is, in reality, very much alive. No less than 84 percent of individuals over sixty-five years are reported to have offspring within an hour's drive,[12] and according to a 1974 Harris poll, over half of this age group had seen one of their children during the last day or so. Relationships with children seem to be strengthened as a result of retirement: "We have more time to be with the kids and the grandchildren."

Americans display a good deal of reciprocity in their aid to the extended family. Traditionally, daughters are especially concerned with the support of their parents, but according to recent data, the gender difference is not so acute as it once was.[13] Indeed, studies indicate that parents at midlife perform more services—babysitting, material and financial aid—than the younger generation gives in return. Most of our retirees spoke of their enjoyment of visiting back and forth with their children. Cliff Wellman is a case in point: "We offer a standing invitation; at least locally the kids are invited to every Sunday dinner. So we have at least two couples and every other week three couples." Likewise, the Hoffmans were eagerly looking forward to their daughter and son-in-law moving into the other half of their duplex.

In several instances the relationship with children is the central driving force. Lois Bennett, a retired nurse, reflects:

"My husband was forty-six when he died. He had multiple sclerosis after he came out of the service and was a vegetable for fifteen years. I took care of him for some four years. Then I had to go in for a hysterectomy, and he went into the VA hospital, but long before he died he came home. I had to feed him, wash him, and take him out of bed with a hydraulic lift. He had worked for several factories off and on—the lift was one of their gifts. . . . My son was four years old and my daughter nine when he took ill. . . . I had to practically fight to have my second child. My husband never wanted more than one. . . . As the years have gone on they have been my salvation. My daughter has two grandchildren, and my son is a pediatrician; indeed, he's professor of pediatrics at a major medical school. . . . I had no problems with my children. People say you have to have a father figure; I'm not sure that's true. Of course, they did have a father, then an invalid one; my son was in junior high and my daughter was nineteen when he died."

Other instances of a close identification with children include Will and Deborah Schulz. He had a career as a government administrator. She was a clerk with a large newspaper, but she considers her main career the raising of seven children, of which one is still at home. However, her main activity over the last fifteen years has been with Birthright, an organization helping pregnant juveniles to prepare for the career of motherhood. A number of situations can become problematic for a parent. For example, because of his heart condition Robard Young felt a deep frustration: "As I was especially close to my two sons it was a disappointment not to be able to play games with them."

If there are children still at home, the father's retirement can be to their advantage. Dottie Fitzgerald, whose husband was one of the youngest of our samples to retire, reflects: "The children have benefited. Their father has been there—especially for my daughter in school—to go to her concerts and the like during the day. Or during the winter, if there's a snow day, he's here to take them out sledding. There's now more communication between them."

A conspicuous aspect of American parent–child relationships is the finances. Harvey Longenbach observes: "One of the things that has struck me as I've seen my buddies at Steel is the way they help their children. One worked hours of overtime even to the risk of his health to put his kids through college. A year after he retired he dropped dead. In my own case I've been lucky and have loaned all my six children at least a few thousand each year to help them buy a house or whatever. Except for one that is out of work, they're all paying me back."

Most of our retirees feel that their main preoccupation in life now has to be something other than their children, as characterized by remarks such as: "When my last child left home, I realized that I had to stand on my own feet." Clearly, few would want to burden their offspring by living with them. This attitude is well entrenched in American society. Only 12 percent of elderly Americans live with an adult child.[14] Only three wives—and no husbands—spoke of ever moving in with their children (i.e., daughter's home, or as one quoted the remark—or cliché—of her father: "Your son is your son until he takes a wife, but your daughter is your daughter all your life"). Still, Adelaide Williams commented: "We've always been a very close family, and I know the boys will take care of us when the time comes that we can't take care of ourselves." On the other hand, Evelyn Cohen, who has an extremely active life, has no desire to live with her children: "When we first moved to Bethlehem, we lived with my son until we found a place. When I did that, the kids were relieved. Or let me put it this way, I can't keep my mouth shut long enough to live with them, plain and simple."

Inevitably, not all parents found their teenage or adult children to be faring satisfactorily. Several mentioned the trauma of marital problems. Walter Koch felt his daughter's divorce to be even more of a blow than his own forced departure from his employer: "It was hell to see her suffer in a misguided marriage, and its termination was for all of us a sense of failure." Norm Reinert, a successful insurance agent, reflects: "We've had general unhappiness with our children. Our youngest daughter just tried to take her life last week. Married to the biggest bum in the world, a con artist. . . . " Other hard-pressed parents, an engineer and his wife, wrestled with their adopted son's alcohol and drug problem:

"Knowing that made my retirement decision a bit harder to make. . . . I went to see the company counselor. I didn't think it was up to me to go see him because I was not the addict, but people told me to see him because he might be able to help. . . . I didn't know how to talk to him about the problems I was having, and I asked him what to do to get my son straightened out, when he should have been talking to me about how to get me straightened out. I was still at the point where I didn't realize that I was the one who was ill."

Several retirees mentioned a radically different approach to certain standards and goals they found in their children: "They don't know the value of money." "God, I could never take debts as casually as they do." "If only they could profit from our mistakes." "Religion doesn't have the same meaning for them as it does for us." "I don't like the way my son and daughter-in-law are bringing up our grandchildren." This theme could also border on envy: "How fast my son has advanced at his company, when I think of how slow it was for me."

In a few instances, a son—rarely, if ever, a daughter—was almost completely estranged. Matt Boyd sees his three daughters with fair regularity, but his one son never recovered from the divorce of his parents and appears only on the Christmas holidays. The Hemphills feel abashed that during four months in Florida every winter they can get together with their son only once or twice: "Maybe I rode him too hard, especially when he dropped out of New York University—I could never forgive him, as I'd almost have given my right arm if my parents could have sent me to college."

If there are anxieties or value clashes, there are also the triumphs. Many sons and daughters had reached professional status, which gave their parents a sense of status and security. As Grace Shoemaker says: "Our daughter has a Ph.D., and she and her husband are doing very well, telling us, 'There's no need for you to leave any money for us.' So we're now enjoying a cruise every winter." Al Johnson went further: "I have four grand coming in to me every month. Most people can live on that, and I do . . . since I got a daughter who lives in a $300,000 home, and my other daughter files taxes on $65,000 income. I told them whatever's left is going in the casket with me."

Variations of the Family Theme

Several couples were childless. Cliff and Bea Thomas made up for their lack of children by "adopting" children abroad, and they are "honorary grandparents" to the children next door. They also work one day at Cedarbrook (the county home for the aged), read on the radio twice a month to the blind, and play an active role in their church. He adds: "We just made up our mind that we would have to rise somehow above our frustration at not having children."

As implied earlier in the chapter, when the children leave home, there is a vacuum. Even though it was not entirely to the satisfaction of Walter, whose postretirement career was highly successful, Irene Koch resolved her frustration by continuing to be a crossing guard, and identified closely with many of the children, especially the latchkey ones: "You can't imagine how these children can grow on you."

In view of the ethnic culture in the Lehigh Valley, familial ties can be strong. We saw that Victor Karlovski, although single himself, belongs to an extended Polish family, returns to the family fold at holidays, and feels strong support from siblings and nephews.

Of course, extended families are not confined to ethnic groups. Norma Chamberlin spoke of her close relationship to her five children. Yet she could share this tie with in-laws. One daughter, widowed very young with four children, continued to live near her late husband's parents in Maine: "I have more satisfaction knowing that she's doing the right thing even though I miss her terribly. Of course, we go there in summer, and with Nick's retirement we're able to interact a good deal more with her and with other members of the family, too."

But other couples can find obstructions in the search for a broader family. Linda Eisenhard reflects on her attempts to be closer to her sister: "She and her husband seem to have no interests. It's her second marriage, and the third for him. I thought maybe this marriage might work out, because he seemed to like to go out to eat and also to bowl. But since they're both retired, he just sits and looks out the window all day long. She finally went and got a part-time job at night. But more and more she is getting to be like him. . . . Why are my sister and I so different?"

The shape of familial ties can be the function of a situation and individual preferences. Nellie Jones, retired director of an employment agency, like her brother and sister, never married. (One may ask whether a given family culture encourages—and another discourages—marriage of the offspring. The Joneses' case is not unique.) They find it most convenient to continue living in the family home together: "We each go our way. My brother enjoys fishing all summer long; my sister is still working. We each have our own set of friends and activities. I enjoy travel, flea markets, and am very active in the local AARP. Still, the three of us do occasionally all go out to dinner together."

That Glorious Detachment: Grandparenthood

Another dimension of the parent–child relationship is grandparenthood. For a variety of reasons grandparenthood has become more relaxed in the last few decades than before. Apparently grandparents tend to intervene less in the way their offspring treat parenthood. A more educated society has learned to permit more autonomy and to find a mix of affection and detachment. Moreover, the involvement of retirees in their own leisure pursuits permits less time for the grandparent role. In other words, a variety of grandparenting styles is available. In their survey, Andrew Cherlin and Frank Furstenberg found that grandparents could be detached, passive, or active.[15] On the whole, however, a number of the interviewees agreed that retirement permitted greater interaction with their grandchildren. In addition, gender differences can be found. In one study, grandmothers found more satisfaction than did grandfathers, but grandfathers tended to be more indulgent.[16] Also, in our interviews the women spoke more of their grandchildren than did the men.

Most of our sample had their children in the "baby boom" period and, in contrast to their own offspring, had an average of three children. As these children were themselves moving into parenthood—often with a maximum of two offspring—several interviewees commented on the enjoyment of their grandchildren. Several spoke of the fun they had in taking their grandchildren on a variety of excursions, from the Jersey shore to Niagara Falls. Others felt frustrated that their grandchildren were at distant points in the country or that their child's divorce prevented them from sufficient contact. At the same time, they were concerned with the overextended lives of their children, as they saw the dual-earner households and the strain this puts on both parents and children.

The Care of Older Parents

For at least a dozen of the sample, the care of their own parents was a problem and was critical in how they viewed their approaching sense of becoming elderly. Decisions as to what to do with their parents were, of course, difficult ones. As one wife reflected: "I'm over at my mother's place three times or four times a week. She can hardly care for herself, but I can't get her to consider going into a retirement center. It all falls on me; my brother lives in New York and only comes around a few times a year. And I don't want to give up my work at the church and other organizations just to take care of her." A former nurse spoke of the pressure when "mother was with us for two winters—she is ninety-two—it especially got to my husband. I simply had to put mother in a home."

All this is different from the extended family of the last century, when three-generational homes were apparently more frequent than today. Yet the interrelationships within the extended family can become as psychologically intense as those our ancestors knew.[17] Possibly there is *more* intensity or bonding today. After all, in previous centuries one could hardly afford to invest one's emotional ties with the other person since death could so easily take the love object away. One observer suggests that the present generation of adults may be caring for their parents in various ways for as long a period as they gave their own children.[18] And as with our own children, we are giving our parents both instrumental and expressive support, as shown in a survey of a large sample of adults aged fifty and beyond.[19] The adult child without a sibling or a nearby sibling is more likely to be drawn into the caregiving role. With the extended longevity of the late twentieth century, a widow may well end up taking care of her widowed mother. Moreover, the quality of the relationship that adult children had with their parents sets the stage for providing care in the upper years.[20]

Thus, the retirees in our sample reflect all aspects of family life in upper age—strong marital bonds, generally close relationships with children and grandchildren, and an increasing realization of the need for care of the parents, coupled with a relatively strong desire for autonomy, both for the individual and the couple. The emotional bonds set in childhood, adolescence, and early adulthood tend to shape the extent of involvement and assistance in the twilight years.

The Drive for Social Links

As we recall, a major frustration of retirees is the loss of social contacts they had on the job; often they mostly miss the friends they once knew. How, then, do retirees make up for this gap? Do they try to hold on to these ties, make new ones, or simply look for distractions? Do they increase their participation in society in one way or another?

Studies point to an increase in informal social participation as retirees try to fill in the void of having lost their friends at work. A national survey revealed that friendship ties are related to feelings of well-being and are especially critical in upper age.[21] Nearly a fourth (24 percent) of our sample said they were more lonely after retirement (72 percent felt no change, and 4 percent were less lonely). Presumably, men are more frustrated at the lack of social links than are women. Research findings suggest that women retain friendships longer into the upper years than do men.[22]

Studies of friendship show our preference for people like ourselves. Obviously, we place our friends in categories; for instance, we think of the difference between "real" and "marginal" friends. Specifically, "older people do not conjure up their definitions of friendship and their ways of organizing sociability out of nothing, but instead build upon patterns established over their life courses."[23] In the words of one of our interviewees, "I kind of guessed which of my work friends I would still have after retirement, and my guesses have proved to be about right. Of course, maybe I had something to do with that." Put in another way, our bureaucratic–industrial society encourages us to move toward "a common lifestyle and extreme flexibility in initiating and terminating social ties."[24]

Moreover, the search for social contacts can also be a means of killing time! Comments revealed that trips to the mall were partly to fill in the day, and partly to have a chance to meet old friends or even make new ones: "We go every Wednesday to the Lehigh Valley Mall and 'people-watch,' and we often run into the same ones we saw a few weeks before."

The single person, of course, has more difficulty in his or her social life. Possibly women have less of a problem than do men. At least in the upper years they seem to maintain closer contact with their friends than do men.[25] Lowell Zettelmoyer, a widowed engineer who had worked in the Arab world for over twenty years, did not find social relationships easy to establish. When his church had split because of the arrival of an ultraliberal minister; he chose to go with the conservatives, but there were few social horizons there. As one might expect, his search was focused on the opposite gender: "I've been able to meet a few people. There was a retired banker I used to lunch with. Now, for a man to meet a male friend is not too easy. I think there are more women floating around. . . . I don't think much of this column in the paper where you search for people. It's gotten to be a sex thing. . . . By the way, I have a girlfriend on weekends, so I do have some friends. . . . "

Lowell had still other observations to make about his experiences with the human condition:

"When I was involved in the Threshold program in the prisons my first student was a prostitute (I guess you'd call her that). It was all very, very enlightening. She did more for me than I did for her. As I said, this was no moralistic program. Threshold simply helps people to make decisions. If you talk to a young lady with a good body and she tells you she can pick up a hundred or two hundred a night on tricks, it's pretty hard to convince her to go to McDonald's to work and break her feet for twenty bucks. . . . I always wondered what became of her, and only last month I happened to be in Allentown on Sixth Street—the twilight zone. Up she came on a bicycle and was about to proposition me. Once she saw me she took off. Now that was a new one, I didn't know they now work from a bicycle."

As a divorcee, Matt Boyd at age fifty-one was also seeking companionship: "I've been through all the groups—Parents without Partners, Singles, you name it. But, oh God, the women over fifty are so set in their ways. There are some nice ones in the late thirties and forties, but they all have one to three children. I just can't go through raising another family, much as I wish I could."

On the whole, the search for social life did not seem to be a major problem. For one thing, because of their European heritage and a tradition of self-reliance, people in the Northeast seem to be less drawn to social participation; that is, social relations are seemingly more impersonal than in other parts of the country. Consequently, the need for friends might be less than in some areas, such as the Midwest or South, where interpersonal relationships are reportedly more open and spontaneous.

The loss of friends from yesteryear has already been noted. Nearly a tenth of the interviewees spoke of the annual dinner or picnic as a means of getting together with their cronies from work. However, for some this would be unacceptable because of the spirit of their departure: "I simply couldn't go back. Then I'd have to see the men who were after my job." And memories of hostile takeovers or the dread of meeting the boss could be a factor.

Some of the sample checked the item "I feel more lonely" and urged any potential retiree to make a lot of friends or join organizations. It seems that society has failed to prepare retirees for this leap into the unknown. Counseling agencies, whether within or outside the employer's realm, might well include this sector of needs in their counseling programs for retirees.

The Role of Organizations

The entry into organizations and volunteer activities is one means of resolving the threat of loneliness, as reported here at some length. Few of the sample considered themselves sufficiently senior to attend the senior citizen centers. Hank Nelson was not only national president of a veterans' association that numbered over eleven thousand members, but a thirty-second-degree Mason, and an elder in his church. In addition, he held down a job as administrative officer, for which he could only receive $9,360, as a larger income would violate Social Security and tax rules. He comments: "I still have my same energy and I enjoy people."

A few wives find their way to LORA (the female contingent of MORA), but occasionally follow their husbands into their organizations—to the point that women are accepted. Men may also follow their wives into their organizations. One wife of a retiree suggests: "Women have less need of a formal organization. They often have a kind of built-in social network." However, most wives are involved in various activities sponsored by organizations, probably because of their desire to be of service as well as to avoid loneliness.

The Marginals

The search for social ties did not always go smoothly. Steve Kovacs found that ethnic lines could prove to be a hurdle. Predominantly Slovak, he encountered some kidding, with an occasional undercurrent of antagonism, on the part of the Pennsylvania Dutch, both on the job and in bars after retirement. Tom Lorenzo, whose family had come to the Lehigh Valley in the 1920s to escape the "godfather" syndrome in an Italian section of Chicago, had thirty-eight years at Steel, ending as a foreman in the alloy department:

"Yeah, I belong to clubs, organizations like the VFW, but they have nothing for a member to go to and enjoy himself. I belong to the Fleas Club—it's a social club for men. They have pool tables and you can play cards. I go there in the evening and have a beer or two. . . . I also belong to the AARP. They meet the first Monday of each month. This is something I should tell you because I attended a meeting, and finding women there I then took my wife a couple of times. . . . But for some reason or other, I don't know what it is, they don't want to socialize with you. You figure you can go there and enjoy it. But it seemed that every time we went there nobody wanted to converse with us."

There are also the relatively self-sufficient. In certain cases, the individual has to find his or her own ways of establishing social relations. Homer Evans retired for health reasons after nearly thirty years as a director of a national service organization. Moving out of New York, he was cut off from his colleagues and now has a universe of friends on several continents through his ham radio. His dialogues became ever more exciting as the breakup of communism established a deeper understanding with ham operators in Eastern Europe. In a somewhat different vein, Mario Moro says: "I used to belong to the Knights of Columbus. I like my freedom. It isn't that I have anything against it. I worked with the Knights for eight years, but I just feel that I have a few years left in my life, and I want to enjoy my life, my way, . . . I listen to my tapes and records. I tape every jazz concert I go to."

Then there are those who seem to be the real loners. Richard Newman had worked over twenty years as a chemist. Heart problems in addition to a takeover of the industrial concern drove him into retirement at age fifty-seven. His mother died shortly thereafter, but he continued to live in their 120-year-old house alone. He finds the reading of scientific and historical books, in addition to the *National Geographic, Scientific American,* and the Smithsonian *Bulletin,* enough to keep him going. He would like to have more physical activity and travel, but health problems won't permit it. He enjoys getting together with his former colleagues every few months, but he has rationalized a life of comparative solitude. It raises the question of how much conditions like health shape our motives as opposed to what comes from within the structure of our personality. There is no firm evidence that being an isolate in the upper years is indicative of poor psychological adjustment.[26]

In these last two chapters we have seen how retirees make their way from a highly structured life into a more flexible life style. For some, the day of retirement is like an escape from prison; for most of our sample, a challenge; for several, a troubled future. Decisions have to be made as to what priorities they have for their leisure time, how to resolve financial uncertainties, or how to cope with health problems. The spouse, children, and an array of interpersonal networks come to the rescue.

In Chapter 8 we examine a number of questions: Can we detect certain personality traits in the response and life histories of our retirees? How do they look at the world? What are their feelings and attitudes toward a changing universe? How do they anticipate their future?

References

1. Barbara J. Logue, "Women at Risk: Predictors of Financial Loss for Retired Women Workers," *Gerontologist, 31,* 657–665, 1991.
2. Ruth A. Erdner and Rebecca F. Guy, "Career Identification and Women's Attitudes toward Retirement, *International Journal of Aging and Human Development, 30*(2), 120–139, 1990.
3. Lois B. Shaw, "Retirement Plans of Middle-Aged Married Women," *Gerontologist, 24,* 154–159, 1984.
4. Elina Haavio Mannila, "Cross-Gender Relationships at Work and Home over the Family-Life Cycle," in Suzanne K. Steinmetz (ed.), *Family Support Systems across the Life Span* (New York: Plenum Press, 1988), pp. 197–212.
5. David L. Guttmann, "The Post-Parental Years: Clinical Problems and

Developmental Possibilities," in W.H. Norton and T.J. Scaramella (eds.), *Mid-life: Developmental and Clinical Issues* (New York: Brüner-Mazel, 1980).

6. Thomas J. Lavin III, "Divergence and Convergence in the Causal Attributions of Married Couples," *Journal of Marriage and the Family, 49,* 71–80, 1987.

7. Charles L. Cole, "Marital Quality in Later Life," in W.H. Quinn and G.A. Hughston (eds.), *Independent Aging: Family and Social Systems Perspectives* (New York: Aspen Publications, 1984), pp. 72–90.

8. Gary R. Lee and Constance L. Shehan, "Retirement and Marital Satisfaction," *Journal of Gerontology, 44,* S226–230, 1989.

9. Michael P. Farrell and Stanley D. Rosenberg, *Men at Midlife* (Boston: Auburn House Publishing, 1981), p. 123.

10. Lee and Shehan, "Retirement and Marital Satisfaction."

11. Thomas T.H. Wan, *Well-Being for the Elderly* (Lexington, MA: Lexington Books, 1985), p. 85.

12. Julia Braun Kessler, *Getting Even with Getting Old* (Chicago: Nelson Hall, 1985), p. 54.

13. Glenna Spitze and John Logan, "Sons, Daughters, and Intergenerational Social Support," *Journal of Marriage and the Family, 52,* 420–430, 1990.

14. Philip Silverman, "The Family," in Philip Silverman (ed.), *The Elderly as Modern Pioneers* (Bloomington: Indiana University Press, 1987).

15. Andrew Cherlin and Frank F. Furstenberg, "Styles and Strategies of Grandparenting," in Vern L. Bengtson and Joan F. Robertson (eds.), *Grandparenthood* (Newbury Park, CA: Sage Publications, 1985), pp. 97–116.

16. Jeanne L. Thomas, "Gender and Perceptions of Grandparenthood," *International Journal of Aging and Human Development, 29*(4), 269–282, 1989.

17. Robert E. L. Roberts and Vern L. Bengtson, "Is Intergenerational Solidarity a Unidimensional Construct? A Second Test of a Formal Model," *Journal of Gerontology, 45,* S12–20, 1990.

18. Ken Dychtwald and Joe Flower, *Age Wave* (Los Angeles: Tarcher Publications, 1989).

19. Alfred Dean *et al.*, "Measuring the Communication of Social Support From Adult Children," *Journal of Gerontology, 44,* S71–79, 1989.

20. Lee B. Whitbeck, Ronald L. Simons, and Rand D. Conger, "The Effects of Early Family Relationships on Contemporary Relationships and Assistance Patterns between Adult Children and Their Parents," *Journal of Gerontology, 46,* S330–337, 1991.

21. Masako Ishii-Kuntz, "Social Interaction and Psychological Well-Being: Comparison across Stages of Adulthood," *International Journal of Aging and Human Development, 30*(1), 15–36, 1990.

22. Karen A. Roberto and Priscilla J. Kimboko, "Friendships in Later Life: Definitions and Maintenance Patterns," *International Journal of Aging and Human Development, 28*(1), 9–20, 1989.

23. Graham A. Allan and Rebecca G. Adams, "Aging and the Structure of Friendship," in Rebecca G. Adams and Rosemary Blieszner (eds.), *Older Adult Friendship: Structure and Process* (Newbury Park, CA: Sage, 1989), pp. 45–64.

24. Eugene Litwak, "Forms of Friendships among Older People in an Industrial Society," in Adams and Blieszner (eds.), *Older Adult Friendship,* pp. 65–87.

25. Pat M. Keith, *The Unmarried in Later Life* (New York: Praeger, 1989), p. 195.

26. Neena L. Chappell and Mark Badger, "Social Isolation and Well-Being," *Journal of Gerontology, 44,* S169–176, 1989.

Chapter 8

Personality, Moorings, and the Life Cycle

Harry Hemphill was in a managerial position with a major airline:

"I was seventeen years old when I went into the Marine Corps. There I learned discipline and authority. But I really wanted to make the U.S. Naval Academy. I couldn't do it because in those days it was a lot different. It was all political; my parents were Republican and the Democrats controlled Kentucky, so I didn't stand a snowball's chance in hell. I stayed in the Marine Corps until 1943 when I applied for flight training and ended up a naval aviation officer in the Navy rather than the Corps.

"After the war, I was in business and advertising, circulation—and very successful. I made a lot of money. But I was terribly unhappy—no airplanes. Airplanes are intoxicating; once you get aviation in your blood, you can't get it out. Because I was so unhappy, I left that job and was unemployed for two to three weeks, maybe a month. I think I almost had a nervous breakdown because I didn't have the security that I had come to know for some time. I couldn't cope at all.

"Finally, I got into the airline business, where every two years you get promoted and transferred. So you name it, I've lived there. And I could walk down to Ninth and Hamilton at PP&L (utility company) or Hess's (department store) and somebody would say, "Hi, Harry!" I liked that because I could be a big duck in a little pond. My name was in the papers. I could associate with the chairman of

Bethlehem Steel, with the president and chairman of the board for Mack Trucks. As the years went by, my ego needed this. That's why I wouldn't leave Allentown for the money.

"But the corporation didn't comprehend that I wanted to stay because I had been one of the team. I had been on the corporate merry-go-round until they offered me a promotion—just the job I wanted. I was going back to Cleveland as a manager. Can you imagine returning to a station as the boss where you were once an agent, with the same people there? It would be a tremendous inflation to one's ego.

"Through the years I was drinking a lot. Whenever we had sales meetings, alcohol occupied a very prominent part of every day. The cocktail party at five o'clock went on for hours and hours. I am not sufficiently wise to conceal my contempt for my bosses. We were in an adversarial position all the time. Again, the alcohol played a big part with this because when we drink a lot, we say things that we wouldn't necessarily say in a sober condition. In any event, there was a very touch-and-go period that lasted a number of years. During that time I soon became a functioning alcoholic. But I didn't know that. I drank more and more, nonetheless. I'd come home and Dora would comment about the amount of alcohol I was consuming.

"In any event, the last three years there were not as much fun as they were before. I kept saying, 'Make me an offer I can't refuse' to the people I thought would have some influence on my retirement. Normally, they gave you an offer to go out at sixty-two instead of sixty-five. It was mandatory at sixty-five then, but I guess they've even thrown that out. I have another opinion on that, because I think the longer people stay in jobs, the longer they are denying the opportunity for young people to rise through the ranks and get some job experience. Now, I understand; there's a time when we outlive our usefulness—we really do.

"So then I retired. I was an alcoholic who was sad, sorry for himself, lost, didn't know what to do, and depressed. From a person who always had a smile on his face, for whom life was always the greatest bowl of cherries, to a man with a severe, lonely depression. I wouldn't go out, I'd just sit there. Dora would say, 'Come on, let's leave.' But I would be afraid that something might happen, that I might miss something.

"After retirement there are no longer any controls—no job to go to, no front to put up, no facade, no nothing. There was just me and this room and that bottle or those bottles. And it went on and just got worse. Of course, the alcoholic himself doesn't realize it; he's the last one to recognize that perhaps something is wrong. But one day my wife said one thing that made the greatest impression on me; it possibly was the thing that began to trigger my thought that I needed help. She said, 'I will not live with a drunk.' Finally I found Alcoholics Anonymous, and like all religions, it doesn't work unless the patient wants to adopt it and is ready.

"My advice for people who are going to retire is to learn how to play. People really haven't learned how to play. I belong to the Lehigh Country Club, so out there we've got people with money, people who have the opportunity to play, and they really haven't learned how in their lives. And when I say play, I don't mean any particular thing. They hang on to their jobs because they don't know what in God's name they would do if they retired. . . .

"My hobby is golf; also, just being at peace with myself is my hobby. I stay occupied with so many things. I do read a lot; I've always been an avid reader, but I'm not handy with my hands and don't particularly care for it.

"I'm very serious when I say I know how much better I am, how much better the quality of life is, that even if I could . . . drink again, I don't believe I would do it. I'm just so much better off now."

* * *

In the last few chapters we have looked at the problems of adjustment, the variety of activities, and the interpersonal involvements of our sample. In the case of Harry Hemphill we find set attitudes and a strong personality—but perhaps more outwardly than inwardly strong. For him, retirement became a means of resolving his problem of alcoholism—four years later in a more recent interview he was still committed to AA. His work history is one more index of work stress and of how the individual may cope—or fail to cope—with it.

In this chapter we turn to the more intricate and perhaps "totalistic" question of how people guide themselves through the life cycle into retirement. We also make some tentative judgments about the dimensions of the self and personality. Of course, any statement about personality has to be considered as hypothetical, especially as no personality inventories were administered to our respondents. Yet the interviews did reveal fairly specific orientations in the way these retirees related to their world and their lives.

In this discussion we ask a number of questions: What are or were the formative influences in their moving through the stages in the life cycle? How do they react to change? Are there certain types or models in the basic responses to life's events? What do these orientations reveal about personality? What are their moorings or belief systems? How do these attitudes relate to their backgrounds? What are the individual's principal concerns? How do they perceive their future?

Aging, the Life Cycle, and the Self

Most of the critical periods of our life are marked by a rite of passage, or a set of socially defined steps by which we move from one phase to another. For instance, we undergo a lengthy period of education, picking up a diploma or two along the way. We are also formally introduced into a particular status in the life cycle such as marriage. While marriage and graduation have clear-cut ceremonies attached to them, many events do not have such rituals. Both the beginning and the end of work fit into the latter case for most of us. There may be a party for the first day on the job, but often we just show up for work; the "ceremony" is filling out paperwork for personnel matters. The last day of work, even when it is as personally momentous as retirement, often receives similar treatment. The retiree cleans out his or her desk and goes to personnel to fill out papers, stopping for informal good-byes and "best wishes" along the way. If he or she is lucky and the retirement is clearly planned, there may be a brief party, maybe even receipt of the proverbial gold watch or its equivalent, and then everyone (else) gets back to work.

So for many shifts in status as we move through life, there is no rigid or stereotyped pattern of change. That leaves it up to us as individuals to "make our own way." We have at our disposal a number of cues to help us make these transitions. As we approach retirement, for example, we have the experiences of others to offer guidance on how we are to adjust to this new phase of life. At whatever juncture of the life cycle, we fundamentally attempt to maintain a degree of ego integrity.[1] This battle to preserve our self-esteem or integrity assumes many forms. Generally, at age sixty—or it may be at forty or fifty—we, as with the young, are conscious of both positive and negative overtones. On one side, we may be aware of less vigor or the onset of health problems and recognize that society confers less status to the old, at least in our contemporary American culture. Indeed, several of our interviewees pointed out that they feel useless or unwanted. This situation stands in contrast to traditional Chinese civilization, which for well over two thousand years conferred prestige and power on the aged—especially the male—and a subordinate position for the young. Regretfully, perhaps, one can't live the first half of one's life in Western society and the second half in pre-1900 China!

On the other hand, entry into the upper years may usher in a sense of relief, a feeling that the pressures are off, that one has succeeded in what one had set out to do, or that the reward of leisure and freedom is now at hand. One interviewee commented: "I don't need to put on any pretenses anymore, I can now be just what I am." In a few instances, the anxiety about retirement gave way to a new sense of accomplishment. As Walter Koch said: "I was so frightened of leaving my job, but now I am accomplishing more in my new career than I ever thought possible."

Erik Erikson and his colleagues pose the question: How does one upper-age person manage "to integrate painful conditions . . . into a new form of psychosocial strength, while another may respond to similar conditions in a fashion that seems to inhibit effective integration and healthy ongoing development?"[2] For one thing, each of us develops throughout life a certain style of adaptation.

At retirement we have several options. Disengagement or activity are two quite different modes of response. In examining various theories of personality and the life cycle, Kenneth Gergen suggests three models: (1) stability—early patterns of responding are more or less fixated for life, (2) orderly change—the individual's adaptation progresses according to stages, and (3) random change—our genetic programming comes to an end by late adolescence, and our life revolves about the situations and often chance factors we encounter.[3] In this connection, most explanations of the life course have centered on the idea of stability and orderly change.[4] Yet, much of how people "feel" their lives to be has to do with particular situations and events.

Throughout life we rely on a number of internal and external controls in order to maintain an equilibrium. That is, we respond both to our inner needs and values and to outside situations and influences. We establish a certain set of roles and personality traits, which have for most of us a fair degree of consistency. Again, rather than disengaging at the moment of retirement, we search for continuity in linking our past with the present and future.[5]

Fundamentally, we are searching for behaviors that are appropriate to our roles. These are to conform to an orderly sequence from childhood to old age. Through the more active or career phase of the life span we are involved in no end of demanding roles, meeting the needs of the job, marriage, rearing children, and community service. These institutionalized roles give way to less clearly defined roles at the twilight of our lives. In other words, we experience the informal, tenuous roles in the early and the late part of our lives, whereas the more rigid institutional roles characterize early and middle adulthood.[6] This lack of structure is a major problem for several of our retirees, as Aldo Carlucci noted: "Those first months were awful and I still find myself at a loss because no one is pushing me."

Coping Mechanisms

We undergo *anticipatory socialization*—we learn in advance how to cope with new situations as they emerge. As George Vaillant asserts, we develop a number of defense mechanisms that facilitate our adaptation to stressful events.[7] As we recall, it was stress of one kind or another that drove over a fourth of our sample into retirement. Moreover, older people tend more than the young to attribute failure to themselves, all of which has the effect of lowering self-esteem and the anticipation of future success.[8]

At the same time, many individuals carry frustrations or maladjustment they felt in the work years on into the retirement period. This particular personality orientation—or one might label it as one more form of consistency or continuity—was found in many of our retirees. We recall that Grace Shoemaker, a former school teacher, who was having her own problems of adjustment (for one, a phobia about driving in her upper years), reflected: "I guess that people who have problems when they retire had problems before they retired."

Most of the sample reported organizing their resources to ward off distress at this new phase of the life cycle. As we have seen, coping mechanisms vary widely across such diverse outlets as alcohol, travel, volunteering, or religious involvement. For most it is a question not so much of killing time but of maintaining self-esteem and a feeling of usefulness. According to a review of research studies, the elderly rely on a number of defense mechanisms in order to sustain an equilibrium. When comparing themselves with younger people, they see themselves as (1) less concerned about their weight, (2) having performed adequately at work, (3) having positive moral values, (4) more inclined to feel adequate in their marital and parental roles, and (5) less likely to admit shortcomings. On the negative side, they see themselves as having poorer health than younger persons.[9] Each of us has a particular style in attempting to hold onto a kind of ego strength in battling the less than flattering images surrounding the upper years. As one retired accountant put it: "I know that I can't hold my own in all the new processes as compared to some of the new kids out of college, but I certainly have more commitment than they do. I'm sure that I can work as many or more hours in a day or week than they can."

According to Daniel Levinson, the life span evolves through a sequence of alternating periods, sometimes resulting in periods of stability that can leave us feeling in a "rut." Consequently, we often have to find a means of breaking out of feelings of stagnation into a phase of renewal.[10] Most important, we have to find a degree of detachment and take inventory: "I sat down one afternoon and made a list of my assets and liabilities and was determined to find some means of making my life worthwhile." Although this technician did not manage to build a new career, as he hoped, he did find a repertory of volunteer activities that brought meaning to his life. Along with the ability to detach oneself, one has to cultivate a sense of humor.[11] Several of our retirees spoke of their search for humor in a variety of ways: comparing their foibles with others, even placing themselves in sitcoms, or at least escaping into them.

The Struggle against Depression

Not all of our sample could maintain their ego integrity. It is difficult enough for the young to avoid despair; the older in our society can hardly do better. Erik Erikson sees mid-adulthood as characterized by Generativity versus Stagnation, and upper age as Integrity versus Despair.[12] These general tendencies can then be coupled with specific stressful events. For instance, death of a spouse can be temporarily very disorganizing, as it was for several of our sample. We must remember that even positive, sought-after events, as retirement often is, are stressful. For Tom Schmidt, retirement itself meant acute depression and suicidal thoughts. As we noted at the beginning of the chapter, Harry Hemphill found that with retirement "the controls were off and my drinking increased until I found AA."

Contrast these reactions to those of Steve Kovacs, for whom retirement was an escape: "I'm feeling better about myself. I think the family is feeling better about me. . . . I used to come home from work and I was emotionally and mentally drained. I know I used to sit there and eat and eat and eat. I think I'm better off now, I don't have that nervous energy. I don't eat as much. I don't feel that compulsion."

It is, of course, difficult to determine the ingredients in each individual that spell the difference between adequate and inadequate mental health, specifically, why some have the capacity to ward off a negative self-image or avoid a sense of gloom. A recent study found little relationship between physical and mental health, although extroversion may play some positive influence in both areas of health.[13] Unquestionably, we found instances of a very positive attitude despite health setbacks. Robard Young, who retired early because of a heart problem, is an example:

"Now my mental attitude about my health is not bad. I have a better quality of life because I feel better physically. Yet it makes my mental problem worse because I could be working and contributing something to society. But when I try to do something on a charitable or volunteer basis, as when I was visiting open-heart surgery patients, it's okay. But then they say to come in at four o'clock the next day. But I never know how I'm going to feel at that time. I remember when we had planned a New Year's party several years ago and I got sick and we lost all our money. We couldn't do it. I talked to my minister about Meals on Wheels or reading books into a tape recorder for blind people. That would be great. I always like to read a book, and I would be helping other people."

The Dimensions of Personality

We have outlined a number of observations about how the person responds to periods of the life cycle, notably the adjustment following retirement. It is in order now to look more closely at the dimensions of personality. We are accustomed to hearing about introversion–extroversion, dominance–submission, and other so-called trait dimensions, but these are based largely on tests. In the present context several dimensions emerged in the interview profiles; these are meant to be suggestive rather than definitive, especially as these characterizations are based on the interviews rather than personality inventories.

Self-Orientation versus Social-Orientation. As the interviews unfolded, it was apparent that the retirees differed in the degree to which they could remove their motivation and feelings from their subjective needs and goals. That is, probably all of us are strongly involved in ourselves ("I am Number One"), but nearly all of us have the capacity to identify with others—at least part of the time.

The distinction between the self-oriented and other-oriented is in part related to the type of career, although individual differences transcend career alignment. Those in business reflect more ego needs, whereas those in service professions—nursing, teaching, and social work—are more focused on their fellow human beings. Engineers, technicians, and blue-collar workers stand somewhere between these two extremes. This fits in with the research findings about the meaning of work for different occupations.

These different values are reflected in comments from several of our retirees. For example, we recall the case of the banker Al Johnson, who bragged of his income but apparently felt little urge to give to charity or his children. Contrast this to the retired teacher Arthur Zavecz, who wanted to enter the Peace Corps. In this same vein, Rev. Donald Siegfried says: "The best part of my ministry has always consisted of helping people adjust to their changing age, and this is true in every decade of life."

Again, it should not be thought that there is any predictable dichotomy. For instance, Lowell Zettelmoyer expressed fairly materialistic values but still found time to work in the Threshold project in the local prison. The same person may move from egocentric to altruistic goals. Most people represent something of both the "I," the self as doer, and the "me," the self as acted upon.[14] That is, from the first year of our life, we act in several ways on society and society acts on us, and this distinction may extend to self-seeking as well as relatively selfless goals. Again, it is a question of detaching ourselves from the situation.

Stability Orientation versus Change Orientation. Another dimension that appeared in the interviews was the range of freedom in self-expression and freedom of action. In a few instances it would seem that the dimension was between constricted and open expression. As with other personality traits, there is a mixture of genetics, socialization, the degree of ego-strength, success or failure in responding to situations, or even chance events occurring over several decades that makes each of us act and react as we do. That is, we have certain inborn tendencies; we also react to events according to what we have observed in our family members and our peers, and we have to make decisions as we confront a problem. No doubt these variables and processes are intertwined.

We have the case of Harry Landon, who had risen from teller to supervisor in a local bank, and who married at forty-four after his mother had died: "I always wanted to get out of the bank but I never felt I could let my boss down, or maybe it was just a habit system at which I felt comfortable. In fact, I wouldn't have left the bank when

I did except for health problems." For someone moving into the Lehigh Valley after living at the more rapid pace of such places as Long Island, New Jersey, or California, the tempo of life styles in this part of Pennsylvania seems overly stable and conservative. The case of Kenneth Kline is another example of stability. He had been at Sears for twenty-four years before moving to the bank from which he was asked to retire, had lived in the same dwelling for thirty-five years, and had made a home for his wife's mother.

In contrast is the profile of Jim Zimmerman, who left AT&T when they placed him on the third shift after contraction of personnel was forced by a business slowdown: "I told my boss and his boss that the deal wouldn't work. I'm Pennsylvania Dutch, German, whatever, and I may procrastinate but once I make a decision, the decision is made. I'm not going to be swayed by someone offering me a little piece of candy. . . . I soon brought myself to go out and look for a job. And as it turns out, tomorrow I have a job as investor counselor." His assertiveness is also shown by a round of construction projects, travel in an RV, and indulgence in a variety of sports and hobbies.

Internal versus External. This dimension overlaps with what is often defined as the constricted and open; however, it refers more to the source of the individual's motivation and explanation of events: Do we act because of our own decision making or because of the influence of others? Do we find life episodes occurring because of what we do about the situations around us? Or do situations simply impinge on us? Naturally a person may show both types of motivation, just as a given person is at one point of time open and at another constricted, or as another person moves daily between ego and other orientations.

Arthur Ferraro well expresses the problem of the individual reacting to the situation:

"They say the loss of income after retirement is the worst thing. I don't think there's any worst part, or maybe it's the moment of retirement or the transition period, and it depends on the type of person you are. If you're the kind of person that can't sit still or enjoy reading a book, then you're going to feel you have to be on the go all the time. I know people who retired and rebuilt their whole home.

They had to be into something. I'm not the kind to sit idle. The best part of retirement is that it forced me to start something. . . . I know one who retired and sits half the time in front of the TV, and the other time he's on the front porch. Another I know hits the bars by mid-afternoon."

The question of ascribing cause and effect to the self or to others is well illustrated among our sample. In reality, most find themselves responding to a situation with no intent of blame, but others could not detach themselves or others from the chain of cause and effect. Robard Young knew that he was not responsible for his heart attacks but still felt guilty that he could not work or do for others what he wished. On the other hand, John Mueller blamed his college for his retirement and was jealous that his colleagues could find consulting and he could not. Because of these resentments he refused to attend campus events, whereas most local emeriti do, at least occasionally. Bitterness is a natural reaction to *forced* retirement, but individual reactions vary markedly.

Many psychologists have found that a specific form of this general internal–external orientation, called locus of control, is a powerful factor in affecting how people think about themselves and also what activities they engage in to deal with changes in their lives. For example, an internal locus of control about health is related to more adaptive strategies of coping with either health problems when they arise or health promotion activities to forestall problems. External locus of control, especially a feeling that powerful others control what happens, is related to low self-esteem and low likelihood of trying to do one's best on intelligence-related tasks. We could go on and on given all the research, but the general point is that internality of feelings about control, at least much of the time, is likely to be related to both adaptive behavior and positive feelings about oneself and the events that happen as one goes through life.

You may remember that we asked in the questionnaire whether or not a person felt he or she had initiated the retirement decision. We found that those who did not feel they had initiated (about one-third of the sample) were less positive in their evaluations of the retirement event and its outcome (that is, the way the retirement occurred and the fact of being retired). This was a very crude measure of control, but it seemed to indicate the importance of feelings of control or choice in adaptation to retirement.

The study of state of Connecticut early retirees verified and extended these findings by including measures that followed this issue more closely. As well as answering the question about initiating the retirement, people were asked to fill out a general locus of control scale and to answer six questions about how much choice they had about various aspects of the retirement: (1) the timing of retirement, (2) the period of time between decision and last day of work, (3) planning and transition, (4) exact date of retirement, (5) choice of successor, and (6) day-to-day activities since retirement. About half of the retirees felt a high degree of choice in all areas except choice of successor.

The results from Connecticut were striking. The question of initiation again was highly related to satisfaction with the process and result of retirement. Although a very general measure did not have large effects, specific questions within it did (this is similar to many findings that so-called global locus of control measures are not as good at predicting activity or satisfaction as are measures that specifically ask about that kind of event). All of the other choice measures, however, except choice of successor, which we would not expect to be related, were very highly related to satisfaction with various specific aspects of retirement. By the way, the evaluation of aspects of choice were also highly related to each other.

This set of results, in combination with those of our main study, indicate several important things about choice or feelings of control. First of all, individuals seem to have a relatively general feeling about being a "chooser" or "initiator" or not. Second, which sort of person one is has important implications for how one reacts to major life events like retirement. High levels of feelings of choice indicate high levels of satisfaction. We should always remember, though, that we cannot directly measure how much choice a person "actually" had, so the relationship between choice and satisfaction may not be so much in the person's head—"I have control over my life"—but may be because some people actually had choice and thus were satisfied and others didn't have choice and so were unsatisfied. Especially in the state of Connecticut study the latter interpretation is unlikely, since everyone was offered basically the same plan with the same

amount of time to choose, but we have to be careful of overinterpreta-
tion. Whatever the interpretation, though, it is crystal clear that any
effort to maximize a person's feelings of control and choice will
enhance the person's reaction to a life event like retirement.

Other Dimensions. There are still other ways by which individuals might be categorized. Gender has already been noted as a relevant variable in determining our response tendencies. Individuals
also differ as to whether they look to the past, the present, or the
future. With a sample of above-average educational level we found
somewhat more future orientation than one might find in a more
blue-collar sample. However, John Mueller, with a Ph.D. degree,
seemed to be more past oriented than present or future oriented until
he discovered new activities. Consequently, in this dimension, as in
others, few generalizations can be made as to social backgrounds and
their reaction tendency.

We must be cautious about categorizing individuals in given
personality modes. Most of us represent too many contradictions.
Remember the case of Al Johnson, a financial consultant for over
thirty years but one who was intrigued with parachuting and hang
gliding and toyed with the idea of leaving his career in financial
management at age fifty-five in order to teach these activities. Yet he
described himself as compulsively meticulous in finances. Although
a devout Catholic with five children, his interviews revealed a person
who felt that the world centered on himself. He saw no reason to
leave his children a cent of his fortune. What seem to us as gross
inconsistencies in the self-image of others can likely be duplicated in
ourselves.

Values and Attitudes

Related to our personality structure is a complex cluster of values, beliefs, and attitudes. We view the universe through a maze of
emotional and cognitive moorings. Partly rational and partly driven
by deep-seated needs, this composite of feelings and beliefs both
propels us and enables us to sort out the unending stimuli and
experiences we encounter. In other words, we have pigeon holes in

which to classify the varied sights, sounds, and images that almost continuously batter our nervous system: "He's Mexican, so he can't be very trustworthy." "He's German, so he'll do an efficient job." "She's young, so she's probably going to make a hasty decision rather than really thinking it over." Generally, attitudes operate in a fairly complicated fashion, as they have evolved over our entire socialization process. In any event, most of us carry a load of stereotypes and impressions.

Attitudes can be latent or overt; that is, they may be fairly unconscious and vague, or they may be very articulate. They are generally pervasive and become the basis of our decisions and actions. In other words, they encourage—or discourage—action in a given direction. They may determine with whom we associate, where we live, or how we vote or spend our time. Some of us can be more flexible in our attitudes—that is, they are subject to change—but more often attitudes tend to be rigid. Presumably, they become more enduring as we grow older, but more important than the age factor is the inner nature of the personality. Most attitudes are rather broad or general; others can be very specific. On the whole, they are more enduring than opinions, which are more subject to change.

Again, let us remind ourselves that there are limits to which attitudes can predict behavior.[15] As implied above, our responses really depend on (1) the totality of our experience over our lifetime—which includes, among other things, our attitudes; (2) our physiological and psychological state at that moment; and (3) our definition of the present situation. For example, our decision about whether to retire or not is a product of these complex events.

We may ask how the attitudinal structure is formed. On the surface, we have already alluded to the conservative life style of the Lehigh Valley—an area that prides itself on its stability and relative security as compared to the frenetic pace of the metropolis—New York, that Sodom and Gomorrah, being the favorite basis of comparison. Moreover, a strong traditionalism operated in the sample. Even the dominance of Bethlehem Steel is almost mystical: "My father and my uncle both worked for Steel. Somehow when I got my accountancy degree I knew that I was expected to apply there for a job. And so I did, and never left."

Not least important in giving our subjects a sense of values are the acute memories of the Depression. These somber images give them a rather critical viewpoint toward finances. Bill Williams recalls how his father lost their farm in the Depression and he and his six siblings lived for several years on a very limited diet. "I dreamt of getting a baseball for Christmas, but more often it was an apple or maybe an orange." Another remarks that the mainstay of their food supply one winter in the 1930s was turnips. There were also sordid histories of unemployment. Cliff Wellman could hardly forget how his father lost his job when the silk mills moved out of Allentown but was lucky enough to get a job as school custodian: "Things were pretty tight as I had two older brothers and a sister. So we four peddled Mom's homemade doughnuts every Wednesday through the neighborhood." Consequently, several interviewees were at a loss to understand the spending habits of their children.

These findings of our study mirror a set of findings in the oft-cited research of Glen Elder in *Children of the Great Depression.* Elder makes a persuasive case that the birth cohorts of people who grew up during the Great Depression, that is, those who were born in the 1910s and 1920s (which is all that *birth cohort* means—a group of people born about the same time), have a unique view of "virtue" that places even greater emphasis on financial conservativeness than does the general American population. Borne from that experience is a serious lack of comprehension of how the "younger generations" can spend without concern for the future. What is lost on these older persons is that only by experiencing the severe deprivation (many of them did and *all* of them were aware of it) can one learn to define morality and virtue in such terms, and, as a matter of fact, they worked very hard to ensure that their children did not have such an "opportunity!" They sowed the seeds of profligacy in their children.[16]

Attitudes are part of the personality of the individual. Some individuals approach the universe in a more critical way than do others. One survey suggests that women tend to be more sensitive to social injustices than men.[17] This capacity is related to intelligence and education, but hinges more on independence, curiosity, and the ability to detach oneself from conventionality or traditions. For instance, the astute Evelyn Cohen found a great deal that was both positive and negative, and left no doubt as to what she disliked. Among other things, she spoke of the inability or unwillingness of the Red Cross to meet an emergency situation in World War II in which she served as a nurse. She decried the public's adoration of the boob tube and specific inadequacies in the Lehigh Valley, such as no mobile library service, which she had seen in New York area communities where she once lived.

The Content of Attitudes

Attitudes are both shaped by and directed toward various factors such as ethnicity, politics, and religion, among others. Yet there are diffuse or general attitudes. For example, we may be either positive or negative toward new ideas or new people. Or perhaps we are simply indifferent about what is new. In any event, attitudes relate to specific classes of experiences.

The Times We Live in

At least a fifth of the sample mentioned the difficulty they had in adjusting to the world of the 1980s or the changes they perceived in society in recent years. Indeed, it was the rate of social change that in part made the "Reagan revolution" possible. From the 1930s to the 1960s an unprecedented degree of social change took place, becoming especially evident during the tumultuous 1960s. Several retirees alluded to the many changes they had seen. Not least was the problem of marital instability. "They go to the altar with the idea that if this one doesn't work out, there's another down the line" was the remark of one former nurse. They also experienced the instability of industry in a community that had been very stable for over a half century: "Many people are trying to get into business for themselves because there is no guarantee. For instance, Mack Trucks has practically left the valley. Who knows where Bethlehem Steel will be in five years. Yet I have faith in AT&T—that they will come back, even though the stocks aren't what they should be." Sally Brown went on to express the anxiety about foreign takeovers, notably by the Japanese.

A number spoke of the lack of commitment they found in the present generation. This often centered on the work habits they saw in younger colleagues as they left their employment. Linda Eisenhard reflects on her last days at the bindery: "One young woman started working in my department and before I knew it she was a supervisor. She soon was trying to run the place. I had been the first one there, but she came in and started to boss everybody. . . . She got away with things we would never think of, like sleeping on the job. I even saw her doing her nails when I came in in the morning—things any of us would have been fired for. . . . and she is still there."

Walter Koch suggested to his minister that he might try to rouse his congregation into more dedication. His minister responded: "I'd be way out of line if I were to preach a sermon on commitment. It's just not in our vocabulary any more." Arthur Ferraro is not alone among the teachers in seeing his students as less able and motivated than what he remembered from his college days, even though he noted that the evening students were more eager than those in day classes: "They're driven to go beyond the expected. Otherwise they wouldn't be there." Other retirees raise similar questions. As college librarian, Kathy Lowell remarked, "They don't know how to study anymore."

Still others point to the indifference and callousness of our society: "When I was young, people seemed to care about others. We walked down the street and we knew almost everyone. Now you scarcely know your next-door neighbor." A chemical engineer said: "When I first went to Roman Hye in Bristol it was a great place to work. Everyone was on a first name basis, but it's a different world today." A few interviewees spoke of the "phoniness" of the present world. "Everything is PR, the image is all that counts. Elections are bought, PAC money and all that. But it shows up in other ways. My alma mater now sends me no end of mail on how great they are. Is it substance or a facade?" Al Johnson couches it in a different way by emphasizing that people shouldn't build up loyalty to an employer, because "the top-level management changes from time to time, so whatever relationships you think you have in the company are all changed."

Specifically, attitudes ranged from complaints about the legal system and the "sue-happy" tone of our society to the high cost of medicine, which more than one retiree saw as related to litigation. Alice Wilson observes: "As a nurse, and I've said it to my neighbor many times, I would never stop at an accident, because people are so darned sue-conscious today. I mean they do have the Good Samaritan law but they'll turn around and sue you to the teeth." In a similar vein, one put it: "Greed is the emblem of the American people today. If you aren't making a salary in six figures, you're regarded as a failure."

In this same context, a retired internist explained:

"Yes, the 1980s and 1990s are an age of greed and corruption, and we M.D.s are often seen as leading the pack, but it's in all occupations. The lawyers, for example, are part of the problem. But don't stop there, just look around. The worker on the assembly line wants twenty bucks an hour, and Iacocca has to have four million a year, and pays at most 31 percent tax; not to mention Stallone who makes twenty million a picture and spreads a cult of violence besides. And the nation is three trillion in debt. Beyond that you think of all the problems of this country that need to be funded."

Others continued with variations of the same theme; for example, a retired professor comments: "In my day we taught four classes and still did research. My younger colleagues feel overworked with two courses." Norm Reinert found it a relevation when he was involved in fundraising for the Cancer Society and his alma mater: "I always thought educated people would have some streak of generosity. The business people are not too bad—they give, if only for public relations. The worst are the doctors and lawyers with few exceptions. Teachers and the clergy are much better but are kind of strapped."

But if our retirees had questions about the present—and only a minority voiced strong complaints—the world of their childhood and youth was hardly the ideal. Adelaide Williams recalls her one-room schoolhouse and considers how lucky the children are today. Charles McLean reminisced about his father, who was not allowed to attend high school because he was underage (he then worked for fifty years at the New Jersey Zinc Company, followed by an early death, which prompted his son to early retirement). A few recalled their early years in the coal country. For example, Sara Timko speaks of her coal town "where you got three dollars for voting Democratic, four for voting Republican, and a teacher could only get a job if the palms of the right board member were greased. It was, after all, the only world we knew, but the Depression drove most of us out to bigger places."

In the world of work, few could overlook the achievements of the postwar period, notably fringe benefits. Roland Eisenhard spoke of his years before joining the staff of the Motor Club: "I earned very little, and the fellow I worked for used to say 'stick with me, let's grow old together and let's prosper.' Well, he prospered and the employees did not, and after fifteen years—this was back in the sixties—with him I had no benefits." Another said, "I remember when I worked over forty-five hours a week and I got no overtime." Adelaide Williams could not get over what she considered the generous maternity leaves after childbirth: "In my time we had to resign and then be rehired."

In other words, despite the inadequacies of the present, no one wanted to return to the past. However, these retirees had, on the whole, found a relatively benign world as compared with some of their ancestors or their cohorts in Appalachia or the urban slum. Also, they were aware that with the coming of age of the "grey lobby," the upper years were blessed with a number of privileges: "With my AARP card I get all sorts of discounts, and here I am with more money in the bank than I ever had before. I should feel guilty, but I know it'll all end someday, especially in the next century when the baby boomers hit their sixties."

Social, Political, and Economic Problems

Notwithstanding a degree of optimism, perhaps even smugness, the interviewees had a range of feelings about what they saw as society's needs and injustices. Although the vast majority were concerned with their immediate problems, several expressed doubts about their country's dislocations. To what degree were these doubts long term or recent ones? The tone of the discussions was that they were long-standing beliefs. Actually, there is no firm evidence as to whether we become more or less conservative in our social attitudes as we grow older.[18]

The fear of inflation was the most common complaint. Steve Kovacs expressed this concern: "The biggest thing I'm worried about is inflation. Since Reagan was in office I kept seeing numbers saying inflation is under control, and all that. I thought as long as that is so now's as good as anytime to retire. In the last three to six months, the way things have gone up, I just can't believe the inflation rate." But when the interviews were done in 1991, property taxes replaced inflation as a major anxiety. The increase in the school tax haunted those on relatively fixed incomes. Stewart Beers was proud that during his tenure on the local school board he questioned what he considered waste—for one, the ordering of the latest textbooks and visual aids "when the ones of a year or two earlier might still be useful." He regretted he could not do anything about the "spiraling of salaries."

On the conservative side was a variety of anxieties: the enormous debt—both national and Third World—the growing number of minorities in the cities, the power of labor unions, among others. Conservatism could take different tones—for one, the awareness that the physical world was changing. Protection of the environment was a strong concern for John Mueller: "I'm watching this I-78 go by me. It's terrible to watch. It's startling the mess they left in cutting through this unspoiled valley of Wilson Township, and I'm thinking of what yet has to be done—not to mention the noise now and what's to come." Several others felt a nostalgia about the Lehigh Valley that used to be. Not least was regret over the decline of the three center cities (especially Bethlehem and Easton), even though many seemed content with the all-year possibility of walking the malls.

On the compassionate or "liberal" side was distress over hunger in the Third World, the homeless, and family disorganization. A recent traveler to Mexico made the point: "I recall my first trips there forty years ago and found beggars in front of every church. Now I see more beggars when I go to New York or Philadelphia than I see in Mexico City." More than anything else, the scope of volunteering points to the strong sympathy that many feel for the disadvantaged as shown by their interest in shelters, the institutionalized, reading to the blind, among other activities. Saul Goldman phrased it this way: "Just look around and see what's wrong in the world. . . . That's why I get on the soapbox and recite what I think: 'There's no hunger in

Washington.' Things like that. There's plenty of people hurting out there."

For those who worked at some level of government, particularly local, attitudes focused on the mysteries of politics. Willard Schultz had worked in city government in Philadelphia, where he had seen the political winds shift when a corrupt regime underwent temporary reform with the entry of the other party into city hall: "It was a kind of new broom. You knew so many years of decadent power politics, and then the broom swept clean for two terms, from about '52 to '61. Then stuff began to get very political from that time on and it's been that way since. There was a lot of political interference. That made the decision to retire not too difficult." As a prison warden, Carl Stouffer found a number of political pressures. Doubts about the political system were voiced by other retirees. Most disturbing for several retirees was the impact of the IRS. "I think that's the one thing everyone's afraid of" was the comment of one-time credit manager Susan Hoffert.

However, relatively few of the retirees voiced any serious protests about the status quo or the value systems of the society. Four of them mentioned working (stuffing envelopes and the like) for the conservative congressman Donald Ritter, who represents the Lehigh Valley district. There was almost none of the "fortress mentality" sometimes found in the attitudes of older people.[19] What seemed apparent was more an indifference to social problems. In part this is because the survey was not designed to investigate the retirees' sociopolitical ideology. A more plausible explanation is that their basic concern is with their immediate needs and the needs of those closest to them. Yet with nearly half being involved in either volunteering or participation in service or related organizations, one could hardly describe the sample as a self-oriented one.

Aging, Death, and the Life Cycle

The interviewees were prompted to reflect on their views of reaching the upper years and the future. Only a few of them thought of themselves as old, but most accepted to varying degrees that they were "past their prime." Sally King was not happy with the rigidity of her peers on AARP excursions: "You get on these day trips and you find that every seat in the bus is reserved. They're like little kids. They have bags on every seat. I'd rather go with a bunch of high school or kindergarten kids. These so-called senior citizens argue and fuss. One-day trips are horrible. They want to stop for breakfast no sooner than you're on the bus." But few others were critical of their peers.

A number regarded aging as a challenge. For example, psychiatric social worker Ruth Schuler was well versed in keeping her equilibrium: "For one thing, I have a young daughter, still at home, that keeps me active. Also, I took an accounting course and I was the oldest one in the class. But I never worked so hard because I was determined that age was not going to be a deterrent to me. . . . I used to teach a course at the hospital to some of the staff, mainly about the myths of old age."

Rev. Donald Siegfried also approached aging positively: "You know one of the real tragedies—and this is my philosophy—I think that our older people represent a great national treasure. They've accumulated wisdom and skills which need to be put to use. You don't have to be a militant like Maggie Kuhn. But you look around at our hospitals and homes for the aged, and look who the volunteers are. The vast number of them are retired people. We couldn't live without them."

A few of the retirees took a humorous stance toward the upper years. Adelaide Williams reports her husband's observation that "If you're wearing a hat, everyone thinks of you as old." On the serious side, others perceived the upper years in view of their experience with their parents. At least a dozen, the wives more than the husbands, spoke of being the principal caregiver of their seniors. Bill Flynn mentioned: "I'm caring for an elderly couple myself. They're dear friends of mine, and I won't get into what I do to help them, but I do. And I see the needs that they have, which the community cannot be aware of because they're not going around and asking people. They need company, they need what I can buy for them with their money, which they aren't going to ask other people to do. . . . Actually what elderly people need is somebody around them who really needs them, loves them, and can give them companionship."

Rev. Donald Siegfried poignantly summed up his thoughts on the confinement and facelessness of many upper-aged in saying:

"Everybody thinks the biggest problem of older people, not necessarily the retired, is either health or money. Actually, the two greatest
problems are loneliness and transportation. . . . This week they had
open house at Cedarbrook (the county home for the aged), and each
time I got to rooms where the patients happened to be eating a meal,
all I could think of was the loneliness. They don't even talk to each
other as they sit at the table. It's very, very sad. When we look at a
woman, she might be newly admitted, and you think that woman
might have had a most useful life with someone and did something
important in her life, and here nobody knows her."

One subject that people generally avoid is death. The topic was
not broached by most of the sample or at least was seldom mentioned
by the interviewees unless they had been through a painful episode
with a spouse or other close relative. Several described their experience of grief. One was Neal Rossi: "After my wife died I didn't
take care of myself. In fact, I was drinking too much. Also, I gulped
down all my meals. But one of the neighbors got a hold of me and
straightened me out—she's the one that decorated my whole apartment here." There were occasionally questions of what would happen if one or the other should go first: "In a way I kind of hope he
goes first, as he would be helpless, but I try not to think about it."

Don Siegfried was struck by how death was more or less taken
for granted by the elderly but had become an increasing preoccupation of the young: "My fellow ministers find their adolescents asking
questions. High schools and colleges are dealing with this question,
even offering courses on death and dying. I had a neighbor who was
mortally wounded in an automobile accident and lived two weeks,
and I had to go tell his mother-in-law. Her daughter was terribly
worried about how her mother was going to take it, but actually she
took it better than her children did."

What Is My Future?

Attitudes about and plans for the last years of their lives were
often a moot point. That is, when the question about the future was

posed, the interviewee had no set answer; most stated that they really have not given too much thought to the question. Yet there were the vague forebodings and occasionally a few "thou shalt nots." On several points there were unrealized ambitions or indefinite plans and even some firm—and some ambivalent—decisions. Mark Cooper, a retired psychologist, mentioned: "I have thought of setting up a counseling service just for people who might want to retire, with the idea that some experts would help me with certain areas like finance. But in the end I guess I'm too lazy to get started." Others had grandiose plans for travel, buying a mobile home, or expanding their time-share plans once they were free from duties with children or parents, or had reached their full retirement benefits—usually with Social Security, which might begin at age sixty-two. Of course, others had initiated these activities even before retirement.

There are always the debates as to where to live. Should we move into a smaller place? Or to the sun cities of the Southwest, or to Florida? "But then, our children are here, and I don't want six months of summer, and I know Mr. So-and-so who moved back because he got tired of humidity and insect life." They are also aware that Florida has now overtaken Pennsylvania in population. Consequently, the restful Gulf Coast is no longer the paradise it once was in their dreams. More fundamental in this thinking was the general rigidity to change: "It just seems more natural for us to stay here."

The question was raised as to whether they would consider a retirement home. Most were clearly putting off dealing with this question as long as they could. As mentioned in Chapter 7, a very few looked forward to living with their children. Others were less than ecstatic with the prospect of an apartment complex with a full-care annex. There was considerable abhorrence about going into a retirement home or even a retirement community. The question of a retirement home had the connotation of a nursing home or "God's waiting room," as Steve Kovacs described it. Still, Alan and Carla Adams had placed their deposit on the new Presbyterian senior community even though they hoped to be in their present home for another decade. Another reflected cynically: "I don't know if I want to trust myself with my children!" Susan Hoffert, a former credit union manager, took a rather practical view: "A retirement home? Okay. It's either the children get the savings or the retirement home does. I would prefer that to being a burden to the children. . . . I had my mother and I know how tough that is. Senility is so hard to handle. Even a physical disability is bad on the children, having to tow someone around in a wheelchair. Oh, no! Children are very kind when you are well."

The age structure in retirement housing was another problem. Jane Kohler draws this picture: "I wouldn't be in one, no way! I had a friend who bought into one—real exclusive. The first month there was never a child around; you never see a baby. When we took her shopping, she would stand and stare at the children. It was just like a prison; it was all old people."

A few drew attention to what to them was an excessive purchase price and the monthly fee. Several recalled their visits to nursing homes. Dorothy Schmidt, who had worked in one of the better ones, said:

"These people lose their identity, they aren't themselves. I doubt that five percent are happy. I read *Modern Maturity* and see from the statistics in retirement villages that the prospects are bad. I don't care even if we're living in a modern area; people are people and they want to be part of their own families. As I've said to my nurses aides, you just wait; things go in a cycle and people are going to be taken care of at home again. Maybe it's gone too far now. I might have been wrong in that, but I have strong hope that the style will change."

Inevitably several in our sample had painful experiences. Arthur Ferraro reflects:

"Only last month when we had to put dad in a nursing home we felt guilty. He had a catheter and all that. He could go on for years. In fact, that is just the point, they do go on for years. They didn't treat him badly. It wasn't one of those horror stories, but you see people in nursing homes when their family can't be there every other day, and you see these people becoming more senile. At first we had a visiting nurse come in several times a week, and we ourselves took turns. He can afford to be there, but how many people can? If it's a county home they can, rightfully so, take whatever property you have."

In somewhat the same vein, Jim Dowd says:

"I think I have friends who would help me to stay in my home. I dread not being useful. My mother went to a home after an amputation. So she went into a nursing home, but while she was still in her home she could take phone calls, order groceries, tell the woman who came in for about six hours a day what she wanted and what she didn't want done. . . . Once she was in the nursing home—not quite as bad as a prison—yet there's control over what you eat, what you do, what time you got to bed, how loud you can play your radio, all that stuff."

There were other complaints—shortage of staff, quality of food —but Don Siegfried, as usual, had a fairly incisive interpretation:

"There are those nursing homes we might call warehouses for the old, but there's another side. The American Association of Homes for the Aging is open only to nonprofit agencies. Another organization exists for the proprietary ones, which most experts agree are not as well run as the nonprofit. But there are good and bad in both groups. Most nonprofit homes are run either by religious or fraternal groups and are generally better. For one thing, they tend to be located in nonurban or semiurban locations. For instance, Allentown is far better off than New York or Philadelphia."

A few in the sample took a fairly realistic stand, knowing their dreams of staying in their home or being invited to live with their children is no way of dealing with the remote future, as Stella Zimmerman sums up: "It wouldn't bother me going into a retirement community. I can't spend my whole life sitting on the porch or watching TV. Keeping up with friends your own age is kind of rough, and I think in a retirement community you would have more opportunity to meet people with your interests and your age, which you don't have otherwise."

In this chapter we have tried to interpret the basic personality orientation of at least some of our retirees. These interpretations must be considered as tentative, but they suggest that there is likely a continuity of overt personality systems from middle adult life into the postretirement years.

It is also significant that the values and attitudes in this sample reflected a conservative outlook based on position in the life cycle and the sociocultural climate of the Lehigh Valley, which for that matter probably reflects most of America. At the same time, there were a number concerned with the social issues of our times.

In regard to their own future there was a reluctance—along with most of us—to think too much about it. Almost universal was the attitude, "I'll stay here as long as I can."

References

1. Susan Krauss Whitbourne and Comilda S. Weinstock, *Adult Development* (New York: Praeger, 1986), pp. 268–269.
2. Erik H. Erikson, Joan M. Erikson, and Helen Q. Kivnick, *Vital Involvement in Old Age* (New York, Norton, 1986), p. 55.
3. Kenneth J. Gergen, "Stability, Change, and Chance in Human Life," in Nancy Datan and Hayne W. Reese (eds.), *Lifespan Developmental Psychology: Dialectical Perspectives on Experimental Research* (San Diego, CA: Academic Press, 1977).
4. David Chiriboga, "Personality in Later Life," Philip Silverman (ed.), *The Elderly as Modern Pioneers* (Bloomington: Indiana University Press, 1987), pp. 133–157.
5. Robert C. Atchley, "Continuity Theory of Normal Aging," *Gerontologist, 29*, 183–190, 1989.
6. Irving Rosow, "Status and Role Change through the Life Cycle," in Robert H. Binstock and Ethel Shanas (eds.), *Handbook of Aging and the Social Sciences*, 2d ed. (New York: Van Nostrand Reinhold, 1985), pp. 62–93.
7. George Vaillant, *Adaptation to Life* (Boston: Little, Brown, 1977).
8. Thomas O. Blank, *A Social Psychology of Developing Adults* (New York: Wiley-Interscience, 1982), p. 157.
9. Matilda W. Riley *et al.*, *Aging and Society: An Inventory of Research Findings*, Vol. 1 (New York: Russell Sage, 1968).
10. Daniel J. Levinson *et al.*, *The Seasons of a Man's Life* (New York: Norton, 1978), pp. 198–199.
11. Lucille Nahemow, Kathleen A. McCluskey-Fawcett, and Paul E. McGhee (eds.), *Humor and Aging* (San Diego, CA: Academic Press, 1986).

12. Erik H. Erikson, *Childhood and Society*, 2d ed. (New York: Norton, 1963).
13. Avron Spiro III *et al.*, "Longitudinal Findings from the Normative Aging Study: II. Do Emotionality and Extraversion Predict Symptom Change?" *Journal of Gerontology, 45*, P136–144, 1990.
14. George H. Mead, *Mind, Self, and Society* (Chicago: University of Chicago Press, 1934).
15. Icek Ajzen, "Attitudes, Traits, and Actions: Dispositional Prediction of Behavior in Personality and Social Psychology," in Leonard Berkowitz (ed.), *Advances in Experimental Social Psychology*, Vol. 20 (San Diego, CA: Academic Press, 1987), pp. 1–63.
16. Glen H. Elder, *Children of the Great Depression* (Chicago: University of Chicago Press, 1974).
17. Douglas Degelman *et al.*, "Age and Gender Differences in Beliefs about Personal Power and Injustice," *International Journal of Aging and Human Development, 33*, 101–111, 1991.
18. Joseph L. Esposito, *The Obsolete Self: Philosophical Dimensions of Aging* (Berkeley: University of California Press, 1987), p. 223.
19. Robert Kastenbaum, "Racism and the Older Voter? Arizona's Rejection of a Paid Holiday to Honor Martin Luther King," *International Journal of Aging and Human Development, 32*(3), 199–209, 1991.

Part IV
Conclusions

Chapter 9

Advice to Others
From Those Who Should Know

The interview with Donald Siegfried, a Lutheran minister, showed that he seemed to be as much interested in others as in himself, as indicated by the number of times he has been cited in previous chapters. As might be expected from his pastoral role, he has considerable sensitivity to people in the upper years:

"I've been interested in gerontology for many years, and I was chairman of our synod Taskforce on Aging, when I was in Maryland. We did a lot of research on aging and came across statistics about General Motors, which had a mandatory sixty-five retirement rule. They did a study of a large sample of production people and a control group of management people, six months before and six months after retirement. The blue-collar people were looking forward to retirement; they wanted to go fishing and hunting and play pinochle, paint their house, and plant a garden. The management people, generally speaking, were regretting it because they had never done anything of this sort. A year later, the positions were reversed. After retirement, the blue-collar people were bored. They had planted their garden, gone fishing, painted their house, and were tired of television and pinochle. The management people were as busy as they ever had been, doing things that they wanted to do rather than what they had to do. So the story is not what you retire from, but what you retire to.

"After my retirement, I guess I felt no more fatigue than the average person would feel. I recovered after I was out for about three or four months, and then went back on a part-time basis, but you don't do that in the ministry. I guess the only thing you can say is that I had gotten to the point in life, and I suppose this is the normal process of aging, whereby I dreaded going out at night, and this was part of my job. I had four to five nights a week of meetings. One of the biggest pluses that I've seen since I retired is that I don't have to do this anymore. I can spend most of my evenings at home, unless I really want to go out.

"Yes, I have plenty of responsibilities, but not the overall responsibility. I don't want to take it; I don't have to, either. Of course, a degree of financial independence is not having to worry about these things. I'm making some money in retirement, but we could live without that.

"I knew I would miss the people, because all of my life I've been involved with people, different from someone who just sits in an office or a laboratory and does that sort of thing. . . . I think part of the hiatus for us was the fact that we were so physically busy. I had a whole string of calls that I had to make. Everybody wanted us for social occasions, and there were parties after parties. Every group in which we were both involved, and we were both very active, had some sort of a party in our honor, you know; plus the fact that we have a lot of stuff, the impediments of forty years and the physical problem of moving 150 miles and getting everything packed up—we were so busy that it just didn't really register. I guess it took us a couple of months before we really realized that we were supposed to be retired. I remember that when I went back to Maryland for our synod's convention in June (which was two months after I retired) I went scurrying about looking for my appointment book, which I always have here. It was about that time that I started to become busier. I had a kind of honeymoon period of adjustment.

"I have dual membership: clerical membership in Maryland and lay membership here. But the bishop of this section of the church happens to be a man whom I have known, well, almost all of his life. He met me in a pastoral meeting and asked me if I was interested in doing some interim ministry for him. I said, 'Well, give me a chance to get my feet on the ground and I will.' And then I started getting supply preaching appointments. Summer was coming on and everybody needed a 'supply minister.' In three and a half years, I supplied in something like forty different churches, sometimes four or five times in the same church.

"I've got a good friend who is a retired minister and lives in Northampton now. He was a pastor at Tamaqua for many years, and he's a very gruff kind of character. It's a typical statement that would come from him—he said when you retire, the first thing you have to learn is that you're no longer a big shot. Now that's the typical hostile remark, but that's the way he felt. I never really thought of myself as being a big shot, but I was in the public eye. We had gone shopping one day, a week or so ago, and we stopped in a restaurant in Quakertown. As we were going in, there was a man there with a wife in a wheelchair, and we offered to help him and he said, 'Oh, I know who you are.' I had never seen the man before in my life that I can remember. He knew who I was, and, as it so happened, our son is an attorney who represented him at one time. My picture is in the paper every once in a while.

"If you look at governmental programs for older people, you'll find that almost invariably they include some kind of transportation. You know, gerontologists talk about the young elderly, the middle elderly, and the fragile elderly, and there are all kinds of nomenclature that I'm sure you're more familiar with than I am—but nevertheless this is more true of course of the older rather than the younger. However, look at how many widows there are; women are much more numerous than men in the elderly group. Look how many widows there are who never drove or who don't drive now or who don't have a car. They are dependent on friends or relatives or someone to provide their transportation. . . . Our society couldn't operate without volunteers, and unfortunately it is becoming less and less popular. People, especially women, are beginning to feel that they should be paid for everything they do. I think that's going to have a big effect.

"I don't think my retirement has placed any tension on our marital relationship. I don't know what my wife said in her interview, but I certainly feel no tension. We have both been very happily married, and I enjoy being with her more of the time and going shopping with her, doing things like that. We do more of that than we used to.

"I know that many people who have chosen to retire to the

Sunbelt find that it was not what they thought it was going to be. And several studies show that for every ten families under retirement age who move to Florida, for instance, seven will move back within a year. And of every ten families over retirement age, three to four of them will move back within a year, and most of them within five years. One of the biggest problems is they miss their grandchildren.

"A very fine couple in my congregation in Maryland retired shortly after we went there. She had been an educator and was director of rehabilitation at the State School for the Mentally Retarded. She had been very active professionally, and when she retired she was terrified at what she was going to find to do. She wanted to get involved with all sorts of things. I said, 'Marie, slow down. You're going to have more to do than you know what to do with.' She got herself involved in too many things, and when they expected too much of her, she had to cut a few of them out. She was terrified at first, running in so many different directions. So I advise all to take it slowly, and make sure what commitments you want to make, and things will come to you. You don't need, in most cases, to go looking for them if you're the kind of person who wants to do things. I think it depends on the person. She was obviously a talented person and one who had been very busy professionally, and people were anxious to have her skills.

"You see, the anthracite region in Pennsylvania—a depressed area that people have moved away from during their working life—is now becoming a place to retire. People are coming back home again, bringing the statistics up. A lot of them are living in a house with upkeep so expensive that they can hardly afford to eat, but this has been home all of their life. Or, they're living in small apartments. They are on their own, they are functioning, and it's good to keep them in their own homes as long as you can. It's better for them and it's super for everyone else. We all have families that we support, social agencies and other people.

"I think another part of the answer is that if you think that you are going to have to go into a retirement facility, the key is not to wait until you're too far gone to go in. We're not talking about nursing homes, now. There are various levels of care. Every expert that I have ever heard in this field who talks about these things says that our nursing homes are full of people that don't belong there. So it's good that there are increasing numbers of boarding homes now, or personal care facilities that do not provide twenty-four-hour skilled nursing facilities."

* * *

One of the questions asked of the interviewees concerned the advice they would give others on the point of early retirement—or retirement in general. The responses reflect the variety of personalities, feelings, and attitudes we have been describing in previous chapters. On the whole, the suggestions reflect a cautious optimism.

Three major pieces of advice emerged from the interviews. First is the kind of general recommendation to take retirement early and learn to enjoy it, including a few cautions. Next most frequently emphasized is how important it is to keep busy in retirement, whether it be in community service, hobbies, exercise, sports, lawn and house care, travel, or another career. A large number feel that being occupied with whatever one chooses is essential to happiness and sound mental health. Or, to put it negatively, a lack of interests, activity, or social contacts results in disaster. The third category is the need to do some financial planning before retirement, though many admittedly had not done so.

Take It and Enjoy It, but Keep Busy!

"Do it" was the advice most frequently heard in the interviews. Indeed, at this point the interviewees are for the most part even enthusiastic about retirement, some to their own surprise. The reasons most often given for their current happiness are a new-found sense of freedom, flexibility, lack of required schedule, and relief from the oft-mentioned pressures in the workplace. "Don't wait," advises a widow. One of the men urges others to "take it as early as you can financially, if you're not in love with your position." Repeatedly such advice as the following is heard: "Enjoy it," "Take it! The earlier the better." One man said, "I wish I'd done it twenty years ago." These remarks came even from those who retired under pressure from their employers or had grave concerns about how they would make out financially or whether they would be happy without contact with fellow workers and career personnel. One man who hated to retire says he'd now like to thank his employer for having pushed him into early retirement! Of course, it must be remembered that most—although not all—participants in this study retired with adequate income or better, and most were in good health.

Interestingly, a former employment counselor for the state of Pennsylvania said most of her clients experienced forced retirement with a sense of guilt. If that reaction characterizes many early retirees, the participants in this study apparently never felt it or overcame any conscious sense of guilt by the time of the interview. Even those who left their offices for the last time with considerable unhappiness— some with anger, hurt, or feelings of humiliation or a sense of not being appreciated or properly rewarded for their years of loyalty to the company—they, too, are feeling somewhat more mellow about retirement. They have reached an accommodation. Many warned that it takes time and effort to adjust—from a month to two years for those in our sample. Others warn that winter is a bad time to begin this adjustment period. One fifth admit they are still not used to being retired.

The following statements reveal the general mode of advice and warnings uttered when the interviewees were asked what advice they would give to others about to retire. Taken together, their collective experience seems to lead them to invite others to "Come on in. The water's fine after you get used to it." And they give tips on how to get adjusted to the change.

For example, Linda Eisenhard was both "pleased and shocked" and somewhat hurt when offered an enticement to retire at age sixty (after eighteen years as a bindery worker and then proofreader in a publishing company). She put it this way: "Be happy in your retirement, because it's wonderful, really. And don't let yourself get bored. I think that's bad, when there are so many things to do now. I think we can find pleasure and something worthwhile in most anything. It doesn't have to be expensive—simply going out to a park and going for a walk, for example. If you find yourself getting bored, then get something to do that you've got to be interested in, even if it's reading—something that will keep your mind occupied."

Planning: Think Positively

Jim Zimmerman, the former department chief, who retired at age fifty-five and whom we met in the opening pages of this study, was offered an early retirement bonus at a time when he was becoming "a little bit unhappy that they weren't utilizing my talents." He became suspicious that trouble lay ahead when he was put on third shift after all those years as a trusted worker and manager. His reactions bear repeating:

"I was not like a few I know who were real happy just to get out. I wasn't looking to get out. I liked working, but I must admit I was looking forward to getting a longer vacation than one week once or twice a year. Now that I'm out I'm enjoying almost every minute of it. I am not going through any emotional shock, but at the same time a person still feels maybe there is something missing. . . . The best part is that I have the freedom to do whatever I want. I'll tell you it's really nice to live like this."

Walter Koch says that when asked to retire at age fifty-five he felt "frustrated if not angry"—his wife added the term "hurt." Yet two years later he was able to say, "It was the best thing that ever happened to me." Having succeeded in finding another line of work (as consultant), he is happy to be earning almost his former salary, and he is working fewer hours. His advice to early retirees is to do some long-range financial planning over the working years, and then in retirement "try to find someplace where you can make good use of your expertise, to do something on a part-time basis so that you feel you have something worthwhile to give the community. Everybody who's reached age fifty-five has some talent, some expertise he can use if he looks around."

Timing the Event

David Lauer, who worked since high school and voluntarily retired on a railroad pension at age sixty-one as a supervisor of switching, now finds himself very busy around the house and very happy. He reflects the feelings of a surprising number of the interviewees about the influence of timing in relation to the seasons: "My main advice is to pick the right time of year. It takes a whole six to eight months to get yourself straightened out and used to retirement before you're holed up for the winter. Once that winter sets in you're pretty well confined to the house. You can't do a lot of things."

Admitting that he has a good pension, he says "I don't regret the fact that I didn't do much financial planning before retirement." He expresses the release he feels in his new sense of freedom: "I don't go beyond next month on the calendar. I don't bother with a watch. I don't check calendars any more. Let the future take care of itself."

A retired head nurse suggests, "If possible you should take a leave of absence first to see what it's like not to go to work, and really think it over." A former professor who still regrets retiring in his fifties advises that when going into retirement one should "try to make some plans for continuity of what you like to do, continuity from the work you are doing—if you like your work—so that the break is only a break for the better." And Mrs. Siegfried expressed this kind of wisdom: "Life is what you make of it. In retirement you have to make an effort. I think too many sit back and wait for things to happen. You've got to meet people half way, and you've got to make some things happen to yourself. There are all kinds of institutions and organizations crying for help. You don't have to have had a background in a lot of things. Even though we don't have time we recently joined the local senior citizens group; they're asking for volunteers. They do a lot of things."

Arthur Ferraro is one who deliberately wanted out of the eight-to-five type of regime, so he opted to retire at age fifty-two. By not following the trend of rising professionals and managers to move to the plush suburbs, but remaining in his central city residence, he could adjust to a lower income. He is intellectually curious and yet committed to volunteering, especially in the teaching area. Unlike members of the academic profession (including the authors of this book), who can gradually disengage themselves from their profession, Arthur had to make a complete break in order to have the life he wanted. Although he does not offer advice, his enthusiasm itself is a kind of model for at least some future retirees:

"I went to Muhlenberg College, got a B.S. in physics. I was married and we had children. Most of the support came from her, because I was away at school two or three nights a week. I was lucky that I didn't have to miss a semester. I really went from 1959–1971. I graduated in '71. That was twelve years' nights. I didn't go summers because if I did I would have just probably gotten burned out and quit. The company paid for my tuition, and I paid for my books. I couldn't beat that. As I was going to school I was getting promotions.

"When I retired I had thirty-four years of Western Electric and AT&T. I was a senior engineer in the engineering department, working on integrated circuits, the development of integrated circuits, packaging techniques, testing, and liability. That's what I retired from. . . . I started young. I think I started in 1951, so that means I was two months away from being nineteen when I started. A year of technical school was all I had. I started in the shop and worked my way up while going to college at night. I got a degree in engineering and worked my way up to engineer senior rank.

"I had to decide about retirement within a month or two. I actually went earlier than the rest. They had until the middle of November to get out, and I wanted out immediately. So I took my vacation at the end of October. I'm the kind of person that if I think about something, and want to do something, I have to push myself to do it, because I may sit there and weigh things too much and talk myself out of it. I'm usually very conservative in that respect. I had pretty well convinced myself that I was going to leave in two years. It wasn't a matter of saying am I going to go at fifty-two or sixty-two. I had pretty well convinced myself that I knew I was going to retire in two years, and so I did.

"AT&T has always been good for trying to keep the retirees informed with periodicals and occasional lunches several times a year. At Christmastime we'll have a luncheon. I don't know how they'll be now, but Western Electric (which was AT&T technology) was oriented this way. They would like to have people working there know other people working there. Now Air Products doesn't do that, but AT&T (Western Electric) always did that. But it's not as much fun working there now. Now it's changing a little bit because it's a new era. Different competition. They were nice people and I miss some of my old friends. Not that you miss the job, but you think about the old jobs you worked on. When I started engineering, I worked on vacuum tubes, so I went from vacuum tubes to transistors to integrated circuits.

"The only thing you have in the beginning is that you feel like you should be going someplace. You don't have a routine, so you need a routine. You do it for thirty-four years and a couple of years in the military, and you're always used to having things routine. So you have to set your own routine, and you start to feel, at least I felt, that you should be doing so. But then I thought I really don't have to be doing anything, I can do whatever I'd like to do, because other people who had retired have told me, 'It's nice to get up in the morning especially if you've had some plans for that day, and if you find it's not nice out, you can just sit and read a book all day.' I love to read, so that's no problem. At first you start feeling like you should be doing something, but then you get past it.

"I think you find later that as you get older, when one spouse dies, the woman usually makes the adjustment much easier than the man does because she has always had the house as her kingdom. She doesn't feel out of control when she's in the house alone. The husbands really feel out of sorts and never really adjust to having the home to themselves.

"One of the reasons I decided to retire so early was that I've seen a lot of cases where people retire in later years and then they couldn't do the things they had hoped to do, not because they died or anything or had serious injuries, but they might have chronic arthritis or something like that, things where you can't be as active. It seems to me the people I saw over the years who had retired at sixty-five and came back to visit, when I spoke to them, seemed to be in better physical health, but not necessarily better mental health.

"Maybe it's the transition period. It depends on the type of person you are. If you're the kind of person that can't sit still and you don't enjoy reading a book or sitting in the backyard, then you're going to feel that you have to be going all the time. I know people who retired and rebuilt their whole home. They had to be into something. It's all right if you can do that, then you won't feel frustrated. If you're the kind of person that likes to just sit and read, as long as you're not frustrated with it, then it's fine. If you find yourself being frustrated because of it, then it's no good. The best part is, at least for me, it forced me to start something new. I feel mentally that I'm in a new situation—something more to look forward to."

Ever a Challenge

We've already reported that close to half of the retirees (42 percent) in this study had taken up postretirement careers, mostly part time, and that almost a third of these say they are happier than in their former positions. Among them, Lew Fitzgerald urges going into business for yourself, as he did upon retirement at age forty-eight. He finds he is much happier with the challenges and flexibility of work as a financial consultant, but warns it takes self-discipline and ability to set time limits if one is one's own boss: "Be a dreamer and don't settle for a lesser goal. Don't look back. The best thing to do is to keep your eyes on tomorrow; yesterday is not going to do anything for you. 'Tomorrow is a promissory note; yesterday is a cashed check,' as the saying goes. In every adversity is a seed of equal or greater benefit."

In other words, we find that positive thinking characterizes the majority of these early retirees. Yet, one nurse, like the professor cited earlier, would like further employment but bemoans the difficulty of finding anything (other than nursing) once one hits fifty-five "no matter what experience you've built up. The jobs just aren't out there."

"Most definitely have something in the pot which you are interested in and can follow through after you retire. I had nothing—no hobbies, no nothing," warned another nurse, Alice Wilson, who had been a pediatric, intensive-care specialist: "Unfortunately, I retired the end of December 1985 and I had that whole winter ahead and did nothing. I read my newspaper, watched TV when I wanted to, cleaned when I felt like it, which wasn't often, and gained weight. If I had thought I was going to retire at that age I'm pretty sure I would have projected to have myself do something. I got really lazy. I was going to put pictures in the album; I didn't do that. I just didn't do what I should have. It took six months if not longer to acclimate myself to the fact that I was retired."

Lois Bennett, a widowed registered nurse, who had had to retire at age sixty-five because of a back injury, advises those who retire: "Just accept retirement. Start living, that's all. Take things as they come. I take one day at a time. I don't get myself all worked up. I get up every day and think, 'Well, O.K., here we go.' I enjoy it, and the next day the same. I think contact with people keeps you a lot more alive. You have to have friends and do things. I take a walk every day, and, of course, I have to do exercises for my back."

Ed Volpe, the former administrator in a vocational–technical high school, left when he sensed the authorities wanted his job for somebody else. He hesitates to give counsel to others but makes this analysis:

"It depends on the individual. Take the individual who has his heart and soul in whatever his job is and then finds the personnel above him no longer cooperate with him. He'd take retirement and never want to see that place again, because whoever they put in there is going to do things that are not in line with what he had done. So stay away from the place. Then there are those who were not happy in their profession and wish they'd done something else. They just can't retire soon enough. They might be the happiest in retirement. Then there are those who had mundane tasks, who didn't have broadening interests; they didn't have time to read or they didn't have a good basic education. They become like the Wanderers Club down here at the corner. You go into their bar at ten A.M. and you find some twenty-five guys will come in; they get a tap of beer and sit there and just look at the walls day in and day out. I'm not sure that kind of person *can* prepare for retirement. So I've never taken on the idea of saying what others should do in retirement."

Ordering Our Priorities

The reasons given by the retirees we studied for attributing great importance to being active in retirement do not support David Ekerdt's thesis that the American work ethic pushes us to excessive "busy-ness" in retirement as a self-defense against others' judgments that we are too old now to do anything or that only those who work are considered worth much.[1] Ekerdt believes that our life style of busy-ness is carried over into retirement years as a justification of retirement. No participants in the current study intimated that they worry at all about what others think of their life style or their contributions to the community. This attitude of openness and adaptability appeared in another study of professional and managerial retirees, who chose to create as much psychological space as they could in their search for new friends and leisure pursuits.[2] Our retirees feel activity in retirement is essential to one's mental well-being and an inherent part of happiness. Even those who dislike retirement at first eventually find that activities help them to adjust and actually lead to a positive assessment of life. For example, Aldo Carlucci, depressed at being laid off at age fifty-eight by the closing of a large industry, strongly expressed his conviction that what finally pulled him out of his negativism was going to seminars and lectures for retirees offered at the community college.

Be a Volunteer

Nurse–educator Alice Stratton felt strongly that a retiree should plan not just to be busy but to be useful through service. Having voluntarily retired at age sixty-seven, ten months previous to the interview, this chairperson of a college department of nursing expressed her conviction about the importance of planning in advance of retirement: "This preparation is especially important if one isn't already involved in community service." She stressed the need to keep alive the sense of importance that workers get from being contributors in their workplace: "If you don't plan it ahead of time you're apt to procrastinate and forget about it. In addition, the volunteer process provides sociability and socialization. Being a contributor is so important—the continuation of being a contributor!"

Then there's the remark of Saul Goldman: "Don't sit back and feel sorry for yourself. Get involved. If you think you're hurting, just take a Meals on Wheels delivery job and see how many people are in really bad shape."

Cliff Thomas, a supervisor in a steel company (who at age fifty-seven took early retirement compensation—a bonus of one half his former salary to be paid to him over a period of twenty-one months), warns: "Those people who never did anything except work and come home and sit down and watch TV and drink beer, they are going to have a rougher time than the person who keeps himself occupied, whether doing things for himself or with friends. I would strongly suggest that anybody who retires should keep active. You can join all kinds of clubs and groups. You can volunteer. There are so many things to do."

Nellie Jones, the former head of an employment office, retired four years earlier at age sixty, comments:

"I think people should think about retirement in advance. You have to have some plans for your time, whether you're going to have a hobby you can pursue, whether you're going to do volunteer work, or part-time work. I think you should have some idea what you're going to do with your time. I think it's a shortcoming in the bureau where I worked that they don't talk about retirement or prepare you for retirement. They prepare people for work for a period of twelve or more years, but they don't prepare them for retirement. Some retirees I know have nothing but golf and a little travel to occupy themselves—no hobbies, no volunteer work. And they become very disillusioned with retirement and wish they were working."

Professor John Mueller, now very busy around his small farm and in community service, admits, "I don't know if I would say I'm retired! Those individuals who are accustomed to mental activity must continue mental activity of some sort."

Yet one man, retired ten years ago at age fifty-five, notes that it can become hard to think of things to fill one's time: "I think it's harder working at retirement than working itself!" Interestingly, though, this glowing picture of the virtues of volunteering is not reflected in the questionnaire comparisons of volunteers to nonvolunteers (or for that matter, workers to nonworkers). Involvement in activities did not result in happier or more satisfied retirees than those who weren't doing volunteer (or paid) work. Certainly, part of the reason is a simple one of matching. Some people need activity to feel alive, others don't. As long as one's activity is matched to his or her needs, the result is positive. And the key to a match is availability and making use of a wide range of options. It is likely, further, that those who do volunteer are more likely to point it out than those who don't and that for many happiness in retirement comes from sources other than volunteering or work.

A handful of persons warned against becoming too busy and thus consuming one of the big advantages of retirement—*freedom*. As the wife of Don Siegfried put it: "Some people are timid about volunteering. They hold back from getting involved because they say it cuts down their freedom, and when they want to go on a trip they're obliged to be sitting at that desk. Organizations must learn to have flexible schedules for volunteers, in order to give them the opportunity to serve." Arthur Ferraro feels a bit pressed by at least eight activities in community and church service, as well as personal hobbies. He admits: "Even when I voluntarily take on something to do, I start to feel it's imposing on my flexibility. Not that I'm going to do anything else that night, but I think my attitude comes with age. One can become a little selfish with one's time that way. I'm beginning to think about whether I really want to have to go out every Thursday night."

And a school counselor, Grace Shoemaker, retired two months earlier at age sixty, explains that she has not undertaken any volunteer work and has turned down an invitation to join a bowling club because: "I haven't felt that I needed something to fill my time. When I do, I will. I've worked for twenty-five years so that I could do what I wanted to do, when I wanted to do it, and I'm enjoying this."

Similarly, former department head George Shafer, now very busy with family, community college courses, travel, yardwork, and the like, and retired voluntarily three years earlier at age sixty-two, put it this way: "I didn't want to become involved in anything. I thought here I was with Western Electric a little over forty-one years—now it's time for me just to relax. I felt if I were a volunteer and helped some organization with management skills it might end up being a full-time job again, because I know I wouldn't drop it till I was perfectly satisfied with what I'd set up for them."

Social Contacts

Several women stressed the usefulness of social engagements and companionship, offering a little different slant from the men. Jennie Fisher, who worked thirty years for General Electric, after ten months of retirement at age sixty-two, emphasizes that it takes effort. "Well, don't sit at home in front of the TV. Get out of the house; do your work and get out. Look for different things to do. If you don't have a friend whom you're going to have lunch or dinner with, plan something. But you have to have a good friend, someone who likes the things you like to do."

The wife of a voluntarily retired man finds from her experience: "It's really, really important that a wife has her own interests and a husband his interests, because you can't totally be with each other twenty-four hours a day and enjoy it. You must maintain your own interests; then the time you spend together is of better quality." And a female psychiatric social worker, retired at age sixty-two after over nineteen years of employment, adds: "One of the things I think is important is that my friends do not come from work. I have a lot of good friends outside. I'm not dependent on people at work for my social life. I think that's important."

Finally, retired insurance agent Norm Reinert observed: "Don't lose your moorings. My friends who decided that their destiny lay in Florida have become isolated from their world. They may enjoy golf, but not seven days a week. My involvement in volunteer work is far more satisfying."

Financial Planning

We recall from Chapter 3 the role that finances play in the adjustment to retirement. Even though many elderly are on the fringes of, if not part of, the economic elite, the retirement plunge usually calls for some financial rearrangements. It is relevant that our sample was largely composed of persons who belonged to a milieu favorable to company pensions: their employment was generally in large companies that accepted unions, and had above-average hourly earnings. Still, nearly all face a reduced income. They also are aware that once they leave the workplace, a return is not too likely.

Though a minority of our interviewees spoke of financial planning in view of retirement (the third distinguishable category among responses of advice), those who did spoke with earnestness about the wisdom of longtime saving investments and planning. An executive who retired at age fifty-five said he became preoccupied with the future about five years before he retired and began running his life and investments like a business: "When in doubt, my advice would be to take retirement. If you can make peace with yourself and do it financially, I think it's the greatest thing in the world."

We return to Walter Koch, the researcher and chief engineer who was terminated at age fifty-five. He believes in planning early in life:

"At age twenty-nine we started planning to retire at fifty-five, putting away money, saving, investing. Otherwise, I don't think I would have had the guts to retire at fifty-five, but this way I didn't have to do things I didn't want to do when the company began to overload me with work and too short deadlines. I think what bothers people facing retirement is they're used to earning some *x* dollars a month, but they don't realize they're spending a large portion on several things that they are not going to spend it on after they retire. For example, I was putting 10 to 15 percent of my money away in some form of retirement savings, and while working you also have a good chunk going into income tax, driving to and from work, buying a noon meal, and all that. So your cost of existence drops considerably.

"I think it would be helpful to make a chart of questions and answers: What do I spend money on now? Will I have to spend that after I retire? What portion of it? I have a feeling a lot of people fear going into retirement. The biggest fear I had was the cost of living and interest rates going up to an inflated percentage that could pretty well wipe me out. People should be helped on understanding the cost of living after retirement. I and my computer would play around figuring out where the money was going, how much of it had to be for certain things, and whether I could make it on less. Also, look for supplemental or part-time work to use one's expertise and earn money after retirement. As a consultant, I'm drawing in almost half the amount of my former salary on top of early retirement benefits and pension."

Machine setter Mario Moro, retired at age sixty-one, said, "I planned for retirement, and everything worked out fine. I tried to get my home maintenance-free beforehand, so now I don't have to spend time doing painting and things like that. Financially, you've got to save for that rainy day. The IRA fund and company stock investment plans are fabulous. Your health, however, is the most important thing."

Gordon Wald, the construction electrician recently forced to retire at age sixty-two because of a severe heart attack, looks back with some regret:

"You should plan to retire when your last child leaves home. That way the money that you used to spend for your children you can balance out for yourself, put it all to your retirement, because you certainly use money when you retire. It's not easy to live off retirement income, especially when you're used to making a fairly decent salary and all of a sudden it stops. I now get for one month (from annuities) what I used to earn in one week in New York City. If I'd known I was going to live this long I'd have taken better care of myself and I probably would have planned financial matters better, but I didn't. I enjoyed myself when I was young and as I got older. Therefore, I'm content with what I'm putting up with, because I have nobody to blame but myself. I'm referring to my health and to not putting more money away."

Al Johnson, the former bank treasurer, had strictly monetary advice to give: "The thing to do is to set aside some money every year."

And Susan Hoffert, a CPA and former manager of a large business's credit union office, answered: "Be sure that you're financially secure, be sure that you're emotionally secure, and that you know what you are going to do when you're at home. . . . The IRA is an excellent way to put money aside, and most companies have a savings plan where if you contribute a dollar they contribute fifty cents. If you get in early on, you would be amazed at what a nest egg you'll have when you retire."

A unique slant to advice on early financial planning comes from electrical-engineer-turned-college-instructor Arthur Ferraro, who had retired at age fifty-two after thirty-four years with the company:

"Start planning retirement when you first go to work, both financially and mentally. You've got to start early laying a foundation for an income in retirement. Savings give you an independence in your late forties and fifties, whereas I've seen people working who must continue to work because they have nothing else. In that case, you're subject to all humiliations on the job when you can't tell somebody, 'No, I don't want to do that.' Having some money around so you know you're not destitute, and thus know that if you had to leave early or retire you could support yourself, gives you a little bit more independence. It also allows somewone in the middle fifties to think about retiring early and taking another career or doing something you really would like to do and couldn't afford before. Now, I'm not talking about 15 to 20 percent of your income, but most of us can save from 3 to 6 percent. Put it away where it can't be touched. Then you'll have independence of thought."

References

1. David J. Ekerdt, "The Busy Ethic: Moral Continuity between Work and Retirement," *Gerontologist, 26,* 239–244, 1986.
2. Tora K. Bikson and Jacqueline D. Goodchilds, "Experiencing the Retirement Transition: Managerial Men Before and After," in Shirlynn Spacapan and Stuart Oskamp (eds.), *The Social Psychology of Aging* (Sage Publications, 1989), pp. 81–108.

Chapter 10

Summary and Implications

It is appropriate that we begin the concluding chapter with the story of Adelaide Williams, who as wife, mother, and nurse, gave of herself and moved into retirement with no trauma. She provides a model of moving into the upper years with a perspective and a sense of humor. With little education beyond high school, she has insight about her husband and sons, and like our other nurses—or for that matter, nearly all our sample—knows she has earned some years of rest and recreation:

"I retired last year at age fifty-six. There are a couple of reasons I retired. The main reason is that my husband is ten years older than I am, so he's been retired for about almost three and a half years. If I worked until I was sixty-two, he would be seventy-two. I've always worked, even when my children were smaller, but I never worked full time when they were small. I waited until they went to school before I considered working more, and we never needed a babysitter or anything. I worked twenty-one years, eleven P.M. to seven A.M., so that we wouldn't need a babysitter. I worked in the labor and delivery room, which is hard work. There's no routine, you know.

"When you go to St. Luke's Hospital, you have to go down a hill to get there, and no matter what, no matter where you live, you'd have to come up the hill. I would find myself coming up that hill going like crazy in my car because I couldn't slow down. On the job I was going, going, going until I was finished, but it was like I was still working. But anyway, what I'm saying is that you're geared the way you work and then all of a sudden you're finished working. But sometimes I realized I was doing this and I'd say, 'Well, I'm finished,' but by the time I'd get home and got out of the car I was so tired I couldn't even walk into the house.

"But besides my husband being older, another reason that I retired is I'm a big person; I've always, all my life, weighed too much, and people have asked me how much weight I lost over the years. They'd say that I looked as if I've lost some weight and how much did I lose. I'd say, 'In a lifetime?' Five hundred pounds at least. As a result, I have two worn-out knees. I've been on my feet all the time, and my husband used to tell friends, family, and people at church all the things I'm involved with. They used to say, 'How do you get everything done that you do and still work?' He'd say, 'Well, it's the sleep that suffers.' I guess I could say that I got myself into the habit of sleeping only about three and a half to four hours a day because I really feel sleep is a waste of time. I only sleep because I absolutely have to. Another thing that entered into retiring was that St. Luke's built a new wing, called the Horizon Wing, and the whole obstetrical department moved to the third floor there. It's beautiful and very nice.

"I thought that I would miss the people that I worked with, and I might have if my life weren't so full of other things. Understand, though, that they are friends and always will be. I am very active at our church, so I really didn't miss my nursing. It was part of me, but I don't really miss it because I do all kinds of crafts like knitting and sewing. Right now I'm altering an old wedding gown for a young girl whose mother graduated the year after me at the hospital. I've been doing craft work for only a little over a month now. I think one of the hardest things about retiring to get used to, for me, was sleeping. I'm not used to sleeping at night. I would call the girls up at work around five o'clock in the morning just to ask how things were going, not because I missed it, but because I was wide-awake.

"I also spend one day a week at Cedarbrook (the county nursing home) as a volunteer. As long as my legs hold out, I'll stay. So far I can stay until the end of the musical program that I'm helping with. It's basically pushing patients in their wheelchairs to choir practice. Some of them don't even know you're there.

"Until May, I was president of our Women's Missionary Society. Now they changed some things and they don't have a vice president anymore, which is what I would really be if they hadn't changed the system. So now my title is director of community missions. We have what we call our 'helping hands,' you know, for people who need help. We have some old people who live in apartments for the elderly and they have to move or they need help cleaning kitchen cabinets and closets. These tasks are for church members, or for anybody else that we know who has a need. It's not a case of my having to do it, but finding people to do it. We also help someone who has just gotten out of the hospital and needs help or meals. We also have a library and a used clothing drive. Most of the clothes get sent out to the Wesleyan Indian Missions in the Dakotas. I also have a recent job as Assistant Sunday School Superintendent. It isn't too much at this point, but within another year or two, our Sunday School Superintendent will feel that he's had enough and I would step in. Once someone said, 'You have too many hats,' and I said, 'Yes, I'm getting rid of some of them.' "

* * *

As we look at retirement—whether Lew Zimmerman in Chapter 1 and his almost compulsive set of interests, Adelaide Williams with her focus on family and church, or the many others we have visited in this book—several features remain as given:

1. *Population.* Persons are living significantly longer with a declining birthrate, leading to an older population.
2. *Marital status.* Over 90 percent of Americans get married at some point in their lives. As we now have the highest life expectancy in history, it means that despite a high divorce rate (nearly 40 percent of marriages end in divorce), more marriages than ever reach the golden wedding anniversary. Moreover, with the survival of more women than men into the upper years, the burden of widowhood falls on women and a small number of adult children who can care for them. It is predicted that by the next century most women will spend more years caring for their parents than they did for their children.
3. *Employment of women.* An ever-growing number of middle-aged women are now in the labor force and are finding

difficulty in meeting the social, psychological, and physical needs of their families, including their own parents.

4. *Expansion of public programs and services.* Governmental and other institutions have taken over many of the responsibilities that once belonged to the family. This intervention by the state is an uneven one, depending on time and place—the current political philosophy in office or the differing social concerns of the region (New York and California versus Louisiana and Arizona, for example).

5. *Secularizing of personal goals.* By the twentieth century most people in Western society were moving toward a viewpoint that our lives are no longer *primarily* rooted in religious purposes. It is not to say that spiritual goals were no longer important, but the search for pleasure and happiness has for most people taken precedence over devotion to a religious commitment.[1] Morality, thus, rests on practical rather than theological principles. Among other implications this shift means that retirement is a commodity to be enjoyed after a lifetime of study and work.

The Meaning of Aging and Retirement

We raised the question in Chapter 8 about how we may look at the aging process. In other words, "just how old is old?" The age of sixty-five has been an arbitrary definition of the beginning of retirement. As Frank Kleiler asks, why can't "elderly" begin at seventy and seventy-five instead of sixty-five?[2] Indeed, suggestions have been made that sixty-eight become the ideal retirement age.[3]

We have never arrived at strict guidelines on how or when specific phases of the life cycle are to be designated. Although we Americans seem to think of forty as the entry into middle age, the British prefer age forty-five. Many of us experience mild crises as we move from one decade to another—the trauma of reaching forty or fifty is perhaps the most often cited hurdle. However, as we have clearly shown in this book, people have quite individual approaches as to how they define their age—mental and physical health being the principal ingredients in this process.

As we define age differently, we are no less individualistic in our approach to retirement, both when we desire to begin it and what we intend to do with it. The famous scientist Dr. Hans Selye is quoted as saying, "I have nothing against retirement as long as it doesn't interfere with my work!"[4]

In assessing the meaning of retirement, both early and on time, we can see that it has several functions. One of these is the development of an upper-age culture, in the same way that the term "youth culture" has emerged over the last forty years or so. Early in this century there evolved an age grading in our society. As we moved from a rural to an urban society, the togetherness of life on the farm, whether in the parlor at home or in the church social hall, began to give way to a consciousness of age groups. Age grading increasingly came to the school system and voluntary organizations from the Girl Scouts to the Masonic lodge. The drive for an institutionalized retirement system earlier in the century and for early retirement in the late 1970s suggests that each age phase of the life cycle has its own rights. As one observer notes: "Age has functioned as a method of integrating the multiple roles and responsibilities individuals assume in modern society."[5]

Still, both society and the individual have their reservations about retirement. Ageism has joined sexism and racism as stereotypes too often assigned to a given group.[6] The "war between the generations" means that this label will be hurled at oldsters when the budget becomes strained and it must be decided how much each group is to receive of the GNP (gross national product).[7] In the mid-1980s, Senator David Durenberger founded the Americans for Generational Equity (AGE) on the basis of a belief that only by dramatically decreasing spending on the elderly can the United States afford to provide adequately for the young. The aging of America, to which we referred in Chapter 1, will require considerable sums spent on the upper-age group. This will hardly reduce the prejudice against the retired population.

Despite the prejudices toward this segment of the population, the general impression of the elderly has not been completely unfavorable. As most of us have observed, it is a mixed set of images. One sees opposing images in TV and advertising.[8] An analysis of TV content shows more unfavorable than favorable themes in regard to the elderly.[9] Moreover, we have all been exposed to the myths about aging, as documented by Ken Dychtwald and Joe Flower[10]:

1. People over sixty-five are old.
2. Most of the elderly are in poor health.
3. The elderly are not as bright as the young.
4. Older people are unproductive.
5. Older people are unattractive and sexless.
6. All the elderly are pretty much the same.

These stereotypes or myths are increasingly fading away. It is significant that despite the national cult of youth, the American public twice elected Ronald Reagan in his seventies to the White House. Although his role in American politics and history will remain controversial, the election did show that the public view of senior citizens is not a static one. More to the point is the accumulation of data on the creativity of those in the upper years. We are familiar with the accomplishments of the elderly: Immanuel Kant wrote his greatest philosophical works in his late fifties and sixties; Giuseppe Verdi composed what many regard as his greatest opera, *Otello,* at age seventy-one and *Falstaff* (which is still in the standard repertory) at eighty. Picasso was still painting at ninety, industrialist–philanthropist Armand Hammer was almost maniacally active well into his nineties, and the list goes on. Individual differences, the environment, and the specific area of creativity may determine this outflowing in the late years.[11]

This century saw the advent of a number of social inventions, in the context of this book most notably, the institutionalization of retirement. As Gordon Streib and Clement Schneider point out, retirement is only possible in a society if three conditions are met: a sufficiently large number of people who survive into the upper years, an economy rich enough to permit these persons to be absent from the work force, and a pension system to lend financial underpinning.[12] Undoubtedly these conditions will continue to be fulfilled in Western society, but the strains will increase, as over a fifth of the population is predicted to be sixty-five years or older by 2020. Also, the spread of retirement in this century was unquestionably related to the declining birthrate, which meant that we could afford to support the dependents at the other end of the life span. Another factor has been the growth of government, especially at the federal level, which can be compared to a large corporation. But mostly it is the affluence of our society that has made for this ability to permit the upper years to be enjoyed with relative freedom from economic want. This is not unrelated to the affluence of American society, not only the comparative income but also our longevity (at least for the middle and upper classes) and a degree of formal education unattained by almost no other nation.

Yet, we cannot escape the reality that at least a minority of the elderly confront a number of serious problems. Many persons still fall through the rather broad cracks—low-income workers with no private pension plan or an unsteady history of employment. Minorities are especially vulnerable as they are usually confined to low-paying jobs that mean a low contribution rate and consequently an inadequate pension.[13] For others, health problems remain paramount. For the retirees in our own study who found less than a happy adjustment, there is the hope of counseling resources. These might range over postretirement career possibilities to coping with deeper psychological problems. Of course, these problems may come in any phase of the life cycle, but if one uses suicide rates or rates of depressive symptoms as a criterion, the upper-aged are especially vulnerable. It is relevant that among our sample were at least two people who felt they could initiate a career for counseling their cohorts. Peer counseling is found to be a fairly effective means of reaching the elderly.[14]

Findings of Our Study

In our survey, we confirmed the positive outlook of today's retirees even though some were moved out of the work force under less than cheerful relations. Among the more salient findings is the lack of a relationship between the age of retirement and happiness in retirement. Generally, however, younger retirees were found to be somewhat more satisfied than older ones. The timing of retirement is important only as it relates to expectations. That is, satisfaction is markedly greater when one can plan one's retirement. Specifically, the longer one has to plan one's retirement, the higher will be his or her satisfaction and happiness. Those who perceive their retirement as more difficult than they had anticipated are also found to be less satisfied and less happy.

What emerges from the questionnaire data more emphatically than any other finding is the importance of a *sense of control.* In other words, if the individual is allowed a maximum of autonomy in planning his or her retirement, the enjoyment of retirement is much more probable.

But beyond the statistical findings coming from the 115 questionnaires are the experiences revealed by the 139 interviewees. We see the ways our respondents plunged into new activities and enlarged their previous scope of hobbies and interests. Not least, their experiences underline the truism that if one has adequate income, health, and a zest for living or a vital set of interests, retirement can hardly fail to be a success—only 15 percent were dissatisfied with their retirement.

Undoubtedly, the first months can be awkward, and for the very early retirees (like Matt Boyd or Lew Fitzgerald) the search for employment may be a somewhat dubious adventure, but if we can judge by our volunteer interviewees the picture is a positive one. The Golden Parachute may be less golden than it was in one's daydreams, but it is there nonetheless!

We have seen throughout this book how the effects of retirement depend in large part on the attitudes of the individuals who retire. Our survey is hardly unique in this finding.[15] Also important are the attitudes of those who offer the retirement plan, expressed in their actions toward their employees who are eligible to retire and, subsequently, those who choose to retire. Although plans may be offered "for the good of the company," most individuals choose to retire based on their attitudes about what is good for themselves. If they feel they would be better off retired, then they will retire. In turn, the feeling about readiness is based on their attitudes—toward the meaning of work and the climate in which that work has been conducted, toward the role and acceptability of leisure in people's lives, and toward themselves.

The Present and Future of Retirement

We have also seen that, most of the time, the current social situation fosters positive attitudes that are favorable toward retiring as early as one can. The current situation, in turn, is partly driven by demographic and economic forces. In order to "conserve capital," many employers have found it necessary to reduce their work force. Positive social attitudes toward retirement have made their jobs easier, because the "golden handshake" was seen as a socially acceptable, humane way to reduce those forces by actually giving people what they want—a chance to engage in a life of leisure! Meanwhile, the growing numbers of older persons have simultaneously made it easy to have appreciable work-force reductions via the "early retirement route" and made following that route increasingly problematic. That is, the economy has been releasing more and more able workers into a part of the life cycle that may prove almost as long as the work years themselves. This situation may require a growing array of resources to be directed toward their care and satisfaction rather than toward the care and satisfaction of the current group of workers or the training and preparation of those who have not yet attained worker status.

What does this mean for the future of society and for the future of early retirement? Will social and economic forces even ten years from now make what we have found about early retirement outmoded, as corporations try harder and harder to find ways to retain, not retire, their older workers?

The answers, as many answers tend to be, are all unequivocal "maybes." Clearly, as we have pointed out, as the baby boom cohort enters their fifties and sixties, it is going to be more and more difficult for the economy to support them with Social Security and the array of programs directed toward people who reach "magic ages" like sixty or sixty-five. It is also going to be increasingly difficult to find enough able, experienced workers from the smaller cohorts to come. Thus, many observers feel that corporations and other employers, such as state and local governments, will rather quickly take a sharp turn away from offering early retirement inducements and instead proffer inducements for continued employment. Already we have seen in American society how certain welfare programs were initiated in the 1960s, expanded in the 1970s, and reduced in the 1980s and early 1990s.[16] These programs, such as Medicaid and food stamps, have affected mainly the financially disadvantaged, with a severe effect on the minority aged, but some, such as the taxability of Social Security payments, have had a wider impact.

Indeed, this may happen, but we must also take into account the attitudes of those who will be attaining ages associated with early retirement as seen in our set of interviewees (that is, the later fifties on average). They have grown up as employees to see that retirement is likely to be a positive experience, allowing for growth opportunities in new directions, including employment under freer conditions than they experienced in their "regular" careers. They have seen that only health and lack of income stand in the way of satisfying retirement. When they get to be fifty-five or sixty, aren't they likely to say, "Now it is my turn"? Indeed, we feel they are. After all, the elimination of mandatory retirement in the 1980s did almost nothing to stem the tide toward early retirement, and most of that early retirement was *not* dependent on a specific inducement plan, but simply on the availability of the opportunity. And, so, it is unlikely that early retirement will simply disappear, even if employers "turn off the taps" of offers too good to refuse, and even if they turn on some other taps of inducements to remain, like sabbaticals or flextime.

Further, even very major efforts to keep people in the work force are likely to increase average work time by at most a few years. That will still leave us with many, many retirees, who will be looking for advice and guidance to those who have gone before, like the retirees who made this book possible by their participation.

What may happen, however, is something that is probably long overdue in our society—a major shift in orientation to what both work and leisure are all about. The best way to keep people from retiring "prematurely" is to make their work lives enjoyable. This, in turn, requires two different strategies—one to increase commitment to work by enhancing the work environment and the other to inject leisure and the potential joys of retiring, which come across so clearly in our research, into one's entire life cycle. On the one hand, technology, management attitudes that attend to the needs and extra work demands of its employees, and a participatory approach to decision making about work environments, assignments, and schedules all can make it less likely that work is just an onerous place to put in one's time for a certain amount of money and more likely that work will be a positive experience. Family care policies, flextime, flexplace, profit sharing, and involvement in management decisions are only a few of the many aspects that can be used to attain these goals.[17] The objective is not to make work "fun" by watering down or doing away with the necessary discipline, structure, and even drudgery of most jobs, but to place the *necessary* elements of control and structure within a broader context that makes employees feel that they—and their activities both on and outside the job—make sense and count for something. On the other hand, employees throughout the life cycle may be more vigorous in demanding that, if they are to work up to a later age than the generation before them, they should be able to develop a well-rounded leisure (in this case simply read "non-work") life as they go along, rather than putting it off until after all participation in the work force. Academia, with its sabbatical programs, offers one model, while the proliferation of adult education programs that are not geared to work advancement but to "life enhancement" can provide another of the mechanisms to develop a sense that learning, working, *and* "taking it easy" can *all* be lifelong. We can move to a society in which involvement among those categories of activity so often compartmentalized and separated can be seen as the norm, and where modulation and movement from one to the other can be much freer than the linear, one-after-the-other model that served well in different times with different social needs and a much different conception of the life span.

What will the future hold? Will we move toward—or away from—voluntary retirement?[18] We don't know. But it is unlikely that it will be so different from the past that we will not be able to take guidance from the experiences and insights of those who have gone before. However retirement is constructed, and whenever it occurs in chronological terms, what we have been learning today will be an important guide, for one thing is sure—for those who have seen retirement and the pleasures it can bring, it will continue to be an important and expected part of the life cycle. And for those who have seen that retirement may have some pitfalls, it will be important to rely on a good road map that can point the pitfalls out and show that, more often than not, there are pathways that avoid the dangers or at least make them less treacherous.

References

1. David R. Young *et al.*, *America in Perspective* (Boston: Houghton Mifflin, 1986), p. 116.
2. Frank M. Kleiler, *Can We Afford Early Retirement?* (Baltimore: Johns Hopkins University Press, 1978), p. 113.
3. William Graebner, *A History of Retirement* (New Haven, CT: Yale University Press, 1980).
4. Edna LeShan, *Oh, To Be Fifty Again* (New York: Times Books, 1986), p. 96.
5. Howard P. Chudacoff, *How Old Are You? Age Consciousness in American Society* (Princeton, NJ: Princeton University Press, 1989), p. 185.
6. J. B. Kessler, *Getting Even with Getting Old* (Chicago: Nelson-Hall, 1980), p. 3.
7. Marvin Cetron and Owen Davis, *American Renaissance: Our Life at the Turn of the 21st Century* (New York: St. Martin's Press, 1989), p. 41.
8. Karin Swisher (ed.), *The Elderly: Opposing Viewpoints* (San Diego: Greenhaven Press, 1990), Chap. 1.
9. Richard H. Davis and James A. Davis, *TV's Image of the Elderly* (Lexington, MA: Lexington Books, 1985).
10. Ken Dychtwald and Joe Flower, *Age Wave* (Los Angeles: Tarcher Publications, 1980), Chap. 2.
11. Dean K. Simonton, "Creativity in the Later Years: Optimistic Prospects for Achievement," *Gerontologist, 30*, 625–631, 1990.
12. Gordon F. Streib and Clement J. Schneider, *Retirement in American Society* (Ithaca, NY: Cornell University Press, 1971).
13. Lodis Rhodes, "Retirement, Economics, and the Minority Aged," in Ron C. Manuel (ed.), *Minority Aging: Sociological and Social Psychological Issues* (New York: Greenwood Press, 1982), pp. 123–130.
14. Bernice Bratter and Estelle Tuvman, "A Peer Counseling Program in Action," in S. Stansfeld Sargent (ed.), *Nontraditional Therapy and Counseling with the Aged* (New York: Springer, 1980), pp. 131–145.
15. Tora K. Bikson and Jacqueline D. Goodchilds, "Experiencing the Retirement Transition: Managerial and Professional Men Before and After," in

Shirlynn Spacapan and Stuart Oskamp (eds.), *The Social Psychology of Aging* (Newbury Park, CA: Sage Publications, 1989), pp. 81–108.

16. Robert L. Clark, "Income Maintenance Programs in the United States," in Robert H. Binstock and Linda K. George (eds.), *Handbook of Aging and the Social Sciences*, 3d ed. (San Diego: Academic Press, 1990), pp. 382–397.

17. Dychtwald and Flower, pp. 194–206.

18. Stanley Parker, *Work and Retirement* (London: George Allen & Unwin, 1982), pp. 162–165.

Appendix A

Research Methods

All respondents who called in or sent a note in response to appeals in the newspaper and on a radio talk show in the late 1980s were mailed a questionnaire (with a stamped return envelope). Of these, over 90 percent were completed and returned. The items, both standardized and open-ended, were directed toward satisfaction with respondents' former work and present situation, conditions of retirement, and changes in their life style and activities. In order to monitor their feeling state, the Bradburn Affect Balance Scale was included.[1] The last item in the questionnaire was an invitation to be interviewed. Of the 115 who completed the questionnaire eighty-seven, in addition to twenty-seven spouses, acceded to an interview. A number had moved away before we were able to reach them for an interview—roughly 9 percent of retirees relocate within the first year of retirement. The interviewees suggested other possible interviewees. During 1990–91 we reinterviewed twenty-two of the original sample to determine what changes had occurred in the years since the original interview. Also, for the purpose of giving broader scope to our sample, we interviewed twenty-five additional retirees during 1990–91. In other words, our total number of interviewees was 139 (or 167 participants if we include those who filled out the questionnaire but did not accede to an interview), representing a broad spectrum of occupations, but weighted more to the white- than to the blue-collar universe.

The Sample

The average age of the subjects at the time of filling out the questionnaire was sixty-three years. The average age of retirement was fifty-nine years, with a range from forty-five to seventy-three. The retirees had been on the average twenty-eight years in their last location, with 41 percent reporting having been with their employer over thirty years—a reflection of the stability of the Lehigh Valley population. Moreover, the average length of time in the last position or job description was over fifteen years.

The sample was 70 percent male. As further indication of the stability of the sample, 80 percent of the sample were married, of which 73 percent had been married over twenty years (6 percent were separated or divorced, 8 percent widowed, 6 percent never married). Of the wives of the interviewees, 32 percent had never been employed outside the home, 17 percent were currently employed, and 50 percent had previously been employed. The traditionalism represented by the sample is further shown in their strong attachment to family life: 86 percent had at least one child (an average of 2.8 children), and 13 percent had one or two children still at home.

As the sample was largely self-selected and represented upper-level occupations, the average educational level was relatively high, considering the age of the subjects. Over 50 percent had at least one college degree, another 20 percent had attended college, and only 4 percent were without a high school diploma. As another symbol of middle-class character—and the shape of a middle-size city—approximately 90 percent owned their homes. Not the least index of the conservatism of the Lehigh Valley was the religious participation: 58 percent attended church almost weekly (62 percent Protestant, 26 percent Roman Catholic, 5 percent Jewish, and 7 percent identifying themselves with another or no religion).

Reference

1. N. B. Bradburn, *The Structure of Psychological Well-Being* (Chicago: Aldine, 1969).

Appendix B

Volunteer Services

The volunteer activities listed below were gleaned from the 87 initial interviews. Statistics represent the number of retirees who said they are or have been volunteers in each area since retirement; the range per person is from no volunteer work up to as many as ten to twelve different volunteer services. The groupings, which are somewhat arbitrary, are listed in two major categories. In subgroups the number of those who served in positions of leadership within organizations of service to others is noted. Most organizations are age or health related.

A. Non-organization-sponsored services
   a. Aiding regularly (at least one day a week) very sick or incapacitated aged relative or friend (6). Also baby-sitting grandchildren (5) (one of whom gave three days a week for employed daughter)
   b. Acting in community theater (1)
   c. Playing guitar in various nursing homes (1)
   d. Refurbishing nurses' private homes in gratitude for former care (1)
B. Organization-related services
   a. Church or temple related (49), including:
      1. Church-run food banks (7)
      2. Church-established park (1)
      3. Church social services and church homes (24), including leadership positions (9), presidents of church boards (2), executive secretary of citywide Sunday

School Association (1), chairman of pastoral search committee (1), church home board and pastor for home (1), teacher of adolescent residents of home (1), and church treasurer (2)

b. Hospitals (12), including:
   1. Long-term care facility for physically disabled adults (4)
   2. State mental hospital (2)
   3. Veterans' hospital (2)
   4. Blood banks (4)
c. Fraternal organizations serving others (17), including:
   1. Elks (2)
   2. Lions (4)
   3. Masons (4)
   4. Rotary (1), as manager of pupil overseas exchange program
d. Community-based service (for general public, not for specific segment) (13), including:
   1. Annual community music festival (2)
   2. Historic Bethlehem (2)
   3. Canal Museum (1)
   4. Public library (2)
   5. Township Commissioner for Public Safety (1)
e. School or college related (8), including:
   1. Public school boards (2)
   2. Consultant for vocational schools and colleges (1)
   3. College class chairman for solicitations and reunion (1)
   4. Hosting foreign college students (1)
   5. College Committee on Gerontology (1)
   6. Multicollege coordination committee on nurse education (1)
f. Veterans' organizations (8), including:
   1. National Commander of China–Burma–India Veterans' Association (1)
g. MORA (Men of Retirement Age) (9), mostly to hear speakers and to socialize, but one gives service 16 hours a week

h. AARP (10), including:
   1. President of local chapter (2)
   2. Program chairman (1)
   3. Pastor for AARP (1)
i. Cancer Society (4), including board of directors (2)
j. Meals on Wheels (8)
k. Alcoholics Anonymous (3)
l. Blind Association (3), including RADPRIN (reading for blind)
m. Company-based service group (9), including:
   1. Secretary (1)
   2. Board of "Valley Volunteers" (1)
   3. Senior Corps of Retired Executives (SCORE) helping entrants into business (2)
n. YWCA, YMCA (9), including:
   1. Nurses on board of directors (2)
   2. Psychiatric social worker on board (1)
   3. Chairman Nominating Committee (1)
o. County nursing home (2)
p. Heart Association (2), including:
   1. Chairman of local, regional, and state (1)
q. Political campaigns (2)
r. Rescue Mission (for homeless) (4)
s. Visiting Nurse Association (2), including:
   1. Giving bereavement counseling (1)
   2. Vice president (1)
t. Special interest (36), including Area Agency on Aging, County Advisory Council, Birthright, Civic Association (now publishes a newsletter), Crime Watch, Educational TV, Emergency Medical Council, Little League, prisoner counseling, Red Cross, Seniors Helping Seniors (legal advice), State Ambulance Corps, State Committee on CPR

Index